Published by OMS / Amazon KDP

This is a work of non-fiction. Any opinions, interpretations, or analyses within this book reflect the author's perspective and are intended to encourage critical thought and discussion.

Who Says This Is Wrong?

Questioning the Foundations of Morality

To those who dare to question

To those who seek truth beyond tradition

To those unafraid to explore the gray areas of morality

May this book serve as a mirror, a challenge, and an invitation to think deeper

Table of Contents

Introduction: Between Shadows and Light

Imagine you're standing in a crowded city square. A man collapses to the ground, gasping for air, his hands clawing at his throat. You glance around—dozens of people see what's happening, but no one moves. A woman nearby clutches her phone, recording the moment rather than dialing for help. A suited businessman hesitates, then walks away. Seconds pass. The man's face turns pale.

What do you do?

Before you answer, ask yourself: What determines the right thing to do in this moment?

Is it your own moral compass, whispering that you should step in?

Is it the law, reminding you that you bear no legal responsibility?

Is it society, which has conditioned you to mind your own business?

Is it the weight of the digital world, urging you to act only if it will be seen?

We live in a world brimming with contradictions, where morality is no longer a fixed guidepost but a constantly shifting maze. Who truly decides what is right and what is wrong?

Is it the whispered traditions of family?

The rigid doctrines of religion?

The ever-changing trends of social media?

The unseen hands of governments and global organizations?

In the past, morality was often dictated by a higher power, cultural norms, or a legal system. Today, however, the line between right and wrong is increasingly blurred by corporate influence, viral narratives, misinformation, and the selective outrage of the digital age. Social media, once a tool for connection, has become the judge, jury, and executioner of our actions. It amplifies fabricated stories, fuels divisions, and manipulates public perception—turning morality into a performance rather than a principle.

People are jailed for crimes they did not commit. Others amass wealth and power while exploiting those beneath them, celebrated as "successful" rather than condemned as unethical. Entire wars are fought under the banner of righteousness, yet history exposes their hidden agendas. Justice has become a commodity, bought and sold to the highest bidder.

This book is not here to dictate morality to you. Instead, it is an invitation—to question, explore, and reclaim your own sense of right and wrong.

Together, we will examine the forces that shape our moral compass, from childhood teachings and religious doctrines to political agendas and corporate interests. We will explore how society distorts morality, how power manipulates truth, and how the "Judgment Core" (JDC)—your internal moral compass—can be refined, strengthened, and made your own.

Can morality exist without law?

If the majority believes something is right, does that make it true?

Should we follow moral codes even when they contradict success, survival, or self-interest?

And most importantly—how do we ensure that our morality, above all else, does not justify harm to others?

Prepare to challenge your assumptions, your inherited beliefs, and even your own instincts.

This is not just a book about morality. It is a journey into the depths of human judgment, a confrontation with the forces that shape our choices, and an exploration of what it truly means to do what is right.

Chapter 1: The Purity of Beginnings – Childhood and Parental Influence

Imagine a newborn child, a blank slate upon which no words have yet been written, no stories told, no judgments made. This child arrives in the world free from the burdens of preconception or bias, their mind a pure canvas ready to be painted with the colors of experience and knowledge. This initial state of purity represents the potential of a human life, unmarred by societal expectations, cultural norms, or personal experiences.

However, as days turn to months and years, the child begins to absorb the world around them, developing an understanding of right and wrong based on what they see, hear, and feel.

1.1 The Role of Parents as Architects of Morality and the Birth of the Moral Compass

Pause for a moment and reflect: Who first taught you to differentiate between right and wrong? Was it the stern voice of discipline or the gentle guidance of bedtime stories about heroes and villains? For most of us, the architects of our earliest understanding of morality are our parents. But as you think back to those lessons, have you ever questioned how deeply they shaped the inner compass that guides your decisions today?

This inner compass—your Moral Compass—is a deeply personal guide that steers your sense of right and wrong, fairness and justice. It is the system you rely on to navigate ethical dilemmas and decide between competing values. At its core lies your Judgment Core (JDC)—the foundation upon which your moral compass is built. The JDC is your internal repository of beliefs, shaped by early experiences, cultural norms, personal reflections, and societal influences. It is the mechanism that evaluates each choice and action, aligning or conflicting with the ethical framework instilled in you.

Parents, as the first teachers, play a pivotal role in shaping this Judgment Core during a child's formative years. They do so not only through direct instructions—teaching honesty, kindness, or respect—but also through their actions. If a parent insists on kindness but responds to setbacks with anger, what does the child truly learn? If they preach honesty yet twist the truth in casual conversation, what does the child absorb? These contradictions are not lost on young minds; rather, they linger, shaping how the child perceives and resolves moral conflicts.

The Moral Compass begins to take form through this intricate dance of words and behaviors. It is not just a list of rules handed down but an evolving guide, influenced by consistency—or inconsistency—in what parents say and do. Parents who exhibit patience, empathy, and resilience in their actions teach far more than words could ever convey. Yet, when their actions contradict their teachings, they risk planting seeds of confusion in the fertile soil of a child's developing JDC.

Children are perceptive observers, absorbing lessons both spoken and unspoken. They learn as much from a parent helping a neighbor in need or showing patience in adversity as they do from explicit moral teachings. But what happens when those lessons conflict? When a parent's actions and words fail to align, does the child's Judgment Core strengthen through questioning, or does it fracture, creating a moral fog that persists into adulthood?

So, we must ask:

- What values did your parents embed in your Judgment Core, and how have they shaped your Moral Compass today?

- When your parents' actions contradicted their words, how did it influence your sense of right and wrong?

- If your JDC was built on their lessons, have you examined and refined it, or do you follow it uncritically?

The Moral Compass is a tool of immense power, but its foundation—the Judgment Core—is forged in the fires of early experience. Parents are not perfect, and their teachings often reflect their own biases, strengths, and flaws. Recognizing this imperfection challenges us to examine the values we've inherited. Are they truly ours, or echoes we've never questioned? If they no longer align with our lived experiences or sense of justice, how do we reshape them?

Your Moral Compass is yours to wield, but its effectiveness depends on understanding its origins. Parents may have laid the groundwork, but you hold the tools to refine it. The question is: Will you let their blueprint define you, or will you take charge of shaping a compass that aligns with the principles you hold dear?

1.2 The Deep Roots of Influence: Shaping the Moral Compass from Childhood

As we delve deeper into the origins of your Moral Compass and Judgment Core (JDC), the profound role of parental teaching comes into sharper focus. Parents, our first guides in the uncharted waters of morality, leave an indelible imprint on our understanding of right and wrong. Through their words, actions, and unspoken cues, they become the architects of our earliest ethical frameworks. But have you ever considered how much of what you believe today is a reflection of their influence—and how much is truly your own?

The lessons parents impart are not confined to what they explicitly teach. A child doesn't merely learn honesty because they're told to tell the truth—they learn it by watching their parents keep promises or own up to mistakes. Similarly, respect for others is not just taught but modeled. A parent who shows kindness to a stranger, patience in the face of frustration, or fairness in resolving disputes is quietly sculpting their child's values. These small, consistent actions become the bedrock of a child's moral reasoning, creating templates for navigating the complexities of the world.

But what happens when the lessons parents teach through their actions clash with the values they espouse? A child told to value honesty but who observes deceitful behavior from their parent may internalize a contradictory lesson: that dishonesty is acceptable in certain circumstances. A parent who preaches equality but exhibits prejudice subtly reshapes their child's worldview, planting seeds of bias that may linger into adulthood.

Parental influence is, therefore, a double-edged sword. It has the power to cultivate virtues like empathy, integrity, and fairness—but it can also propagate flaws, such as dishonesty, prejudice, or aggression. The Moral Compass forged in childhood is not static; it evolves, challenged by new experiences and shifting societal norms. Yet the foundational framework laid by parents often exerts a lingering pull, shaping how individuals approach ethical dilemmas long after they've left the parental sphere.

This influence is deeply intertwined with cultural and societal contexts, which parents themselves navigate and interpret for their children. In some cases, parents may perpetuate harmful norms simply because they reflect the societal values of their time. In others, they may consciously resist such norms, instilling in their children a critical awareness of systemic flaws and the courage to challenge them.

As children grow, the opportunity to reassess and recalibrate their values emerges. Yet, this process of questioning is neither automatic nor easy. It requires reflection and courage to confront the biases, contradictions, and inherited beliefs that shape the JDC. How often do we pause to examine whether the values we live by are genuinely ours or remnants of lessons absorbed in childhood?

Consider your own journey:

- What values did your parents model through their actions, and how have they shaped your Moral Compass?

- When their actions contradicted their teachings, how did you reconcile the difference? Did it leave your Judgment Core clearer or more clouded?

- As an adult, have you critically examined these inherited beliefs, or do they continue to guide you unchallenged?

The influence of parents is undeniable, but it is not immutable. As adults, we bear the responsibility of scrutinizing the frameworks we've inherited. Are the values embedded in your Judgment Core a reflection of your own principles, or do they echo lessons you've never questioned?

Parental teachings are the first brushstrokes on the canvas of your Moral Compass, but the picture is never complete. With each new experience, you hold the power to revise, refine, and realign your sense of right and wrong. The question is: Will you accept the framework you were given, or will you take charge of reshaping it to reflect the person you aspire to be?

This is your journey—a path of inquiry and introspection. The compass may have been set by your parents, but only you can decide where it will lead.

At the heart of this parental influence lies the Judgment Core (JDC)—the foundation upon which a child's moral compass is built. In these formative years, every lesson, every act of kindness or discipline, becomes a drop in the reservoir of their ethical reasoning. Whether consciously or unconsciously, parents shape not just behavior, but the internal decision-making framework that will guide their child long into adulthood. But how much of this core remains intact? How much is later rewritten by external forces?

The Gentleman Thief

New Rochelle, New York – 1960.

In a quiet suburb just north of Manhattan, the Abagnale house on Elm Street stood like any other—white shutters, clean hedges, a flag hanging just right. But inside that home, a boy was learning a different kind of patriotism. Not the kind that honors truth and justice—but one that salutes charm, appearance, and winning at all costs.

Frank William Abagnale Sr. was the kind of man who could sell snow in winter. He wore tailored suits and spoke with the slow confidence of someone used to getting his way. People liked him. Trusted him. Believed in him. Especially his son, Frank Jr., who watched his father not just with affection—but with reverence.

"I idolized my father," Frank Jr. would later say. "He could talk anyone into anything. He was always in control. To me, he was the definition of success."

Frank Sr. didn't teach with lectures—he taught by example. And that was the problem.

Whenever a bill collector called, he'd smile and say, "You don't need to tell them the truth. Just tell them what they can live with."

When a deal started falling apart, he'd remind Frank Jr., "Always look like you know what you're doing. People will believe the suit before they believe the story."

When his son mimicked him—flattering strangers or joking his way out of consequences—he didn't correct him. He clapped him on the back and laughed.

"People see what you show them, Frankie," he once said. "You don't need to be honest—you just need to be convincing."

These weren't just offhand remarks—they were blueprints. In the absence of values like honesty, accountability, or humility, young Frank's Judgment Core (JDC) formed around a different foundation:

- Deception is a tool.

- Appearance is more important than truth.

- Rules are flexible—if you're clever enough.

Even as life at home began to unravel, Frank Sr. continued praising the very traits that would soon become his son's greatest weaknesses. When young Frank was caught forging a note at school, his father didn't scold him.

He smiled.

"You've got the gift, kid," he said. "Just make sure you use it wisely."

Frank Jr.'s world collapsed when his parents divorced. He was 15. The charm of his father remained, but the structure vanished. His father, now broke and bitter, leaned harder into denial and nostalgia. His mother was distant. No one was watching.

That same year, Frank began forging checks—first small ones, like altering figures on his father's gas card to buy food. But the rush it gave him—of control, of cleverness—was intoxicating. He felt powerful.

By 16, Frank had dropped out of high school and left home. With just $200 in the bank, he realized checks were more valuable than cash—if you could manipulate them. He studied routing numbers, magnetic ink, and bank patterns. Using false names and IDs, he opened dozens of accounts in different states and began printing counterfeit checks.

Over the next few years, Frank would cash more than $2.5 million in fraudulent checks.

But banking wasn't enough.

At 17, Frank became a Pan Am pilot—at least on paper. He forged an FAA license, printed a fake pilot ID, and got his hands on a uniform. With nothing but confidence and forged credentials, he "deadheaded" on over 250 flights, logging two million miles across 26 countries.

"I never flew a plane," he later admitted. "But I flew in one almost every day."

Being a pilot gave him access—and respect. It made cashing fake checks in distant cities easier. And no one questioned a man in uniform.

Frank moved to Georgia and became a pediatric supervisor, using a fake Harvard degree and forged records. For 11 months, he worked night shifts, managing residents and staff at a local hospital. He didn't perform procedures, relying on real nurses to handle the medical side. But he was convincing.

"It gave me respect," he said. "And if you're respected, you're not questioned."

Confidence became a substitute for competence. Another lesson learned.

In Baton Rouge, Louisiana, Frank posed as an assistant attorney general. He had forged Harvard Law credentials and passed the Louisiana bar exam after studying hard—passing on his third attempt.

Wearing suits, quoting case law, and carrying himself with authority, no one suspected him.

By age 20, Frank had built a life around lies—each one more elaborate than the last. But this wasn't random rebellion. It was a performance rooted in a corrupted value system.

His father never told him to lie, cheat, or steal. But he applauded the traits that made those things possible:

- Charm over truth

- Confidence over competence

- Winning over integrity

In the vacuum of moral clarity, praise became permission.

Frank was finally arrested in France at age 21, then extradited to the U.S., where he was sentenced to 12 years in federal prison. He served five, after striking a deal with the FBI to help expose fraud.

But the real reckoning came later.

"My father never taught me right from wrong," Frank admitted. "He taught me how to fake right. And that was worse."

Frank Sr. loved his son. But love without guidance is like wind without direction. In his admiration for charm, his obsession with image, and his quiet approval of deception, he built a Judgment Core founded not on ethics, but on illusion.

This story is not just about crime. It's about what happens when parents shape their child's morality around performance rather than principle. When the appearance of goodness is rewarded more than its practice, the result is a moral compass that spins in circles—always pointing toward what looks good, never what is good.

Let me know if you'd like this exported into a clean Word/PDF format, or if you want help adding a final discussion prompt to fit your book's structure.

The Silent March: Ruby Bridges' Story

New Orleans, Louisiana — November 14, 1960.

The morning was unusually crisp for Louisiana. Six-year-old Ruby Bridges clutched her mother Lucille's hand tightly as they stood on the front steps of their modest home. Across the street, a black sedan idled, its engine humming softly. Inside were the federal marshals assigned to escort Ruby to her first day at William Frantz Elementary School, one of the first all-white schools to be desegregated in New Orleans.

Ruby's wide, curious eyes betrayed no fear, but Lucille could feel the tremor in her daughter's grip. As the car door opened, Lucille bent down and looked her daughter in the eye. "Keep your head high, baby," she whispered. "You're walking for more than just yourself."

As they approached the school, Ruby saw the crowd for the first time. A sea of angry faces. Shouts rose like waves crashing against the car. She couldn't make out the words, but she could feel their hatred. Adults held signs scrawled with threats and slurs. Federal marshals flanked Ruby as she stepped out, their towering frames a stark contrast to her small, white dress.

Behind that dress stood years of hard choices and deep convictions.

Lucille Bridges was no stranger to the cruelty of racism. Born in Tylertown, Mississippi, she grew up under the grip of Jim Crow laws —a system of legalized racial segregation in the Southern United States that lasted from the late 19th century into the 1960s. These laws mandated "separate but equal" facilities for Black and white Americans, but the reality was far from equal. They entrenched racial injustice and restricted everything from education and healthcare to housing, voting rights, and transportation.

Lucille's childhood was marked by exclusion and limited opportunity. But her spirit remained unbroken. She believed in the dignity of every human being and in the transformative power of education. She was determined that her children would have the chances she never did.

She and her husband Abon had wrestled with the decision to let Ruby attend William Frantz Elementary. They knew the risks—violence, isolation, harassment—but also understood the weight of the moment. "If not us," Lucille had said during one of their late-night conversations, "then who? Someone has to go first."

In the days leading up to Ruby's first day, Lucille would sit with her daughter every evening after dinner. "You're as good as anyone in that school," she told her. "You deserve the same education, the same dreams." But she also offered her daughter tools to protect her heart.

"When they scream, pray. When they threaten, pray. Prayer isn't giving in—it's how we keep our strength. It's how we stay clean inside."

Lucille was building something deeper than resilience. She was cultivating what the Bridges family called strength of spirit, but what we might now understand as Ruby's Judgment Core (JDC)—the internal moral compass that would help her navigate a world poisoned by hate.

Each morning, the federal marshals arrived on schedule. Each morning, Ruby walked past the mob—calm, quiet, head held high. Inside, the hostility didn't end. Teachers refused to instruct her. White parents pulled their children from classrooms. Ruby sat alone, day after day, with Barbara Henry—the only teacher willing to defy the boycott.

Lucille could only watch from home, praying that her daughter would endure what no child should ever have to.

That evening ritual became sacred. Lucille would sit by Ruby's bed, holding her small hands, asking about her day and reminding her, again and again, of the larger purpose. "You're a bridge, Ruby. A bridge to a better world."

One day, as Ruby walked toward the school, a woman in the crowd spat at her feet. Ruby froze. Her breath caught in her throat. The noise around her blurred into static. Then Lucille's voice echoed in her mind: "Pray for them."

So Ruby did. She closed her eyes for a moment and whispered a prayer. Then, she lifted her chin and walked forward, her steps as steady as ever. In that instant, grace became her shield, and her mother's voice, her armor.

Years later, Ruby would reflect on how deeply her parents, especially her mother, shaped her Judgment Core. From her father, she learned perseverance. From Lucille, she learned compassion, forgiveness, and moral courage—the power to choose grace over anger, purpose over fear.

Her experience taught her that morality is not fixed by rules alone, but built through reflection, intention, and the courage to resist injustice. Her JDC blended resilience with empathy, integrity with understanding—a compass she would carry into adulthood as a civil rights advocate.

Ruby's walk into William Frantz Elementary became one of the defining images of the Civil Rights Movement. Her presence in that classroom cracked the foundation of segregation in public education. Over time, her courage helped inspire nationwide conversations and legal actions that accelerated school desegregation.

Her story became part of the curriculum in American schools, not just as a tale of bravery, but as a lesson in moral leadership and the power of individual action. Through books, documentaries, and public speaking, Ruby dedicated her adult life to advocating for educational equity and racial justice.

In 1999, she established the Ruby Bridges Foundation, aimed at promoting tolerance and creating change through education. She believed that children, if guided by empathy and understanding, could heal divisions long embedded in society.

Today, Ruby's impact lives on in integrated classrooms, diversity programs, and in every child who learns that doing the right thing often means standing alone—but never in vain.

Ruby Bridges' story is more than a chapter in history—it's a blueprint for change. It shows how the moral courage of one small girl, shaped by the unwavering love and values of her mother, helped dismantle a system of injustice.

In the hostile streets of 1960s New Orleans, a child walked a path no child should have to. But with each step, she carried the lessons of a mother who knew that true strength lies in grace—and that true morality demands both conviction and compassion. Ruby's journey reminds us all: the smallest steps can leave the deepest footprints on history.

1.3 Beyond the Nest: Expanding the Judgment Core

As we grow, the morality instilled by our parents—the initial framework of our Judgment Core (JDC)—faces its first true test: the encounter with broader perspectives. What happens when the neatly defined lessons of childhood collide with the complexities of the outside world? Can your moral compass remain static, or does it evolve under the weight of new influences?

The family home, while foundational, offers a limited lens. Parents, no matter how well-intentioned, can only impart values shaped by their own experiences and biases. But morality, as life will teach us, is rarely confined to a single set of beliefs. The moment we step beyond the boundaries of familial influence, we are thrust into a sea of diverse viewpoints—each with the potential to challenge, enrich, or even upend our understanding of right and wrong.

Take, for instance, the subtle tension between generations. Grandparents, often rooted in traditions, might emphasize the steadfastness of cultural norms, while a progressive aunt or uncle introduces ideas that seem to contradict those foundations. A grandparent might assert, "This is how it's always been," while a younger relative asks, "But should it still be this way?" These differing voices do more than confuse—they illuminate the vast spectrum of moral beliefs, urging us to question and refine our own.

The classroom becomes another arena for moral growth. Here, teachers emerge as guides, presenting structured lessons on fairness, justice, and diversity. A discussion on historical injustices might force a child to reconsider notions of authority or fairness learned at home. A teacher who champions curiosity and critical thinking offers a subtle yet powerful counterpoint to rigid moral doctrines. In these moments, children begin to glimpse the layered complexity of ethical questions and develop the tools to navigate them.

Peers, too, leave their mark. A debate with a friend over fairness in a playground game might seem trivial but lays the groundwork for understanding compromise, perspective-taking, and conflict resolution. These interactions, free from the hierarchical structure of parent-child relationships, provide a unique space to test and negotiate moral beliefs.

Mentors—coaches, religious leaders, or community figures—further expand this moral dialogue. A coach emphasizing teamwork and resilience, a spiritual leader preaching compassion and service, or a community activist demonstrating courage in the face of injustice—they all serve as living examples of moral values in action. Each one introduces new facets of morality, allowing the JDC to grow more nuanced and adaptive.

This exposure to varied viewpoints is not merely a developmental milestone—it is a necessity. It fosters a moral framework capable of flexing under the weight of life's complexities. A child who learns to see the world through multiple lenses gains the capacity to navigate situations where the answer is neither obvious nor simple. This adaptability shields against the pitfalls of rigid thinking, equipping them to recognize and challenge biases, even those inherited from their parents.

Through this journey, children also discover the malleability of morality. They learn that what is deemed ethical or just in one culture may be viewed entirely differently in another, and what is acceptable today may be condemned tomorrow. This realization demands humility: an acknowledgment that no single perspective holds all the answers and that morality itself is a dynamic, evolving construct.

Consider your own moral journey:

- How often do you question the lessons you absorbed as a child? Do they still serve you, or have they become constraints?

- Have you embraced the perspectives of those outside your immediate circle, or do you resist viewpoints that challenge your core beliefs?

- When faced with conflicting values, how do you determine which path aligns with your Judgment Core?

The evolution of your JDC is both a personal and a collective endeavor. Moving beyond parental influence is not a rejection of their teachings but an acknowledgment that no single source can define morality. By engaging with diverse perspectives, we cultivate a moral compass capable of navigating the ever-changing landscapes of life.

But the question remains: Will you seek out these broader viewpoints, daring to challenge the boundaries of your inherited beliefs? Or will you let the framework you were given dictate the entirety of your moral path? The choice to expand and refine your Judgment Core is yours alone—but its impact will ripple through every decision you make.

The Dual Compass: Maria's Journey in São Paulo

São Paulo, Brazil, 2005. The streets of São Paulo pulsed with energy as Maria Oliveira stepped off the crowded bus and made her way to her new high school. It was her first week at Colégio Elite, one of the city's top institutions, and she was nervous. Coming from a family of modest means and deep-rooted values of compassion and community, Maria wasn't sure how she'd fit in among the school's ambitious students.

Her parents, Helena and João, were both teachers who dedicated their lives to uplifting others. They believed in collective welfare and regularly involved Maria in community service. She spent weekends volunteering at local shelters or distributing food to underprivileged families. Helena often said, "Maria, our worth is measured by what we give, not what we take." These lessons were etched deeply into Maria's moral compass, shaping her belief that helping others was life's highest calling.

But Colégio Elite was a different world. Here, the students valued competition over collaboration, self-reliance over collective good. For the first time, Maria's Judgment Core—a deeply internalized framework built on empathy and sharing—was about to be challenged.

In early 2006, Maria joined the school's prestigious debate club, hoping to expand her skills and gain confidence. It was there that she met James Miller, a sharp-witted and fiercely independent student with an uncanny ability to dominate arguments. Born to British expatriates, James had been raised with a philosophy starkly different from Maria's. His parents, after years of financial struggles, had taught him the value of self-interest and assertiveness.

During their first debate, the topic was polarizing: "Is self-interest the key to societal progress?" Maria argued passionately for the collective good, drawing on examples from her upbringing, where community and empathy fueled positive change. James, however, countered with precision, painting self-interest as a driving force for innovation and progress. His arguments were compelling, rooted in his own experiences and his belief that survival often required prioritizing oneself over others.

Maria left the debate unsettled. She had always believed in the strength of her values, but James's words lingered. Was self-interest truly selfish? Or was it a survival mechanism, as James claimed? Could compassion coexist with ambition? These questions nagged at her, pushing her to confront the limits of her upbringing.

One afternoon, determined to understand James's perspective, Maria approached him. They sat beneath the sprawling shade of an old jacaranda tree on campus. "James," she began hesitantly, "your argument yesterday—it made me think. Why do you believe self-interest is so important?"

James's eyes softened as he recounted his story. His family had moved to Brazil when he was a child, seeking better opportunities after losing everything in a financial collapse. "My parents taught me that no one was going to hand us a better life," he said. "We had to fight for it ourselves. Self-interest isn't about selfishness—it's about survival. It's about ensuring a better future for yourself and your family."

Maria listened intently, her own worldview shifting with each word. For James, assertiveness wasn't about greed but about resilience in the face of adversity. She began to see that his perspective wasn't at odds with hers—it was simply born from a different set of experiences.

As Maria continued in the debate club, she began experimenting with integrating James's perspective into her own. During a debate on education reform, she argued for policies that balanced individual opportunity with collective investment, earning praise from her peers for her nuanced approach.

Maria also started to apply these lessons to her personal life. At first, it felt unnatural to prioritize her own needs, but over time, she learned that self-care wasn't selfish. Setting boundaries didn't mean abandoning her compassion—it meant respecting herself as much as she respected others.

One pivotal moment came when Maria had to choose between helping organize a community fundraiser or preparing for an important academic competition. Torn, she sought her mother's advice. Helena surprised her by saying, "Maria, you've already done so much for the community. It's okay to choose yourself this time. Remember, you can't pour from an empty cup."

Maria chose the competition and excelled, realizing that pursuing personal goals could enhance her ability to help others in the long run. This decision marked a turning point in her Judgment Core, blending the values of self-advocacy with her deeply ingrained sense of empathy.

By 2008, Maria had become a leader within her school. Her peers admired her ability to balance ambition with compassion, blending assertiveness with inclusivity. She spearheaded a project that provided mentorship for underprivileged students, ensuring they had access to resources while also encouraging her classmates to contribute. Maria's leadership style was collaborative, yet firm—rooted in her belief that personal success and collective good could coexist.

Her interactions with James and others like him had reshaped her Judgment Core. She no longer saw self-interest as the enemy of compassion but as a tool that, when wielded responsibly, could complement her values. Maria understood that morality wasn't about choosing one approach over another but about finding harmony between seemingly opposing principles.

Maria's journey illustrates the transformative power of stepping beyond the confines of one's upbringing. Her parents' teachings laid the foundation of her moral compass, but it was her exposure to diverse perspectives that refined it. Through her experiences, Maria discovered that the values we are taught at home are not immutable truths but starting points for a lifelong process of growth and understanding.

Today, Maria works as an advocate for educational reform in São Paulo, blending her passion for community welfare with the assertiveness she learned to embrace. Her story is a testament to the importance of challenging our beliefs, listening to others, and allowing our Judgment Core to evolve as we encounter new ideas and experiences.

The Unraveling of Entitlement: Tommy's Journey

Cambridge, England, 2004. It was a chilly autumn morning in Cambridge when ten-year-old Tommy stood by the bay window of his family's sprawling estate. He watched as their housekeeper, Mrs. Hale, meticulously tended to the flowerbeds in the garden. "She's diligent, isn't she?" Tommy remarked innocently to his father, William, who sipped his morning tea with the poised air of a man who believed the world revolved around him.

"She's doing what she's paid to do, son," William replied with a dismissive wave. "People like her exist to serve people like us. Remember, Tommy, we are better than them. It's in our blood."

This was not the first time Tommy had heard such words. William, a man steeped in the traditions of Britain's upper class, had built his identity around notions of social superiority. To him, wealth and lineage were not just markers of success—they were the foundation of moral worth. From as early as Tommy could remember, his father reinforced the idea that they were inherently better than others due to their "superior heritage."

By the time Tommy was 12, he had absorbed these teachings into his very being. He treated his schoolmates from modest backgrounds with disdain, dismissing them as unworthy of his attention. At the prestigious private school he attended, he refused to collaborate with peers whose parents weren't business executives or aristocrats.

This sense of entitlement also extended to his interactions at home. The gardener, Mr. Finch, was invisible to Tommy, and he mimicked his father by never acknowledging the man's presence. The housekeeper, Mrs. Hale, was spoken to only when Tommy needed something. He viewed the staff not as individuals but as tools, a perspective that his father fostered at every turn.

In 2012, Tommy's world shifted dramatically. At 18, he enrolled in a new school in London, renowned for its academic rigor and diverse student body. Unlike the insular environment of his previous schools, this institution was a melting pot of cultures and social classes. Here, Tommy met Javier, a quiet but confident student from a modest background. Javier's father was a mechanic, and his mother worked in a small café—facts that initially made Tommy view him with disdain.

Their first encounter was during a group project. Tommy, accustomed to taking control, attempted to assert dominance, expecting Javier to fall in line. But Javier was different. He didn't argue or fight back; instead, he calmly listened, contributed his ideas, and encouraged others to do the same. Tommy noticed how others in the group respected Javier—not for his background, but for his ability to foster collaboration and elevate everyone's contributions.

One day, Tommy faced a challenge that exposed the cracks in his confidence. A particularly complex math problem left him stumped during a study session. Javier, noticing Tommy's frustration, quietly offered his help. At first, Tommy hesitated, his pride urging him to reject the offer. But Javier's approach was disarming—there was no judgment or condescension, only a genuine desire to assist.

"Let's tackle this together," Javier said, his tone calm and encouraging. For the first time, Tommy felt a sense of equality he hadn't experienced before. Javier's kindness and intelligence stood in stark contrast to the values Tommy had been taught to admire.

That small act of kindness planted a seed of doubt in Tommy's mind. Over the weeks that followed, he found himself observing Javier more closely. Javier's humility, empathy, and quiet strength contradicted everything Tommy had been conditioned to believe about status and worth. He began to question his father's teachings, wondering if the "superiority" William so often spoke of was an illusion.

The realization came one evening as Tommy reflected on his interactions with Javier. He thought about how his father's lessons had shaped his worldview, turning him into someone who judged others based on wealth rather than character. For the first time, he felt ashamed—not of others, but of himself.

By 2014, Tommy's perspective had shifted dramatically. As he prepared for university, he actively sought out diverse friendships, engaging with classmates he would have dismissed just a few years earlier. He discovered that many of them possessed talents, insights, and perspectives that enriched his life in ways he hadn't thought possible.

Tommy's encounters at his new school reshaped his Judgment Core (JDC), the internal compass that guided his moral decisions. Where his father's teachings had once been the foundation of his JDC—rigid, elitist, and dismissive—his experiences with Javier introduced empathy, respect, and the recognition of intrinsic human value.

This transformation wasn't instantaneous, nor was it easy. Tommy struggled to reconcile the conflicting lessons of his upbringing. But as he interacted with people from different walks of life, he realized that true worth lies not in status but in character.

In the years that followed, Tommy made a conscious effort to challenge the biases ingrained in him. He acknowledged the privilege of his upbringing but rejected the entitlement that had come with it. When he returned home to visit, he treated the staff with a newfound respect, engaging with them as equals rather than subordinates.

William, however, remained unyielding in his views. "You've gone soft," he remarked one day when Tommy helped Mrs. Hale carry a heavy basket of laundry. But Tommy no longer sought his father's approval. His Judgment Core, once shaped by his father's narrow worldview, had evolved into something broader, kinder, and truer.

1.4 Conclusion: The Purity of Beginnings – Childhood and Parental Influence

A young child sits at the kitchen table, watching a parent quietly slip a few extra bills from the household jar. "Don't tell anyone, "The parent says with a wink. "This is our little secret."

The child doesn't question it. They smile, feeling trusted. What they've just learned isn't about money—it's about morality. About loyalty over truth. Silence over integrity. And just like that, a new path is drawn on the child's inner map—the one we call the Judgment Core.

We are all handed a map in childhood. Drawn by the hands of those who raised us, it is shaped by their beliefs, limitations, fears, and hopes. At first, we trust it completely. We walk its roads believing they are the only way.

But as we grow, we begin to encounter roads unmarked, landscapes that challenge the outlines we inherited. And we are left wondering:

Was the map ever complete? Was it ever fully ours?

This is where the Judgment Core begins to awaken—not as a set of fixed instructions, but as a living, breathing guide that demands reflection.

Upbringing can be grounding—or confining. For some, it instills resilience. For others, it imposes invisible limits. What matters is not just what we were taught—but whether we've examined it.

- Can you remember the first time something you were taught as "right" didn't feel that way?

- Are you still carrying values that have never been tested, only inherited?

- Have you ever found yourself defending an idea, not because it aligns with your beliefs—but because it's familiar?

Sometimes, what we call "instinct" is merely repetition. And what we call "truth" is just a comfortable echo.

To question your upbringing is not disloyal—it is brave. It honors your early lessons while allowing them to evolve.

Picture yourself standing on a narrow bridge.

On one side: the values you were given.

On the other: the person you are becoming.

Below lies uncertainty—questions, conflict, maybe even loss. But ahead lies clarity. Growth. A morality crafted by reflection, not repetition.

Your Judgment Core is not a fixed inheritance. It is a framework that can—and must—be reshaped.

So now, the moment turns inward. Ask yourself:

- What beliefs do you hold today that were never yours to begin with?

- Which parts of your moral compass have you never questioned?

- Are you willing to release teachings that no longer serve your evolving self?

- Do you follow your Judgment Core—or simply follow tradition?

And most importantly:

Are you the author of your values… or the custodian of someone else's?

This isn't an ending—it's an invitation.

You were given a map. But now, the world has changed.

And so can you.

Will you follow paths drawn for you, or will you take the pen and redraw the lines?

The compass you inherited was only the beginning.

Where it points next is entirely up to you.

So ask yourself:

Is your Judgment Core guiding your future… or guarding your past?

The answer doesn't lie in what you were taught.

It lives in what you choose—starting now.

Chapter 2: Community Influence – The Wider Family

You're walking through a bustling marketplace in a town you have never visited before. The scent of fresh spices lingers in the air, voices rise and fall in an unfamiliar rhythm, and every action around you follows an unspoken order—where to walk, how to greet a stranger, even the proper way to exchange money. At first, you mimic what you see, blending into the crowd without questioning why things are done a certain way. But then, a moment of hesitation: You witness an elderly vendor being shortchanged, yet no one intervenes. You pause, unsure— is this an accepted practice here, or is it simply something people have stopped questioning?

This is the silent power of community. It teaches, shapes, and directs our sense of right and wrong—sometimes without us even realizing it. From the moment we step beyond our family home, we are absorbed into a broader collective, a world of shared customs, expectations, and unspoken rules. Communities act as extended families, larger networks that provide structure, belonging, and identity. But just as they offer support and a sense of purpose, they also imprint their biases, traditions, and moral contradictions onto us.

Now, ask yourself: How much of your moral compass was crafted by the community around you? Do you live by its values because they align with your true beliefs, or because they were handed down to you as unquestioned truths? Communities create a framework for what is considered "acceptable," but does that mean they are always right?

History is filled with examples of communities normalizing practices that later generations would condemn. Slavery, discrimination, unjust laws—all were once upheld by societies that believed them to be morally justified. But at the same time, communities have also been the birthplace of great moral revolutions, challenging outdated norms and forging new paths toward justice.

So, where do you stand?

- Have you ever followed a rule simply because "that's just how it's always been done"?

- What happens when your personal values clash with the expectations of your community?

- Do you have the courage to challenge a norm that no longer serves justice, or do you accept it to avoid conflict?

This chapter will explore the unseen forces that shape your Judgment Core (JDC)—not just through your family's influence, but through the collective voice of the community. It is a voice that can either guide you toward wisdom or trap you in unquestioned conformity. Will you listen, challenge, or redefine it? The choice is yours, but the answer will determine more than just your actions—it will shape the very foundation of your moral compass.

2.1 The Mysterious Power of Collective Norms

From the moment we step beyond the threshold of our family homes, we enter a vast and intricate web of societal expectations—a world where unseen threads of collective norms silently guide our actions and choices. These norms, woven together by schools, religious institutions, peer groups, and the communities we inhabit, act as both compass and constraint. But what are these norms really? Are they rules meant to unite and protect, or invisible chains that shape us without our consent?

The power of collective norms is undeniable. They are not arbitrary; they are designed to foster cooperation, maintain order, and uphold the shared values that bind communities together. Yet their influence is subtle, creeping into our lives through unspoken rules and age-old traditions. Have you ever questioned how deeply these norms shape your own Judgment Core (JDC) and moral compass?

Consider this real-life example:

In the highlands of Papua New Guinea, the Fore people once practiced endocannibalism—ritualistically consuming the bodies of deceased relatives. This custom wasn't rooted in violence or malice but in love, honor, and spiritual connection. It was believed that consuming the dead allowed their essence and wisdom to live on within the family. For generations, this practice was normal, sacred, and unchallenged.

It was only later, when researchers discovered that the ritual was spreading the fatal disease kuru, that the community began to question its morality. But this raises a profound ethical question:

If no one believed it was wrong at the time, was it truly immoral?

And what current practices do we accept today—simply because our communities say they are right?

This is the unsettling power of norms: they can cloak even the most controversial behaviors in moral acceptability when reinforced by tradition and belonging.

Schools often serve as the first architects of these societal rules, crafting lessons that extend far beyond the curriculum. In the classroom, students learn about honesty, teamwork, and the consequences of their actions on others. Through group projects, playground dynamics, and even the enforcement of seemingly minor rules, children begin to understand the value of respect, fairness, and collaboration. Schools prepare individuals not just for academic success but for integration into the broader social fabric. But do they also unwittingly plant the seeds of conformity, teaching us to prioritize compliance over questioning?

Religious institutions add another layer to this tapestry, offering moral frameworks that have endured for centuries. Rituals like communal prayers, festivals, and acts of charity do more than reinforce faith—they embed virtues such as compassion, humility, and selflessness. These shared experiences create a profound sense of belonging, reminding individuals that their moral choices ripple through a larger collective. But when tradition clashes with evolving societal values, do these institutions adapt, or do they anchor us to outdated practices?

And then there are social circles—the informal but potent shapers of behavior. Peers set unspoken standards, teaching lessons about loyalty, kindness, and the cost of betrayal. Peer approval becomes a powerful force, often stronger than explicit rules, guiding individuals to align with the values of their group. Have you ever wondered how much of your moral compass is genuinely yours, and how much has been sculpted by the silent influence of your social circle?

While collective norms foster unity and identity, they also have a darker side. They can perpetuate biases, enforce conformity at the expense of individuality, and uphold practices that no longer serve the common good. Consider norms that silence dissent, marginalize minorities, or prioritize tradition over progress. How often do we blindly follow these norms, mistaking them for immutable truths?

Even in the mundane—attending a communal meal or public gathering—implicit rules guide our behavior. We share food, speak politely, and engage respectfully, all without questioning why. These practices reinforce values like generosity and cooperation, but they also lull us into accepting the status quo. Do we ever pause to question whether the norms we follow still align with our evolving Judgment Core, or do we simply obey out of habit?

Collective norms shape not just individuals but entire communities. They provide structure and predictability, but they also carry the weight of generations, passing down both virtues and flaws. Their power lies in their subtlety, shaping our actions without our conscious awareness.

But here's the challenge: Are these norms still serving their purpose, or have they become relics of a time long past? Can you identify which norms enrich your moral compass and which distort it?

- When was the last time you questioned a tradition or expectation you've followed without thought?

- How do you distinguish between norms that foster unity and those that suppress individuality or perpetuate harm?

- What happens to your Judgment Core when you choose to defy a collective norm? Does it strengthen, or does it falter under the weight of disapproval?

The power of collective norms is as mysterious as it is profound. They shape us, define us, and bind us to one another. But their true influence is revealed only when we dare to question them. Will you take the path of least resistance, or will you challenge these unseen forces to ensure they align with your evolving sense of justice and morality?

The choice, as always, is yours—but the impact of that choice will ripple far beyond you

While parents lay the foundation of the JDC, communities act as sculptors, chiseling away at this core with cultural norms, traditions, and societal expectations. The beliefs of those around us become benchmarks against which we measure our own values. Yet, the question arises:

Is the JDC being refined—or is it being overwritten?

Are we embracing morality, or merely inheriting it without question?

Let me know if you'd like this integrated into a document or formatted for a chapter layout.

The Secrets of Greenwood

Greenwood, Appalachia, Summer 1968. Tucked into a quiet valley surrounded by the dense, whispering forests of the Appalachian Mountains, Greenwood seemed like a town untouched by time. The cobblestone streets, lined with clapboard houses and painted shutters, exuded charm, and the locals prided themselves on their tight-knit community. It was a place where everyone knew each other's name and history. But Greenwood's beauty masked a peculiar tradition—one that would haunt young Ben Harris for the rest of his life.

Every summer, Greenwood came alive with its annual festival, a week-long celebration of history, unity, and shared values. The festival culminated in a grand parade, followed by a closing ceremony that was as old as the town itself: the outing.

On this night, under the light of lanterns strung across the town square, secrets were revealed. Any wrongdoing, indiscretion, or hidden truth was expected to be publicly disclosed. What had started in the 19th century as a way to encourage honesty had evolved into a spectacle that often bordered on cruel public shaming. The townspeople justified it as necessary for preserving integrity and trust, but for many, it was a source of dread.

Ben Harris, 15 years old in the summer of 1968, had grown up hearing stories of these outings. His father, Jack, a local carpenter, spoke of them with pride. "The outing keeps Greenwood honest," Jack often said, his voice heavy with conviction. "Secrets rot communities, son. Honesty cleanses us." Ben had believed this for as long as he could remember. It was the way of Greenwood, and who was he to question it?

That summer, Greenwood buzzed with anticipation as the festival approached. Ben spent most of his days with his closest friend, Sarah Wilkes. The two had been inseparable since they were children, exploring the woods, building forts, and dreaming about the future. But one afternoon, as they sat by the riverbank skipping stones, Sarah's usual lively demeanor seemed subdued.

"Ben," she began hesitantly, "I need to tell you something." She explained, her voice trembling, how she had broken a window at the town library while playing with her younger brother. She hadn't meant to do it, but fear of punishment had kept her silent. "Promise me you won't tell anyone," she pleaded, her blue eyes wide with worry.

Ben nodded solemnly, though unease crept into his chest. Sarah's secret conflicted with everything he'd been taught about the importance of transparency. Over the next few days, the weight of her confession gnawed at him. Could he keep this secret without betraying the values his parents and the town had instilled in him? Or would his silence make him complicit?

The night of the outing arrived. Lanterns swayed in the summer breeze as townsfolk gathered in the square. Ben's heart pounded as he sat with his parents, who watched the proceedings with solemn approval. One by one, people stepped forward to confess their missteps—lost tools returned late, debts unpaid, small arguments aired for all to see.

As the ceremony continued, Ben's mind raced. He glanced at Sarah, who stood with her family across the square, her shoulders stiff with tension. Torn between loyalty to his friend and the town's unyielding moral code, Ben's pulse quickened. It's for the greater good, he told himself, rising to his feet.

When he revealed Sarah's secret, his voice wavered, but the crowd erupted. Gasps and murmurs rippled through the square. Sarah's face crumpled in disbelief, her cheeks flushed with humiliation. Her parents looked stricken. What Ben had thought would be a brief moment of catharsis turned into a torrent of whispers and judgment. The betrayal etched itself into Sarah's eyes, and Ben knew, even before the ceremony ended, that their friendship was over.

The following days were unbearable. Sarah avoided Ben, and her parents refused to meet his gaze in town. For the first time, Ben felt the outing's true weight—not as a tool of integrity, but as a weapon of shame. The ceremony, which he had revered, now seemed cruel and misguided.

That summer, Ben's once-unquestioned belief in Greenwood's traditions began to crumble. He realized that the outing didn't foster trust; it bred fear and resentment. People didn't confess their secrets willingly—they did so out of dread, knowing their neighbors would expose them if they didn't. The practice fractured relationships instead of strengthening them, creating wounds that never fully healed.

As Ben grew older, he reflected on the experience with growing clarity. By the 1970s, when he moved to a nearby city for college, his view of Greenwood had transformed. He began to study how communities shape their values, questioning the blind adherence to traditions that seemed noble on the surface but caused harm in practice.

Ben came to understand that his Judgment Core—his internal moral compass—had been shaped by Greenwood's rigid norms. But that summer had also sparked its evolution. He realized that morality wasn't about unwavering loyalty to rules or traditions. True morality required empathy, critical thinking, and the courage to challenge harmful practices, even when they were deeply ingrained.

Years later, Ben would return to Greenwood, not as a participant in the outing but as a quiet observer. He watched as the tradition continued, though its participants seemed fewer with each passing year. The town remained picturesque, but the shadows of its rituals lingered. Ben's heart ached for the friendships and trust that had been lost to the outing over generations.

Ben's story is a reminder that community norms, no matter how well-intentioned, must be scrutinized. Traditions like Greenwood's outing may claim to uphold integrity but can often mask deeper issues of control and fear. For Ben, the loss of his friendship with Sarah became a turning point—a painful but necessary step toward developing a more nuanced and empathetic Judgment Core.

In the end, Ben learned that honesty, while essential, should never come at the expense of kindness or trust. And as he walked the streets of Greenwood one last time, he hoped that future generations would have the courage to forge a more compassionate path.

2.2 The Mysterious Shadows of Normalization

Imagine a world where the unthinkable is commonplace, where acts that might seem abhorrent from an external perspective are accepted without question. How does this happen? How do communities, sometimes over generations, turn the unethical into the ordinary? This is the power—and peril—of normalization. It shapes not only individual choices but the very Judgment Core (JDC) of entire societies, embedding harmful practices so deeply into the fabric of daily life that they become invisible.

Normalization operates like a slow, creeping shadow, blurring the line between what is and what ought to be. It is a mechanism so powerful that it can transform the collective conscience of a community, reshaping moral compasses to align with practices that might, under different circumstances, be recognized as deeply harmful or unjust. But who decides what becomes normal, and what happens when the status quo is a cage?

When a behavior is normalized, it ceases to feel like a choice; instead, it is perceived as the natural order of things. People follow these norms not out of conviction, but because they have been conditioned to believe that deviation is unthinkable—or even dangerous. This creates moral blind spots, where individuals and communities fail to question practices that perpetuate harm.

The danger is clear: once a behavior is normalized, it gains a shield of resistance. Even in the face of overwhelming evidence of harm, these practices persist, defended by tradition, necessity, or fear of change. Have you ever wondered how many of your beliefs or actions are shaped not by conscious choice but by the invisible force of normalization?

Throughout history, some of the gravest injustices have thrived under the shadow of normalization. Consider slavery, a practice that once permeated societies across the globe. For centuries, it was justified through false narratives of economic necessity and racial superiority. Entire legal and cultural systems were built around it, reinforcing its acceptance. It took centuries of struggle, war, and moral reckoning to begin dismantling slavery's grip—but its scars remain, a haunting reminder of how normalized harm leaves a legacy that echoes through time.

Or take the chilling practices of human sacrifice in ancient cultures. For some, the ritualistic killing of others was seen as essential to appease gods, secure harvests, or ward off calamity. These acts, incomprehensible to modern sensibilities, were deeply rooted in the cultural and spiritual norms of the time. The unquestioned acceptance of such practices highlights how normalization can cloak even the most extreme behaviors in a shroud of righteousness.

Closer to the present, the caste system in certain societies exemplifies how normalization can institutionalize discrimination. Caste-based hierarchies, often justified by religious and social traditions, have inflicted systemic exclusion and suffering on millions. Despite legal reforms and advocacy, the remnants of these normalized injustices persist, reminding us how deeply such beliefs can be entrenched in collective consciousness.

But normalization isn't confined to the past or to distant cultures—it thrives in today's world as well. Look at corporate exploitation: unfair labor practices, environmental destruction, and the prioritization of profit over well-being are often accepted as "just the way things are." Rationalized through economic pressures or competitive markets, these practices desensitize us to their human and environmental costs.

Have you ever paused to consider how often you accept such realities as inevitable? Are we complicit in perpetuating cycles of harm simply because they have become the norm?

The power of normalization lies in its subtlety, in the way it operates unnoticed by those it affects. It silences dissent, marginalizes challengers, and creates a self-sustaining cycle that resists change. But cycles can be broken.

The first step is awareness—a willingness to shine a light on the shadows of normalized practices. Education is a vital tool in this process, offering diverse perspectives and encouraging critical thinking. By understanding historical contexts and engaging in ethical reasoning, individuals can begin to see the cracks in the facade of normalized behaviors.

Empathy is equally essential. It allows us to step outside our own experiences and understand the impact of normalized practices on those who are marginalized or harmed. When we see beyond the comfortable veil of "this is how things are," we begin to ask the deeper, harder questions:

- What practices have I accepted without question?

- Do the norms I follow align with my moral compass, or have I been conditioned to ignore their harm?

- What am I willing to risk to challenge what others consider normal?

The danger of normalization is not just its ability to obscure the truth, but its capacity to make us complicit in harm without even realizing it. It is a silent force that shapes not only our actions but our beliefs, binding us to the status quo.

But here's the mystery: what else might be hidden in plain sight, normalized by the world around you? Are you prepared to question what you've been taught to accept? And if you uncover an unsettling truth, will you have the courage to challenge it—or will you let the shadow of normalization continue to define what is right and just?

The answers lie not in what has been normalized, but in your willingness to see beyond the surface and align your Judgment Core with the principles of fairness, empathy, and justice. Are you ready to ask the uncomfortable questions and confront the world as it is—not as you've been conditioned to see it?

The Silent Revolution of Kalira

Kalira, Northern India, 1925. In the shadow of the Himalayan foothills lay the secluded village of Kalira, shrouded in mist and ancient traditions. A cluster of stone houses with sloping roofs encircled the village square, where life ebbed and flowed in a rhythm unchanged for centuries. But beneath its serene exterior, Kalira hid a darker reality: a tradition that ostracized certain families, marking them as "impure" and barring them from the heart of village life.

For Meera Devi, a 12-year-old girl from one of these excluded families, the weight of this tradition was all too familiar. Her family's home, at the edge of the village, bore a faded symbol etched into the stone above the door—a mark that set them apart. She had never been invited to a festival, and at school, her classmates whispered behind her back, ensuring her solitude. The elders, with their flowing robes and stern faces, claimed these customs protected the village's purity and prosperity. To Meera, this was simply the way of the world.

In the summer of 1928, on a dusty afternoon, Meera's father, Shyam, returned from a trip to the nearby city of Dehradun. In his hands, he carried something forbidden but precious: books. Meera's father, though burdened by tradition, had always believed in the power of knowledge. These books spoke of equality, dignity, and justice—concepts alien to Kalira but intoxicating to Meera.

By the dim light of an oil lamp, Meera devoured the stories and ideas within those pages. She read of leaders and thinkers who challenged societal norms, of communities that valued character over lineage. Each word chipped away at the foundation of beliefs she had been taught. For the first time, Meera began to see her family's treatment not as fate but as an injustice.

In the spring of 1930, Kalira received a visitor who would change the course of its history. A man from the city, dressed in simple khadi clothes, arrived carrying only a small bag and a voice full of conviction. He introduced himself as Ramesh, a teacher and advocate for social reform. The elders reluctantly allowed him to speak in the village square, and the entire community gathered to hear him.

Ramesh spoke of unity, fairness, and the need to rise above divisions. "We cannot prosper as a society if we deny dignity to some while elevating others," he said, his voice ringing clear against the mountains. Meera stood at the edge of the crowd, her heart racing. His words echoed the ideas she had read about, and for the first time, she saw a glimmer of possibility: her village could change.

After the speech, Meera approached Ramesh, her small frame trembling with both fear and excitement. "How can someone like me make a difference?" she asked. Ramesh knelt to her level, his expression kind but resolute. "Change begins with a voice willing to speak the truth," he said. "Even in the face of resistance."

Inspired by Ramesh, Meera began speaking out against the exclusionary practices of Kalira. Her first act of defiance was small but symbolic: she invited a group of children, including her ostracized cousins, to share a meal in her family's courtyard. The act sent ripples through the village. While some parents forbade their children from attending, others allowed it out of curiosity. Meera's small rebellion did not go unnoticed by the elders.

Word spread quickly, and the backlash was swift. Elders visited her home, warning her father that Meera's behavior threatened the village's harmony. But Shyam, emboldened by his daughter's courage, stood firm. "What kind of harmony comes from division?" he asked. His defiance only deepened the tension in the village.

Despite the growing resistance, Meera continued her efforts. She spoke to her classmates, shared her books with curious neighbors, and sought out others who questioned the status quo. Over time, she won a few quiet supporters—young people like herself who dared to dream of a different Kalira.

In the winter of 1935, Meera finally had her chance to confront the village council. Standing before the elders in the dimly lit hall, she held her books tightly against her chest. Her voice, though shaky at first, grew steady as she spoke of fairness and unity. She quoted passages from ancient texts that emphasized compassion and justice, countering the elders' claims that their practices were rooted in tradition. She argued that true prosperity came not from exclusion but from the strength of a united community.

The council room fell silent. The elders exchanged uneasy glances. For the first time, the immovable wall of tradition seemed to waver. Then, something unexpected happened: a young farmer named Ravi stood up. "Meera is right," he said, his voice firm. "These practices do more harm than good. It's time we let them go."

One by one, others joined him. The momentum grew, and by the end of the meeting, the council reluctantly agreed to abolish the ritualistic exclusion. It was not an overnight transformation, but it was a beginning.

In the years that followed, Kalira slowly shed its old ways. Families once marked as "impure" began to participate in festivals and gatherings. Children who had grown up as outcasts now sat side by side with their peers in school. The change was not without its challenges, but it was undeniable.

Meera's journey had not just transformed her village—it had reshaped her own Judgment Core. Once rooted in acceptance of the status quo, her moral compass had evolved into something stronger, guided by principles of fairness and empathy. She realized that the values she had been taught were not immutable truths but constructs that could—and should—be challenged when they caused harm.

By the 1940s, Meera had become a respected teacher, dedicating her life to spreading the lessons she had learned. She often spoke of Kalira's transformation, not as her triumph, but as an example of what could happen when people chose courage over complacency.

The mark above her family's door had long since faded, replaced by the warmth of neighbors who had once turned away. Kalira itself became a symbol of change, proof that even the most entrenched traditions could be rewritten by those brave enough to question them.

Meera's story remains a powerful testament to the strength of an individual's Judgment Core when nurtured by knowledge and compassion. It is a reminder that while community norms can shape us, they do not define us—and that true progress begins with the willingness to ask: Is this the best we can be?

2.3 The Dance of Independence and Conformity

Imagine standing at a crossroads where two powerful forces pull you in opposite directions: the comforting embrace of conformity and the daring call of independence. This is not merely a choice of behavior but a profound struggle of the soul, a tension that shapes the Judgment Core (JDC)—the internal compass guiding our moral and ethical decisions. How do you navigate this delicate balance? And how often do you silence your inner voice to blend into the crowd?

From our earliest days, conformity promises safety, belonging, and identity. As children, we learn quickly that adhering to group norms earns us acceptance, while deviation often invites rejection or ridicule. In the classroom, for example, students may mimic the attitudes or prejudices of their peers to avoid being ostracized. At home, the subtle pressure to align with family values reinforces this lesson: fitting in equates to approval.

But what happens when this instinct to conform demands a betrayal of our personal values? How often do we act against our beliefs, telling ourselves that blending in is easier than standing apart?

Conformity is not inherently wrong. It weaves the fabric of communities, fostering cooperation and shared identity. Yet, its shadow lies in the suppression of authenticity. The cost of belonging can be high when it demands silence in the face of injustice or complicity in behaviors that conflict with one's moral compass.

This creates a dissonance—a quiet, gnawing discomfort as outward actions clash with inner convictions. Have you ever felt that unsettling tug, knowing that the path you're on aligns with the group but not with yourself?

Adolescence and early adulthood often spark a rebellion against conformity, a period of questioning and exploration. It is during these years that the inner voice grows louder, challenging the norms we once accepted without question. Alternative viewpoints beckon, offering glimpses of a broader world and a chance to realign with values that feel uniquely ours.

But independence is not a rejection of all that we inherit; it is a refining process. It requires courage to selectively adopt the values that resonate and discard those that don't. True independence lies not in isolation but in the ability to stand firm in one's beliefs while remaining open to growth.

Choosing independence often comes at a cost. The road is strewn with disapproval, subtle alienation, or even outright rejection. Communities value cohesion, and stepping outside the accepted boundaries can mark you as a disruptor. Yet, the strength of one's convictions is tested in these moments. Are you willing to face the storm to remain true to your moral compass? Or will you retreat into the comfort of conformity, leaving your authenticity behind?

The journey between independence and conformity is not about choosing one over the other but about mastering the dance between them. There are moments to align with communal norms for harmony and moments to assert independence for integrity. This dynamic balance shifts over time, molded by experience, reflection, and growth.

What happens when you find the courage to redefine the values you've inherited? How do your actions shape not just your Judgment Core, but also the collective norms of your community?

The interplay between independence and conformity is not a one-way street. When individuals challenge outdated norms or uphold values that inspire others, they contribute to the evolution of their community's moral landscape. In this way, the act of forging an independent moral compass becomes a transformative force, shaping not just the individual but the collective as well.

So, where do you stand?

- Do you conform to the values of your community out of conviction, or out of fear of rejection?

- Have you silenced your inner voice to fit into a mold that feels foreign to your true self?

- When faced with the tension between belonging and authenticity, how often do you choose the latter?

The struggle for independence and conformity is an eternal dance—one that challenges us to question, to grow, and to redefine. It is through this tension that we refine not just our own Judgment Core but also the moral fabric of the world around us. Will you accept the norms you've inherited, or will you dare to challenge them, knowing that your choices shape more than just your life—they shape the collective conscience of your time?

Aria's Choice: The Scientist Who Defied Tradition

Soleto, Southern Italy, 1999. In the small, sun-soaked town of Soleto, nestled in the olive-strewn hills of southern Italy, tradition ran deeper than the roots of its ancient trees. Soleto was a place where families gathered under terracotta rooftops to share stories, recipes, and values passed down for generations. For young women like Aria Bellucci, life followed a well-trodden path: marriage, children, and devotion to the household.

At 17, Aria already felt the weight of expectations. Her mother, Bianca, often reminded her, "A woman's strength is in her family, Aria. There's no greater purpose." Her father, Lorenzo, echoed these sentiments, proud of his family's adherence to tradition. Yet, Aria's heart longed for something more. Beneath her quiet demeanor lay a fierce curiosity about the world beyond Soleto's cobbled streets. She excelled in school, often surprising her teachers with her aptitude for science. Her room, cluttered with dog-eared books on biology and physics, was a testament to dreams that stretched far beyond the town's borders.

By 2001, the clash between Aria's ambitions and her community's expectations reached a tipping point. That spring, she received a scholarship offer from a prestigious university in Rome to study biology. The news arrived in a crisp envelope that smelled faintly of ink and hope. For Aria, it was a promise of freedom, of stepping into the future she had always envisioned. But the joy of acceptance was shadowed by fear.

Bianca's face fell when Aria shared the news. "Rome?" she whispered, the word heavy with disapproval. "What good can come from leaving your family? Your place is here, Aria. You have responsibilities." Her father's silence was even worse, a quiet storm brewing in his eyes.

The village murmured about her scholarship as though it were a scandal. "She's chasing selfish dreams," one elder scoffed at the market. "It's a betrayal of her roots," another added. Yet not everyone dismissed her ambition. Nonna Rosa, her grandmother, pulled Aria aside one evening. "You remind me of myself when I was your age," she said, her wrinkled hands clutching Aria's. "But I didn't have the chance you do. Follow your heart, child. The world is bigger than Soleto."

With her grandmother's words echoing in her mind, Aria made her decision. On a warm September morning in 2001, she boarded a train to Rome, carrying little more than a suitcase and the hopes she dared to nurture. As the hills of Soleto faded into the distance, Aria felt a mix of exhilaration and loss. She knew her departure marked more than a geographical shift—it was a fracture in the life her family and community had mapped out for her.

In Rome, Aria found herself awash in a sea of new ideas. The bustling streets, lined with ancient ruins and modern cafes, reflected the coexistence of tradition and progress. At university, she met people from different walks of life, each with their own stories, beliefs, and aspirations. The rigid notions of gender roles she had grown up with began to feel like relics of another time. For the first time, Aria encountered women pursuing careers, challenging norms, and living lives untethered from convention.

Yet, the transition wasn't seamless. Aria grappled with guilt and loneliness, especially during holidays when she remained in Rome while her family gathered in Soleto. Letters from her mother often carried a bittersweet tone, filled with updates on the town and subtle reminders of what Aria was missing. "The Ferragosto festival wasn't the same without you," Bianca wrote in one letter. "But I suppose your studies keep you busy."

The disapproval of her parents and community weighed heavily on Aria's mind. At times, she questioned whether she had made the right choice. But as she delved deeper into her studies, her doubts began to fade. She realized her passion for science wasn't just a career aspiration—it was part of who she was. The more she learned, the more she felt aligned with her true self.

By 2003, Aria began to see her upbringing in a new light. The values of her small town—loyalty, family, and tradition—had their merits, but she also saw how these norms could stifle individuality and limit opportunities. Her Judgment Core (JDC), the internal compass guiding her decisions, began to evolve. She no longer accepted Soleto's values as absolute truths but as one lens through which to view the world. Rome offered her another lens, one that valued personal freedom, intellectual exploration, and gender equality.

Aria's journey wasn't about rejecting her roots; it was about integrating the best of both worlds. She learned to appreciate the strength her family had instilled in her while also embracing the independence she discovered in the city. Her new moral compass was more nuanced, balancing respect for tradition with a commitment to personal growth.

In 2006, armed with her biology degree and a newfound sense of purpose, Aria returned to Soleto for the first time since leaving. Her arrival was met with mixed reactions. Some villagers still viewed her as a renegade, while others—especially the younger generation—saw her as an inspiration. Her father greeted her stiffly but with a glimmer of pride in his eyes. "You've changed, Aria," he said, his voice gruff. "But maybe that's not a bad thing."

Aria used her education to bring something back to her community. She worked on local agricultural projects, helping farmers adopt sustainable practices to protect their olive groves. Over time, even the staunchest critics began to acknowledge her contributions. She had not abandoned her roots; she had enriched them.

Aria's story is one of transformation—not just of herself but of those around her. She proved that challenging norms doesn't mean rejecting them outright but reexamining them to create space for growth and progress. Her journey reshaped her Judgment Core, teaching her that morality isn't static but a dynamic interplay between tradition and individuality.

By forging her own path, Aria became a beacon for others in Soleto. She inspired young girls to dream beyond the confines of their small town, showing them that independence and community could coexist. Her legacy lives on in the olive groves of Soleto and the hearts of those who dare to ask: What if there's more?

2.4 The Dual Nature of Community Influence: A Mirror or a Mask?

Communities—vibrant, interconnected webs of shared stories, traditions, and values—shape us in ways we often fail to notice. They are sanctuaries of belonging, teaching us the language of solidarity, justice, and empathy. But beneath their comforting embrace lies a duality, a shadowy complexity that challenges the very fabric of our Judgment Core (JDC)—the internal compass guiding our sense of right and wrong. Are communities the mirrors that reflect our highest ideals, or are they masks that obscure our moral clarity?

At their best, communities are beacons of unity and purpose. They rally together in crises, remind us of the power of collective action, and foster an environment where individuals feel valued and protected. In these moments, communities illuminate the potential of human connection, reinforcing values of mutual respect and shared responsibility.

Picture a neighborhood coming together after a natural disaster, rebuilding homes and spirits side by side. The unity in such acts reflects the profound good that communities can inspire. Through rituals, shared narratives, and collective goals, they teach us that we are stronger together, bound by threads of solidarity that transcend individual interests.

But what happens when the shadows of conformity and prejudice creep into this collective?

Communities are not always forces for good. Beneath their surface lies a quieter, more insidious influence—the pressure to conform, even when conformity demands the surrender of personal values. In communities rooted in exclusion, prejudice, or rigid traditions, the need to belong can become a trap, ensnaring individuals in a web of harmful ideologies.

Imagine a community that upholds discriminatory beliefs—where silence about injustice is praised as loyalty, and questioning the status quo is seen as betrayal. In such spaces, the warmth of belonging comes at a steep price: the suppression of critical thought and the silencing of moral instincts.

Have you ever felt the weight of this pressure, the tug-of-war between fitting in and staying true to yourself?

The power of communities lies in their ability to normalize behaviors—both noble and destructive. What begins as subtle alignment with communal values can grow into unquestioning acceptance of harmful practices. When unethical behaviors are cloaked in tradition or loyalty, they lose their sharpness, becoming part of the everyday fabric of life.

How often do we excuse injustice, not because we believe it is right, but because it has become routine? Think of systemic discrimination, corruption, or abuse that persists under the guise of tradition. When communities prioritize cohesion over ethical clarity, they create environments where dissent is stifled, and harmful norms are perpetuated.

Navigating the dual nature of community influence demands a careful, reflective approach. It requires the courage to examine the values we inherit, the wisdom to discern when conformity aligns with integrity, and the resilience to stand apart when it does not. This is no simple task. The pull of belonging is strong, and the cost of standing alone can be isolating.

But consider this: What happens when you accept community norms without question? Does your silence make you complicit in perpetuating harm? And when your Judgment Core whispers that something is wrong, will you have the courage to listen?

Communities offer strength, connection, and purpose, but they must be engaged with critically. True moral growth comes not from blind conformity but from a nuanced understanding of when to embrace communal values and when to challenge them.

- When does loyalty become complicity?

- How often do we trade authenticity for acceptance?

- Can we shape our communities to reflect our highest ideals, or will they shape us into reflections of their flaws?

The dual nature of community influence asks us to confront uncomfortable truths about the spaces we inhabit. Do your communities uplift your moral compass or obscure it? When faced with the choice between belonging and integrity, what will you choose?

Communities are powerful forces, capable of shaping the individual and the collective. But the ultimate responsibility lies with you. Will you let your community define your moral boundaries, or will you redefine them, ensuring that your Judgment Core remains your true guide?

The Silent Shift in Fairview:

In the picturesque town of Fairview, nestled in the rolling hills of the United Kingdom, life in the late 1990s seemed untouched by the currents of change. The townspeople prided themselves on their loyalty to tradition, an unspoken code that bound everyone together. Loyalty wasn't just a value; it was the foundation of Fairview's identity. Questioning the collective was not merely frowned upon—it was seen as betrayal.

Liam Walker, born and raised in this insular community, grew up with these values ingrained in every fiber of his being. From church sermons to school assemblies, the message was clear: belonging means conformity. In Fairview, loyalty meant protecting the community's traditions at all costs, even if it meant shutting out those who didn't fit the mold.

But the story of Fairview took an unexpected turn when Liam, a bright and curious young man, left his hometown in 2005 to attend the University of Edinburgh. There, amidst the cobblestone streets and ancient architecture, Liam encountered a world vastly different from Fairview. University life exposed him to a mosaic of cultures, ideas, and perspectives that made him question the moral foundation of his upbringing.

One particular class on social ethics altered the course of Liam's thinking. The professor, a sharp-eyed woman named Dr. Harriet Lane, led a discussion on groupthink and blind loyalty. She shared chilling historical examples, such as the Salem witch trials and McCarthyism, where communities, in their unwavering commitment to tradition, had committed grave injustices. These stories stirred something deep within Liam. For the first time, he saw shadows of his own community in these cautionary tales.

Dr. Lane posed a question that lingered in his mind long after the lecture ended: "What happens when loyalty to tradition blinds us to justice and compassion?" Liam began to wrestle with this question, seeing his hometown in a new, unsettling light.

In 2007, Liam returned to Fairview for a break. It was during this visit that the defining moment of his story unfolded. A town meeting was called to discuss a divisive issue: a proposal to allow an immigrant family to settle in Fairview. The family, fleeing hardship in their homeland, sought refuge in the quiet village. Yet, resistance to their arrival was strong.

The meeting hall buzzed with whispers of discontent as older residents voiced their opposition. "They don't share our traditions," one elder declared. "They'll change our way of life," said another. Their arguments, though cloaked in concern for the community, were laced with prejudice and fear of the unfamiliar.

Liam sat in the back row, the weight of his upbringing battling with his newfound understanding of inclusivity. The room felt stifling, but as the murmurs of agreement grew louder, Liam realized he could no longer remain silent. Gathering his courage, he stood up.

His voice, steady but resolute, broke the tense silence. "I know how important tradition is to Fairview," he began, "but tradition isn't meant to be a wall that shuts people out. It's meant to be a foundation that grows stronger as we build on it."

He spoke of the richness diversity could bring—new skills, fresh perspectives, and the chance to weave empathy into the fabric of Fairview's identity. "This family isn't here to take anything from us," he said. "They're asking for a chance to contribute, to share in what makes this town special."

His words hung in the air like an uninvited guest. Some faces were etched with discomfort, others with quiet contemplation. The elders whispered among themselves, their expressions resolute. But Liam noticed something in the eyes of the younger attendees: a glimmer of curiosity, a hint of agreement.

In the weeks following the meeting, Liam's boldness became the talk of the town. Though many resisted his perspective, others began to question the rigid norms that had defined Fairview for generations. For the first time, conversations about inclusivity and change began to surface.

The council eventually voted to allow the immigrant family to settle in Fairview. It was a narrow victory, but it signaled a shift in the town's collective mindset. The family's arrival sparked a cautious but hopeful dialogue about what it truly meant to belong in Fairview.

Liam's story is more than a tale of courage—it is a profound exploration of the Judgment Core (JDC) at work. His journey illustrates the tension between loyalty to one's community and the pursuit of higher ethical principles. The Judgment Core challenges us to ask:

- Fairness: Is our loyalty to tradition serving justice, or is it excluding those who seek acceptance?

- Empathy: Are we acting out of fear or compassion? Are we willing to see the humanity in those who are different from us?

- Accountability: Do our actions reflect the best of our community, or are we perpetuating harm under the guise of protecting it?

Liam's stand against the status quo not only shifted the moral compass of Fairview but also served as a reminder that true loyalty lies in challenging the community to grow, not in preserving its flaws.

The immigrant family's integration into Fairview was not without challenges, but it marked the beginning of a new chapter for the town. Over time, Fairview learned that embracing change did not erase its identity—it enriched it. Liam's courage to confront his community's fears and prejudices planted the seeds of a more inclusive future.

His story leaves us with a question to ponder: When faced with the choice between loyalty to tradition and the courage to challenge it, where does your Judgment Core guide you?

2.5 Conclusion: The Judgment Core and the Paradox of Belonging

You're sitting in a room filled with people you've known for years—family, friends, colleagues. A comment is made. It's unjust, maybe even cruel. You know it in your gut. Your heart beats faster. You want to speak, but something stops you. Not fear exactly—something deeper. Something like obligation. Loyalty. Belonging.

And just like that, you stay silent.

Not because you agree, but because you've been conditioned to protect the comfort of the group over the discomfort of truth.

That moment—subtle, invisible to others—was not about weakness. It was about programming. It was about your Judgment Core (JDC), the internal compass built not just by your thoughts, but by the collective voice of your community. And like so many before you, you followed it without even knowing whose voice was guiding you.

Communities shape us in ways that rarely announce themselves. Their beliefs seep in through the traditions we repeat, the silences we inherit, the stories we are told about "us" and "them." Over time, these collective codes imprint themselves onto our personal sense of right and wrong—sometimes without a single word of debate.

We think we are making free choices.

But are we?

Or are we simply echoing what we were taught, calling it conviction?

So now, the mirror turns inward.

- Which parts of your moral compass did you choose—and which parts were handed to you without question?

- What norms have you upheld simply because they offered safety in numbers?

- Have you ever disagreed quietly and conformed loudly?

- What if your silence has been interpreted as agreement?

- What does it mean to belong when that belonging requires self-betrayal?

Here is the paradox:

Communities offer love, safety, identity.

But they can also teach prejudice, reward conformity, and punish independent thought.

And so, the real question becomes:

If the communities that shaped you were flawed, what does that mean for the Judgment Core they helped build inside you?

Will you follow it blindly?

Or will you inspect its roots, test its truths, and revise where necessary?

Your Judgment Core is not a life sentence. It is a living framework—one you can update, realign, and reclaim.

You have inherited a map.

But you hold the pen now.

So ask yourself, and ask boldly:

- Will you let your community dictate your morality?

- Or will you dare to shape your Judgment Core by your own evolving truth?

The answers won't come easily. They're not meant to.

But the future of your moral self—the truest version of your compass—depends on whether you ask them at all.

And perhaps, just perhaps, your willingness to ask... is the beginning of real belonging.

- How does your government shape your beliefs—through genuine ethical guidance, or through silent conditioning?

By the end of this chapter, you may find that the government is not just a referee of morality—it is a player in the game, actively molding the boundaries of right and wrong. But the real question is: Do you trust it to be the final judge of your moral compass, or do you dare to question its authority? The answer may not be simple, but it will define not only the society you live in but the person you choose to be..

3.1 Laws: Society's Compass or a Political Tool?

Laws are more than a set of rules; they are society's attempt to articulate and enforce shared values. By defining acceptable behavior and prohibiting the unacceptable, laws provide a roadmap for navigating the complexities of daily life. Ideally, they protect fundamental rights, foster social order, and promote collective well-being. When fair and justly applied, laws act as a tangible reflection of a society's moral and ethical beliefs.

Beyond their role in ensuring compliance, laws also educate. They shape societal attitudes over time, setting norms that influence how people think and act. For example, laws that promote equality and prohibit discrimination do more than punish offenders—they gradually challenge biases, shift public perceptions, and encourage acceptance of marginalized groups. Through this process, laws become agents of moral evolution, expanding what society considers fair and just.

However, the effectiveness of laws in shaping morality hinges on their perceived fairness and alignment with the ethical standards of the people they govern. When laws are equitable and consistently enforced, they bolster trust and encourage adherence. Citizens are more likely to respect laws that resonate with their own sense of right and wrong.

On the other hand, when laws are seen as unjust, inconsistently applied, or driven by ulterior motives, they can erode public trust and breed moral dissonance. For instance, a law that benefits a privileged few while oppressing others challenges the legitimacy of the legal system, leading people to question whether legality truly equates to morality.

This disconnect between legal requirements and personal beliefs can create a complex landscape where individuals feel torn between obeying the law and following their conscience. This chapter will dissect such conflicts, highlighting the critical role governments play in either reinforcing or destabilizing the Judgment Core (JDC).

Laws do more than reflect society's current moral standards—they actively shape them. By codifying principles and enforcing accountability, laws can serve as a mirror of collective beliefs while also acting as a catalyst for progress. They balance individual freedoms with communal needs, offering a structured approach to resolving the inevitable conflicts that arise within a diverse society.

Take, for instance, landmark legislation that challenged entrenched inequalities or expanded civil liberties. These laws not only changed behaviors but also redefined societal values, illustrating the law's capacity to propel moral progress. This chapter will explore these examples in depth, examining how they influence the moral compass of individuals and communities alike.

In this chapter, we will conduct a comprehensive analysis of the intricate relationship between laws, governance, and morality. We will examine how governments and their legal frameworks influence the Judgment Core (JDC)—the internal system each person uses to navigate ethical dilemmas. We will delve into the following questions:

- How do laws shape societal norms and individual morals?

- When do laws align with ethical principles, and when do they diverge?

- What happens when the government's definition of right and wrong conflicts with personal or cultural beliefs?

Through historical examples, contemporary case studies, and philosophical reflections, this chapter aims to shed light on the government's role as both a guardian and a challenger of moral clarity.

In essence, laws occupy a unique and powerful position in the moral fabric of society. They are both a product of collective values and a mechanism for evolving them. However, their effectiveness depends on how well they align with the ethical aspirations of the people they govern.

As we unravel the complexities of this interplay, this chapter seeks to illuminate the profound and sometimes paradoxical influence of government and law on our moral compass. By understanding these dynamics, we can better navigate the gray areas of morality and strengthen the alignment of our Judgment Core (JDC) with principles of fairness, justice, and empathy.

Shadows of the Law:

The chill of a Cape Town morning in June 1950 seemed to bite deeper than usual, but Samuel Mokgale hardly noticed. The carpenter's hands were steady as he crafted an intricate wooden chair in his modest workshop in District Six. His young son, Peter, played nearby, his laughter blending with the hum of life in the vibrant, multiethnic community. It was a world of colors, sounds, and cultures, woven together by shared dreams and struggles.

Then came the notice—a single sheet of paper nailed to Samuel's front door. The words were cold and bureaucratic, but their meaning hit like a thunderclap: "Under the Group Areas Act of 1950, this area is now designated for white residents. You must vacate your property within 60 days."

Samuel read the notice twice, his heart sinking. He had heard rumors of the government's plans to segregate neighborhoods, but he had dismissed them as distant political talk. Now, it was here, in his home, in his life. Within weeks, the Mokgales were forced to leave the bustling streets of District Six for Langa Township, a barren settlement on the edge of Cape Town. Their new home was a hastily built shack, with no electricity, no running water, and no promise of better days.

Peter, once full of laughter, grew quiet in Langa. The vibrant community he had known was gone, replaced by overcrowded shacks and dusty streets. Samuel tried to reassure his family, but the weight of displacement hung heavy. It wasn't just the physical hardship; it was the cruel message etched into the law—that their presence in District Six was not just unwanted but illegal, as if they were intruders in their own land.

The years rolled on, and the apartheid government tightened its grip. In 1953, another blow came in the form of the Bantu Education Act. In Soweto, a young girl named Thandiwe Ndlovu sat in a dimly lit classroom, her hands clutching a tattered schoolbook. She dreamed of becoming a doctor, imagining herself treating the sick and bringing hope to her community. But her dreams were not part of the government's plans.

Thandiwe's school curriculum was abruptly changed. Math and science lessons disappeared, replaced by rote teachings on household chores and manual labor. The government's justification was clear and chilling: "The black man must be trained to serve." Thandiwe's teachers, underpaid and demoralized, did their best to resist. Some slipped books into her hands after class, whispering, "Read this when you can." But the system was unyielding, designed to keep her aspirations small and her opportunities limited.

For Thandiwe, the message was as suffocating as the walls of her overcrowded classroom. The law had made her dreams seem not just difficult but almost foolish, as if wanting more for herself and her people was a transgression.

By the 1960s, apartheid had become a well-oiled machine, controlling every aspect of life for non-white South Africans. In Johannesburg, Jonas Nkosi, a factory worker, felt its suffocating reach. One afternoon, his employer, a white shopkeeper, called him into the back office.

"Jonas," the man began, avoiding eye contact, "I have to let you go. It's not personal—it's the law."

Jonas clenched his fists. The law, always the law. It was a phrase he had come to hate, used to justify every injustice. How could something so deeply wrong be called legal? And yet, the law shaped every interaction, forcing people like Jonas into silence, resignation, and despair.

For white South Africans, the law was a shield, a justification for privilege. For black South Africans, it was a weapon, cutting into their lives and leaving scars that would last generations. It twisted the moral compass of the nation, embedding the idea that legality equated to righteousness—a distortion that corrupted the Judgment Core (JDC) of an entire society.

But oppression breeds resistance, and by the 1970s, the cracks in apartheid's foundation began to show. Thandiwe, now in her thirties and an underground activist, found herself in the heart of the Soweto Uprising on June 16, 1976. Thousands of students marched through the streets, protesting the forced use of Afrikaans in schools. They carried placards reading, "We demand equal education!"

When the police opened fire, chaos erupted. Thandiwe saw Hector Pieterson, a 13-year-old boy, fall to the ground. She rushed to help, but it was too late. Hector's lifeless body became a symbol of apartheid's brutality, a rallying cry for those who refused to accept a world defined by unjust laws.

That night, as she sat in a dimly lit room with fellow activists, Thandiwe felt a fire ignite within her. The law had stolen homes, crushed dreams, and taken lives, but it could not kill the spirit of those who fought for justice.

In 1994, the world watched as South Africa transformed. The oppressive laws of apartheid were dismantled, and Nelson Mandela, a man who had spent 27 years in prison for his resistance, became the nation's first black president.

Samuel Mokgale, now an old man, sat in his small home in Langa, watching the inauguration on a borrowed television. Tears streamed down his face. He thought of District Six, of Peter, who had moved to another country to escape the crushing weight of apartheid. The laws that had once dictated every facet of their lives were gone, replaced by a new constitution that promised equality, dignity, and hope.

The legacy of apartheid remains a stark reminder of the power of law to shape morality—for better or for worse. In South Africa, the legal framework of apartheid had twisted the nation's Judgment Core, normalizing injustice and perpetuating suffering. But the people's resistance, their refusal to accept that morality and legality were the same, had ultimately triumphed.

The story of apartheid is not just a tale of oppression; it is a testament to the resilience of the human spirit and the power of collective will to realign a nation's moral compass. It leaves us with an enduring question: how do we ensure that the laws we create guide us toward justice rather than chaining us to oppression?

Chains in the Shadows:

The summer of 1705 in Virginia was unforgiving. The sun hung low, casting long shadows over the endless tobacco fields. Josiah, a 12-year-old boy with wide, solemn eyes, crouched in the dirt, his small hands deftly picking the leaves that would be sold for profit by a man who owned his life. He worked in silence, the sting of the overseer's whip fresh on his back. For Josiah, freedom was not even a concept—it was an absence, a hollow space where hope should have lived.

The plantation's overseer patrolled the rows with a slow, deliberate pace. To him, Josiah was not a boy but a tool, one of many whose worth was measured in pounds of tobacco picked and hours worked. The overseer didn't feel guilt or pity; he had the law on his side. The Virginia Slave Codes of 1705 decreed that Josiah was property, no different than the horses in the stable or the plows in the barn. To the white families in the plantation house, this was the natural order. If it was legal, it had to be right.

But for Josiah, the weight of the law wasn't just in the chains around his wrists. It was in the way the overseer looked through him, the way even the other enslaved people seemed resigned. The law didn't just govern behavior—it seeped into hearts and minds, shaping the way people understood the world, their place in it, and each other.

Thousands of miles away, in the bustling docks of London, the air carried the smell of saltwater and the distant clang of ship bells. It was 1788, and Thomas Griffith stood at the pier, watching the crew unload his ship, The Golden Venture. Thomas had built his fortune in the transatlantic slave trade, his wealth derived from the labor and suffering of countless enslaved Africans.

Thomas had heard murmurs of abolitionists in Parliament. Men like William Wilberforce were growing louder, calling the trade an abomination. But Thomas dismissed them. "Parliament has regulated the trade," he said to a colleague over a glass of brandy that evening. He was referring to the Slave Trade Act of 1788, which dictated how many slaves could be crammed into a ship and what rations they should receive during the voyage. To Thomas, these laws were proof that his business was not only legitimate but moral.

"Legal," he repeated to himself, as if the word could erase the images of shackled men and women, the cries of children, the smell of death that lingered in the ship's hold. If it's sanctioned by the Crown, how can it be wrong?

By the time Sarah Jenkins escaped her plantation in Georgia and fled north, the world felt different—but not safer. It was 1850, and the Fugitive Slave Act had turned the entire United States into a hunting ground for people like her. Even in free states, she was not free. Every face in the crowd could belong to a bounty hunter; every knock at the door could mean capture.

One night, as Sarah and her son Samuel hid in the cellar of a Quaker family's farmhouse, she tried to calm him. "Why do they hate us?" Samuel asked, his small voice cutting through the darkness.

Sarah didn't know how to answer. How could she explain that the law, which was meant to protect, had been twisted into a weapon? That morality had been contorted to fit the desires of men who saw her as less than human? Instead, she whispered, "Because they don't know any better. They think the law makes them right."

The words tasted bitter. Even as she said them, she knew they weren't entirely true. The law didn't just guide people's actions; it reshaped their hearts. It made them believe that cruelty was justice, that oppression was order.

In a grand courtroom in Missouri in 1857, the nation's moral compass fractured further. Dred Scott stood quietly as the judge delivered the ruling that would define him—not as a man, but as a possession. "African Americans, whether free or enslaved, cannot be citizens of the United States," the judge intoned.

For Scott, the decision ended years of fighting for his freedom. For the nation, it was a stark reminder that the law was not a reflection of justice but a tool for those in power to maintain their grip. Outside the courtroom, a crowd had gathered, their murmurs growing louder. Some cursed the ruling, while others nodded solemnly, convinced that the Supreme Court had upheld the natural order.

The law is the law, they told themselves. And in their minds, the law had become synonymous with morality.

It wasn't until the summer of 1833 that change came to the British Empire, though even then, freedom came with conditions. In Westminster, Parliament finally passed the Slavery Abolition Act. The cheers in the streets of London were loud, but they didn't reach the plantations of Jamaica, where Samuel Abrahams, a former slave, stood in a sugarcane field, still working for his master under the guise of an "apprenticeship."

"They call this freedom," Samuel said, his voice heavy with bitterness. His hands were raw, his back bent under the weight of the cane. The chains had been removed, but the exploitation remained. "They've just given it a new name."

In 1965, on a bridge in Selma, Alabama, John Lewis marched with hundreds of others, their feet pounding against the pavement as they demanded the right to vote. The air was thick with tension, and when the state troopers raised their batons, the crowd braced itself.

The first strike fell, then another. Blood mixed with sweat as Lewis stood his ground. "The law is wrong," he said later, his voice steady despite the bruises. "And we must change it."

The story of slavery, upheld by laws on both sides of the Atlantic, is a chilling reminder of how legal frameworks can distort a nation's moral compass. Laws like the Virginia Slave Codes, the Fugitive Slave Act, and the Jim Crow statutes didn't just govern behavior—they shaped beliefs, embedding injustice into the Judgment Core of entire societies.

But the resistance of people like Josiah, Sarah, and John Lewis reminds us that morality does not have to bow to legality. The fight for justice is not easy, but it is necessary, proving time and again that laws can be rewritten, hearts can be changed, and the arc of the moral universe, though long, bends toward justice.

3.2 The Shadows of Justice: Challenging the Limits of Legal Systems

In the stillness of a courthouse, beneath the imposing architecture and the weight of tradition, lies a question that whispers through the silence: Is this justice? The law, revered as the bedrock of order and fairness, promises to uphold the principles that bind a society together. But beneath its polished surface, cracks run deep, revealing contradictions and flaws that force us to confront an unsettling truth—what is legal is not always just.

Take the tension between the letter of the law and the spirit of justice. Laws are crafted to provide clear guidelines, drawing sharp lines between right and wrong. Yet life is rarely so simple. Imagine a young woman, Clara, who steals food to feed her hungry child. The law sees theft and prescribes a mandatory sentence; Clara sees survival. Her circumstances, desperate and complex, find no place in the rigid framework of mandatory minimum sentencing. The judge's hands are tied, bound by a system that values consistency over compassion.

The gavel falls. Six months in prison. Clara's crime is minor; her punishment, severe. Justice, once promised, feels distant—its spirit suffocated by the rigidity of the law.

This rigidity is not an isolated flaw; it is a systemic feature, one that often leads to outcomes that defy proportionality. While mandatory sentencing was designed to deter crime, it frequently becomes a blunt instrument, ignoring the nuances of individual cases. Can a system that punishes without understanding ever truly serve justice?

And then there is the matter of bias—an insidious shadow that darkens the courtroom. Legal systems are meant to be blind, treating every individual equally under the law. Yet, time and again, the scales tip toward those with power, wealth, or privilege. A wealthy executive caught in an insider trading scheme walks free with a fine, while a young man from a marginalized community, caught with a small amount of drugs, faces years behind bars. Both committed crimes, yet their punishments diverge, exposing the stark inequalities embedded in the system.

What does it say about justice when it bends to the weight of money and privilege? When fairness becomes a privilege itself, accessible only to those who can afford it?

Even as society evolves, the law often lags behind. Consider environmental protections weakened by corporate lobbying, or antiquated statutes that fail to address modern realities. Laws that once seemed just can become relics, their continued existence a testament to inertia rather than morality. And yet, these outdated laws remain enforceable, their authority unquestioned simply because they exist.

Does this contradiction—laws that are valid but no longer ethical—diminish the very foundation of the legal system? When public sentiment shifts but the law does not, whose interests does the system serve?

For many, the barriers to justice are not just philosophical—they are tangible, towering, and insurmountable. The cost of legal representation, the labyrinthine complexity of the system, and the sheer time it takes to resolve disputes leave countless individuals without recourse. A single mother fighting an unjust eviction might face a landlord armed with expensive lawyers, her case doomed before it begins. A wrongfully accused man might languish in jail, unable to afford bail, while his wealthier counterpart secures his freedom within hours.

And then there are the invisible contradictions that quietly persist in homes and workplaces. Consider the laborers and housemaids who agree to grueling conditions: 12-hour workdays, seven days a week, with no holidays. When questioned, the employer confidently asserts, "This is what we agreed on." The veneer of legality is used to mask exploitation. But is an agreement truly just if it arises from desperation, inequality, or the lack of viable alternatives? What does it say about a system that permits such arrangements under the guise of mutual consent?

If access to justice depends on resources, can the system ever claim to be fair? How many voices are silenced, not by the strength of the law, but by the weakness of those who cannot navigate it?

These contradictions—the rigidity of rules, the biases in enforcement, the lag behind societal values, and the inaccessibility for the vulnerable—reveal a deeper truth about legal systems. They are human creations, shaped by the hands of lawmakers, judges, and enforcers. And like all human creations, they are imperfect. The Judgment Core of a society, the internal compass that guides its sense of right and wrong, is often distorted by the very laws meant to reflect it.

So, the question lingers: What happens when legality and morality collide? Do we accept the system's flaws as inevitable, or do we challenge it to rise to a higher standard? When the law fails to serve justice, do we have the courage to demand change?

As you walk past a courthouse, hear a verdict, or read about a law, let these questions take root. For justice, true justice, requires more than obedience to the letter of the law—it demands a relentless pursuit of its spirit. And that pursuit begins with you.

The Silent Shadow of the Law:

Laws are meant to protect, to safeguard dignity, rights, and the sanctity of life. But what happens when the very systems designed to shield us twist into instruments of oppression? What happens when the law becomes a mask, concealing the unchecked brutality of those who wield authority? These are not abstract questions; they are the haunting realities that demand our attention.

On May 25, 2020, the streets of Minneapolis bore witness to an act that would reverberate across the globe. George Floyd, a Black man, was arrested for allegedly using a counterfeit $20 bill—a trivial offense. Yet, his fate was anything but trivial. As he lay pinned beneath the knee of a police officer for nine excruciating minutes, Floyd's desperate cries, "I can't breathe," echoed through the night, falling on deaf ears. The officer's blank expression betrayed the chilling confidence of someone who believed their actions would face no consequence.

The law, in its rigidity, allowed this. Protocols might justify force in certain scenarios, but where is the line when a non-violent offense ends in death? The legal protections afforded to law enforcement cloaked the act in procedural legitimacy, even as Floyd's life slipped away. How can a system claim justice when it permits such disproportionate responses?

Floyd's death sparked protests in over 60 countries, forcing the world to confront the grim truth: legality does not equal morality. In the United States, Black individuals are three times more likely than white individuals to be killed by police, according to data from Mapping Police Violence. Is this a failure of the law, or does the law itself perpetuate these outcomes?

Thousands of miles away, in the occupied territories of Palestine, a similar narrative unfolds daily, though it often escapes the global spotlight. Since 1948, Palestinians have lived under an occupation that enforces two separate legal systems: one for Israeli settlers, governed by Israeli civil law, and another for Palestinians, subjected to Israeli military law.

Under this dual framework, Palestinians—including children as young as 12—face detention without due process. According to Defense for Children International - Palestine (DCIP), between 500 and 700 Palestinian children are arrested by Israeli forces each year. These children are often subjected to harsh interrogation tactics, physical abuse, and prolonged detention. Since 2000, over 13,000 Palestinian children have been arrested. Their only "crime"? Existing in a system designed to suppress.

But it doesn't end there. Reports from the Women's Centre for Legal Aid and Counselling (WCLAC) document cases of rape and sexual violence committed against Palestinian women by Israeli police and soldiers. These crimes, heinous and deeply personal, rarely see justice. The legal system offers little recourse for victims, instead perpetuating a culture of impunity. What does justice mean in a world where the powerful escape accountability, and the vulnerable are left to suffer?

The cases of George Floyd and the ongoing injustices in Israel and Palestine force us to confront the uncomfortable truth: the law, when wielded without accountability, can become a weapon. It can justify the unjustifiable, excuse the inexcusable, and protect the powerful at the expense of the powerless.

How do we reconcile this contradiction? How can a system designed to uphold justice allow such glaring failures? These incidents underscore a critical gap between what is legal and what is moral. Does the fact that something is sanctioned by law automatically make it right?

The global outrage following these events is more than a reaction—it's a demand. People across the world are questioning the frameworks that allow such injustices to persist. They are asking:

- Why do protocols permit lethal force in non-violent situations?

- How can laws prioritize security or control over human dignity?

- What reforms are needed to ensure accountability and equality under the law?

Justice demands more than adherence to legal frameworks. It requires a commitment to ethical principles that elevate the dignity, rights, and humanity of every individual. The stories of George Floyd and the Palestinian children detained without cause remind us that the law must evolve—it must serve the people, not subjugate them.

So, the question is not just What is legal? but, What is just? And more importantly, What will we do to bridge the gap between the two?

3.3 When Laws Betray Justice: A Call to Question the System

Laws are the framework upon which societies build their ideals of order, fairness, and protection. They promise to safeguard human dignity, ensure equality, and maintain peace. But what happens when these promises unravel? What happens when laws, influenced by power, bias, or outdated norms, serve not justice but oppression?

Laws are not infallible. They are human constructs, shaped by those who hold the reins of authority. But here lies the paradox: laws designed to protect can just as easily harm when wielded as tools of control. When power corrupts the law, can it still claim legitimacy?

Legal systems, in theory, are impartial, yet in practice, they are often at the mercy of political, economic, and social agendas. The wealthy and powerful lobby for laws that serve their interests, bending the framework of justice to fit their needs. Corporate influence has led to environmental laws that prioritize profit over sustainability and labor laws that neglect the rights of workers.

If laws favor the powerful at the expense of the vulnerable, can they still be called just? Who holds the system accountable when it betrays its foundational promise of fairness?

The world evolves, but laws often lag behind, rooted in norms that no longer reflect contemporary values. Consider how privacy rights are threatened by digital surveillance in an age where data is more valuable than oil. Laws designed in analog eras struggle to protect individuals from modern exploitation.

Can a legal system that clings to outdated principles adapt to the ethical challenges of today? What happens when the pace of change outstrips the reach of justice?

Justice is meant to be blind, but often, it peeks through its blindfold, favoring some while marginalizing others. The inconsistent application of laws—based on race, gender, socioeconomic status, or political affiliation—erodes public trust. A wealthy corporation avoids consequences for environmental destruction, while a marginalized individual faces harsh penalties for minor infractions.

How can we trust a system where justice is for sale? If the law is not applied equally, is it truly justice, or merely an illusion of it?

Injustice doesn't always arise from malice; sometimes it stems from inaction. The inability of legal systems to adapt to new challenges—

whether technological advancements or global crises—creates gaps that leave individuals unprotected. As digital surveillance expands unchecked, as climate change accelerates, as AI redefines industries, legal frameworks remain stagnant, unable to address these emerging threats.

Who is responsible for ensuring that the law evolves with the times? And when it fails to do so, who bears the consequences?

When laws fail, it is the vulnerable who pay the price. Those marginalized by race, gender, or economic status often bear the brunt of systemic flaws. These failures deepen social divides, disempower communities, and erode the very social contract that binds societies together.

When individuals lose faith in the law, what replaces it? Can trust ever be restored in systems that have repeatedly let them down?

Addressing these failures demands more than minor adjustments. It requires a fundamental rethinking of how laws are made, enforced, and interpreted. It requires recognizing that justice is not static—it must evolve to meet the needs of society. This means challenging entrenched biases, limiting the influence of economic power, and ensuring that laws prioritize human dignity over profit or control.

But this transformation raises questions:

- Can a system built on power ever truly be reformed?

- What role do individuals play in holding these systems accountable?

- Is it enough to challenge the flaws, or must we envision entirely new frameworks for justice?

As you navigate the world, consider the laws you live under. Do they protect the vulnerable, or do they serve the powerful? Do they reflect the values of today, or are they relics of another time? Most importantly, when the law fails to uphold justice, what will you do about it?

Justice is not inevitable. It is a choice—a commitment to fairness, equality, and dignity. The question is not whether the law is just, but whether we demand it to be.

Laws dictate behavior, but do they define morality? The JDC exists beyond the boundaries of legality, compelling individuals to weigh law against justice, duty against conscience. Throughout history, countless figures have stood at this intersection, torn between what is lawful and what is right. When the legal system fails to align with moral truths, does the JDC compel us to challenge it—or conform?

The Deep Divide: A Tale of Oil, Protest, and Justice

Gulf of Mexico, April 20, 2010, The calm waters of the Gulf of Mexico reflected the pale moonlight as the crew of the Deepwater Horizon oil rig carried out their routine operations. To the workers onboard, this was just another day at sea—another night drilling for black gold. But beneath the surface, hidden by layers of corporate oversight and ignored safety warnings, disaster was brewing.

At 9:45 PM, the unthinkable happened. A blowout—an uncontrolled surge of oil and gas—ignited, transforming the rig into a fiery inferno. Explosions ripped through the platform, claiming the lives of 11 workers and sending millions of gallons of crude oil gushing into the ocean. Over the next 87 days, the Gulf became a graveyard for marine life, its waters choked with a slick of death that spread across thousands of miles.

BP, the oil giant behind the operation, scrambled to contain the spill. Public apologies were issued, and billions of dollars were pledged in settlements. But as the smoke cleared and the oil washed ashore, the true scope of the disaster became evident: ecosystems ravaged, livelihoods destroyed, and communities left to grapple with the aftermath.

Executives sat in polished offices, crafting press releases and negotiating fines. They knew they would pay billions, but to BP, it was a cost of doing business. No one would go to jail, and the company's operations would continue. The law, it seemed, offered them an escape—a shield against accountability. But was it justice?

North Dakota, October 27, 2016. Hundreds of miles away, a very different battle was being fought. On the wind-swept plains of North Dakota, members of the Standing Rock Sioux Tribe and their allies gathered at the edge of the Missouri River. Their mission was clear: stop the Dakota Access Pipeline (DAPL), a project that threatened to contaminate their water supply and desecrate sacred land.

Among the protesters stood Maya Ironcloud, a young Sioux woman who had grown up hearing stories of her ancestors' connection to the land. To her, the fight wasn't just about the pipeline; it was about preserving a way of life and standing up to centuries of exploitation.

The camp buzzed with the energy of resistance, but tension hung heavy in the air. As construction crews pushed forward, the protesters formed human barriers, chanting prayers and holding signs. They called themselves Water Protectors, vowing to defend their land peacefully.

Then came the crackdown. On the morning of October 27, militarized police arrived in force. Helicopters buzzed overhead, and armored vehicles rolled onto the camp. Maya watched as protesters were sprayed with tear gas and rubber bullets, their cries drowned out by the roar of machinery. By nightfall, over 140 people had been arrested, including Maya, charged with trespassing and rioting.

Her crime? Standing on her ancestral land, protecting the water her people had relied on for generations. The legal system, which should have protected her rights, instead branded her a criminal.

BP's fines and settlements totaled over $20 billion, the largest environmental penalty in U.S. history. Yet, the company rebounded, its executives untouched by the devastation they had caused. The spill became a line item on their balance sheet—a financial setback, not a moral reckoning.

Maya, meanwhile, faced the harsh consequences of her resistance. She spent weeks in jail, her criminal record now a barrier to employment and housing. Her story was one of many; hundreds of protesters faced similar fates for their role in defending the land and water.

The juxtaposition was glaring. BP had caused irreversible damage, yet its leaders walked free. Maya had sought to prevent harm, yet she was punished. How could a system designed to uphold justice allow such disparities?

The stories of BP and Standing Rock reveal a deeper crisis—a fracture in society's Judgment Core. The legal system, which shapes our sense of right and wrong, seemed to favor power over principle. Laws held corporations accountable in dollars, but not in deeds, while individuals fighting for justice faced severe repercussions.

These cases challenge us to question the morality embedded in our legal frameworks. When does legality diverge from justice? When does the pursuit of profit outweigh the protection of people and the planet?

As the oil slick fades from memory and the Standing Rock arrests recede from headlines, the questions remain. Who does the law truly serve? Can a system that punishes protectors and shields polluters claim to be just? And what role must we play in recalibrating the scales of justice?

These are not just stories of the past; they are warnings for the future. The Deepwater Horizon spill and the protests at Standing Rock remind us that justice is not guaranteed—it must be fought for, defended, and demanded. Will you stand on the sidelines, or will you challenge the system to align with the core principles of fairness and dignity?

3.4 The Shadows of Obedience: The Power and Peril of Authority

Authority is a force that hums quietly in the background of our lives, shaping our actions and beliefs from the earliest moments we can remember. As children, we are taught to trust and obey—parents, teachers, police officers—those who represent the structures of power that govern society. This obedience is presented as virtuous, a cornerstone of order that keeps chaos at bay. But have you ever stopped to wonder: When does respect for authority become blind compliance? And at what cost?

Authority, after all, is a double-edged sword. Its power lies in its ability to command deference, to simplify the complexities of governance by ensuring that rules are followed without constant conflict. Without authority, society might crumble under the weight of endless disputes and fractured norms. But here lies the paradox: while authority can maintain harmony, it can just as easily become a tool for oppression. When does the stability it promises morph into the chains of control?

Imagine a classroom where the teacher's word is absolute. Most students comply without question, trusting that the authority figure knows best. Now imagine that same obedience applied to laws and leaders. What happens when those in power misuse their authority to enforce rules that are unjust or oppressive? History is rife with examples: regimes that demanded obedience to discriminatory laws, governments that silenced dissent, and institutions that perpetuated harm under the guise of maintaining order.

Think of the Nuremberg trials, (military tribunals held after World War II, from 1945 to 1949, to bring to justice key members of Nazi Germany's leadership who were responsible for war crimes, crimes against humanity, and crimes against peace) where individuals justified their heinous actions with a chilling phrase: "I was just following orders." The weight of authority had extinguished their ability—or willingness—to question the morality of their actions. If you were in their shoes, would you have the courage to resist?

The power of authority over obedience is not just a societal construct—it's deeply psychological. Consider the infamous Milgram experiment, where participants, under the guidance of an authority figure, administered what they believed were painful electric shocks to another person. Despite hearing screams of pain, many continued, simply because they were told to do so. The results were unsettling: ordinary people were willing to harm others when instructed by someone they perceived as an authority.

What does this tell us about ourselves? How often do we suppress our moral instincts to conform to authority, even when it conflicts with what we know to be right?

The challenge, then, lies in striking a delicate balance. Authority is necessary to maintain societal order, but blind obedience can perpetuate injustice. When faced with a law or directive that conflicts with your sense of right and wrong, do you comply to avoid conflict, or do you challenge it?

How often do we stop to question the laws we follow or the figures we revere? Do we accept their directives simply because they come from a place of power, or do we evaluate their alignment with our ethical principles?

To prevent the misuse of authority, societies must foster a culture of accountability and constructive questioning. This begins with education—not just teaching individuals to respect authority but empowering them to challenge it when necessary. A healthy society is not one where people blindly follow orders; it is one where they feel confident to ask, "Is this just? Is this fair?"

Imagine a world where laws and practices are constantly scrutinized, not to undermine order, but to refine it. Where dissent is not silenced but encouraged as a pathway to progress. Where obedience is not expected blindly but earned through trust and alignment with ethical values.

Would such a world be chaotic, or would it be stronger, its moral foundation reinforced by collective vigilance?

Authority shapes the Judgment Core of a society—the internal compass that guides our sense of right and wrong. But what happens when that compass is skewed by unquestioned obedience? When does respect for authority suppress the very courage needed to challenge injustice? And how do we teach ourselves—and each other—to discern the line between justified compliance and moral surrender?

The next time you encounter a rule, a directive, or a figure of authority, ask yourself:

- Does this align with my moral values?

- Am I complying out of fear or convenience, or because I truly believe it is right?

- What might happen if I question this authority?

Authority is necessary, but it is not infallible. It must be earned, scrutinized, and, when necessary, resisted. The real strength of a society lies not in its ability to enforce obedience but in its willingness to embrace accountability. The question is: Will you be the one to ask, 'Why?'.

The Milgram Experiment: A Dark Mirror to the Judgment Core

In the sterile corridors of Yale University in 1961, an experiment unfolded that would unravel the secrets of obedience and challenge the very fabric of morality. Behind closed doors, ordinary individuals faced a test—not of knowledge, but of conscience. Would they listen to their moral compass, or would the voice of authority drown it out?

Participants, drawn from all walks of life, entered the experiment with little idea of what lay ahead. They were told they would play the role of a "teacher," tasked with administering electric shocks to a "learner" seated in another room. The learner, of course, was an actor, and no real shocks were delivered. But the participants didn't know that. Each mistake the learner made on a memory test would require the teacher to increase the voltage of the shock—a mere 15 volts at first, but rising to a stomach-churning 450 volts.

As the experiment progressed, the learner's responses grew desperate. Cries of pain, pleas for mercy, and eventually eerie silence filled the room. The participants hesitated. They turned to the figure of authority—the experimenter in a crisp lab coat—for guidance. And with simple phrases like, "The experiment requires that you continue," and "You have no other choice; you must go on "the authority figure pushed them forward.

What happened next shocked even the researchers. 65% of participants continued administering shocks all the way to the maximum voltage of 450 volts. Many did so reluctantly, visibly distressed, sweating, trembling, even pleading to stop. But they obeyed. Why? Because an authority figure told them to.

They weren't sadists or sociopaths. They were ordinary people—teachers, salesmen, clerks. Yet they overrode their moral instincts, trusting authority over their own ethical judgment.

The Milgram experiment revealed a chilling truth: authority has the power to distort the Judgment Core, the internal compass that guides our sense of right and wrong. Participants weren't blind to the learner's suffering; they heard the screams. They felt the tension between their actions and their morality. Yet they acted against their values, swayed by the perceived legitimacy of authority.

This raises unsettling questions: How often do we silence our moral compass in deference to authority? Do we obey laws, rules, or orders simply because they come from a figure of power, even when they conflict with our ethical beliefs?

The implications of the Milgram experiment extend far beyond the lab. Think of the countless historical and contemporary examples where individuals have followed harmful orders: soldiers committing atrocities in war, employees enforcing discriminatory policies, citizens turning a blind eye to injustice.

Were they evil? Or were they, like Milgram's participants, victims of authority's influence, acting not out of malice but obedience?

The experiment challenges each of us to reflect on our own Judgment Core. If placed in a similar situation, would you have the strength to resist? Would you defy authority to uphold your ethical beliefs, even at great personal cost? Or would the lab coat's quiet commands overpower your conscience?

These questions are not hypothetical. They resonate in everyday life, in the choices we make, the rules we follow, and the authority we trust. When does obedience become complicity? And where do we draw the line between following orders and standing up for what is right?

The Milgram experiment is more than a psychological study—it's a mirror, forcing us to confront the fragility of our moral compass in the face of authority. To strengthen our Judgment Core, we must ask ourselves:

- Do I question authority when it conflicts with my values?

- How do I balance respect for rules with my responsibility to challenge injustice?

- Am I prepared to act against authority when it asks me to betray my ethical principles?

The experiment's haunting legacy is a reminder that morality isn't passive; it demands vigilance and courage. Will you have the strength to listen to your moral compass when authority tries to silence it? Or will you, too, succumb to the quiet power of the lab coat?.

3.5 The Shadows of Law: A Call for Critical Reflection

Laws, the silent architects of society, shape the boundaries of acceptable behavior and establish the framework for social order. They are the invisible threads weaving together the fabric of justice—or, at times, injustice. But have you ever stopped to ask: Are all laws just? And what happens when they are not?

On the surface, laws appear neutral, even noble. They claim to embody fairness, safeguard rights, and protect the collective good. Yet, beneath their polished veneer lies a complex reality. Laws are not immutable truths but human constructs, shaped by power, influence, and sometimes, deeply flawed values. Can we truly trust them to guide our moral compass, or must we hold them to a higher standard?

Fairness is the bedrock of justice. A fair law applies equally to all, free from discrimination or favoritism. But history—and the present—tell a different story. Consider laws that once enforced segregation or denied women the right to vote. These were legal frameworks, yet they perpetuated inequality and oppression.

Does the mere existence of a law justify its morality? If fairness is the standard, how many of today's laws would withstand scrutiny? And if they wouldn't, why do we continue to obey them?

Empathy is a rare and fragile quality in legal systems. Too often, laws focus on control rather than compassion, ignoring the human impact of their enforcement. Think of policies that criminalize homelessness or deny asylum to refugees fleeing danger. These laws might maintain order, but at what cost to human dignity?

Should laws prioritize structure over the well-being of individuals? Can a society claim to be just if its legal system lacks empathy? And what does this say about our own moral compass when we accept these laws without question?

Laws should serve the collective good, reflecting the needs and values of society as a whole. Yet, far too often, they are tools of privilege, benefiting the powerful at the expense of the vulnerable. Corporate lobbying, political agendas, and economic incentives frequently shape legislation, creating policies that prioritize profit over people.

How can we trust a law written with hidden motives? Do we blindly accept its authority, or do we challenge its origins and implications? Whose interests are truly being served?

The power of law lies in its authority, but that authority can be dangerous when wielded without accountability. Laws have been used to control, oppress, and silence. Think of anti-protest laws, censorship policies, or statutes that criminalize poverty. These aren't relics of the past—they're realities of the present.

Do we have the courage to question laws that conflict with our ethical principles? Or do we risk becoming complicit in their enforcement, choosing comfort over conscience?

History offers a powerful response to unjust laws: civil disobedience. From Gandhi's salt march to the civil rights sit-ins, acts of peaceful resistance have challenged oppressive systems and sparked transformative change.

But civil disobedience comes with a cost—ostracism, imprisonment, even violence. Would you be willing to pay that price for what you believe is right? And if not, how do you reconcile that with your own Judgment Core, the inner guide that tells you right from wrong?

Ultimately, the call for a critical approach to laws is a call to examine our own Judgment Core. Laws may provide structure, but they are not infallible. They must be evaluated against higher principles—fairness, empathy, and justice. This requires personal responsibility, the courage to question authority, and the willingness to act when laws fall short.

- Do you question the laws you follow, or do you accept them as unchallengeable truths?

- When a law conflicts with your moral compass, do you have the strength to resist?

- How do you balance respect for societal order with the need to confront injustice?

The law's authority is powerful, but it is not absolute. It can shape our world for better or worse, depending on how we engage with it. Will you blindly follow, or will you challenge it to reflect the values of justice and humanity? The answer lies not in the law itself but in your willingness to hold it accountable to your moral compass. The real question is: Are you ready to take on that responsibility?

The Unbroken Thread of Justice: Rosa Parks, Martin Luther King Jr., and Nelson Mandela

On a cold December evening in 1955, Rosa Parks sat quietly on a Montgomery bus, her body weary from work—but her spirit unwavering. Around her, segregation laws governed every interaction, woven so deeply into everyday life that most people followed them without question. When the bus driver ordered her to give up her seat for a white passenger, silence fell. Everyone knew the rule. Everyone knew what she was supposed to do.

But Rosa didn't move.

That small, still act of defiance sent shockwaves far beyond that bus. Her refusal ignited the Montgomery Bus Boycott, a 381-day protest that shook the city's infrastructure and awakened the moral conscience of a nation. Behind the scenes, a young pastor named Martin Luther King Jr. stepped into leadership. With conviction and clarity, he reframed the boycott as more than a local protest—it became a moral reckoning.

King believed that unjust laws are no laws at all. Drawing from theology and philosophy, he argued that legality must be grounded in higher principles—justice, dignity, and equality. His message, rooted in nonviolence and love, reached far beyond Montgomery. Through marches, sermons, and speeches, he challenged a nation to confront the chasm between its laws and its values.

Thousands of miles away, another battle raged—this one under the brutal grip of apartheid in South Africa. There, Nelson Mandela fought a regime that didn't just segregate—it systemically erased the rights and humanity of Black South Africans. They were denied land, denied freedom of movement, and forced into "homelands" under the illusion of separation.

Mandela, like King, began with peaceful resistance. But as the state answered peaceful protest with violence, Mandela co-founded Umkhonto we Sizwe, an armed resistance wing. His decision wasn't driven by hatred, but by the painful conclusion that the system could not be dismantled with petitions alone. In 1962, he was arrested. Two years later, sentenced to life in prison.

From his cell on Robben Island, Mandela refused conditional release. Each offer came with the demand that he renounce the cause. He refused. Like Parks and King, he followed his Judgment Core, even when it meant enduring isolation, injustice, and the loss of decades.

The lives of Rosa Parks, Martin Luther King Jr., and Nelson Mandela are bound by a common thread: the refusal to obey laws that violated human dignity. Each of them understood something profound—that legal does not always mean moral.

They lived under systems that weaponized law to uphold inequality. And they chose to resist, not with ease, but with unflinching moral clarity. Their actions ask us:

- Who decides what is right?

- And when the law contradicts justice, which do you follow?

Laws, after all, are human constructs. They reflect the dominant values of the time—values often shaped by those in power. Segregation, apartheid, slavery—all were legal, yet profoundly unjust. These systems were not outliers; they were normalized through legislation, accepted by many, and enforced with chilling precision.

So what of today?

What practices are protected by law now—only to be condemned by future generations?

Parks was arrested and endured years of harassment. King was imprisoned, threatened, and ultimately assassinated. Mandela lost 27 years of freedom. And yet, they emerged—not broken, but stronger. Their sacrifice was immense—but so were their victories.

- The bus boycott ended segregation on public transport.

- King's leadership paved the way for the Civil Rights Act of 1964.

- Mandela was elected South Africa's first Black president, dismantling apartheid peacefully.

They did not follow the path of least resistance. They followed their Judgment Core, even when it cost them everything.

And now, the burden of choice shifts to us.

- When we see laws that harm, will we comply or question?

- When injustice wears the mask of legality, will we look away—or confront it?

- Do we obey because it is easier… or because it is right?

The bus in Montgomery. The marches in Selma. The prison cell on Robben Island. These were not just symbols of protest—they were sites of moral reckoning, where law was tested against conscience.

The lives of Parks, King, and Mandela force us to see that justice is not handed down—it is demanded, defended, and fought for, one courageous choice at a time.

So now the question is yours to answer:

- When faced with injustice, will you stand in silence…

- or will you follow your Judgment Core, even if it means standing alone?

3.6 The Contradictions of the logic behind some laws

In the intricate web of U.S. laws, a peculiar contradiction unfolds in the treatment of youth autonomy. Minors are deemed too young to make certain decisions—purchasing alcohol, smoking cigarettes, or gambling—because society recognizes their cognitive and emotional immaturity. Yet, in several states, these same minors are granted significant autonomy over life-altering medical decisions, such as gender-affirming hormone treatments and even irreversible surgeries. This paradox forces a profound question: How does the legal system decide which choices minors are capable of making, and why are these decisions so inconsistent?

The protective logic behind restricting minors from substances like alcohol and tobacco is clear. Society seeks to shield them from harm, understanding that their decision-making abilities are still developing. Yet this caution appears absent when it comes to medical interventions that permanently alter their bodies. Gender-affirming treatments, such as hormone therapy and surgery, can result in irreversible changes—infertility, altered physical characteristics, and lifelong hormone dependency. And in many cases, these decisions are made without the involvement or consent of parents.

Proponents of such policies argue that granting autonomy in these cases respects minors' rights to address gender dysphoria and prevents mental health crises like depression and anxiety. Critics, however, question whether adolescents—still grappling with cognitive and emotional growth—can truly comprehend the long-term implications of these decisions. How can a 15-year-old be considered too immature to buy a pack of cigarettes but mature enough to make decisions that will affect their body and identity for the rest of their life?

This question becomes even more poignant when examining the real-world stories of individuals who have undergone these procedures as minors and later experienced regret. Nathan, a teenager from Los Angeles, provides one such example. At 15, Nathan began to question his gender identity, influenced by social media, peers, and school counselors. Encouraged by his environment and with the consent of his parents, Nathan started puberty blockers and hormone therapy. Initially, these treatments provided relief, making him feel as though he was taking control of his identity.

But as the years passed, Nathan's sense of relief turned to doubt. By the time he turned 18, he had undergone partial gender-affirming surgery, but instead of feeling empowered, he was left questioning the decision. "When I was a child," he reflected during an interview, "I would choose a $2 candy over a $1,000 payment because I lacked the maturity to understand long-term consequences. How could I have been considered mature enough to make such a permanent decision?"

Nathan's feelings of regret weren't just about the physical changes but about the emotional and psychological pressures he faced during adolescence. He later argued that children and teenagers often experiment with identity as a natural part of growing up and that such exploration shouldn't be met with irreversible medical interventions. For him, the legal system's permissiveness felt like a betrayal, failing to protect him from making decisions he now feels he was too young to fully understand.

His story highlights a critical flaw in the way laws address youth autonomy. On one hand, minors are shielded from choices deemed risky; on the other, they are granted profound decision-making power in contexts with permanent consequences. This inconsistency reveals a deeper issue: laws, as human constructs, are shaped by societal pressures, political agendas, and cultural norms. They are imperfect reflections of the societies that create them, often failing to balance protection and autonomy consistently.

Nathan's experience isn't unique. It underscores the broader complexities of adolescence, a time marked by exploration, identity formation, and emotional turbulence. It also raises urgent questions: Are current laws sufficiently aligned with what we know about adolescent development? Do they adequately safeguard minors from hasty, irreversible decisions while allowing space for exploration and growth? And how do we, as a society, reconcile these contradictions in a way that respects both protection and autonomy?

These questions take on even greater significance in the context of regret. While supporters of gender-affirming treatments emphasize their importance in addressing mental health challenges for transgender youth, stories like Nathan's challenge us to consider whether the current legal framework provides enough safeguards. Regret doesn't just highlight personal struggle—it calls into question the ethical foundations of laws that grant such autonomy to minors while restricting it in other areas.

As society grapples with these contradictions, one thing becomes clear: the need for thoughtful, nuanced reform. Laws cannot remain static in the face of evolving societal values and emerging challenges. They must reflect a deeper understanding of maturity, decision-making capacity, and the potential for long-term consequences. This is not just a matter of legislation but a test of our collective Judgment Core, the internal compass that guides our sense of fairness, morality, and justice.

If the goal of the legal system is to protect while empowering, we must ask: Are we truly serving minors by granting autonomy in some areas and withholding it in others? Are we prioritizing immediate affirmation over long-term safeguards? And how can we create a framework that balances protection, autonomy, and empathy?

Nathan's story is a cautionary tale but also an opportunity—a chance to critically evaluate how laws address youth rights and decision-making. It challenges us to engage deeply with these questions and to advocate for systems that align more closely with ethical principles and the realities of adolescence. The answer lies not in absolutes but in our willingness to question, reflect, and evolve. The question remains: How do we ensure that our laws protect the most vulnerable while respecting their potential for growth and self-determination?

3.7 Conclusion: A Reckoning Between Law and Judgment Core (JDC)

You're standing at a crossroads, two paths stretching before you. One is smooth, well-paved, and marked with signs declaring "Legal. Approved. Sanctioned." The other is rocky, uncertain, and shadowed by the weight of defiance, yet whispers the haunting question: "But is it right?"

Which path do you take?

Laws have long been the architects of societal order, shaping behavior, defining justice, and dictating morality. Yet, history has shown us that legal systems, for all their claims of righteousness, are neither infallible nor inherently just. They have been used to oppress, exclude, and silence just as often as they have been used to protect and uplift.

But if laws do not always define morality, then what does?

That answer lies within you—within the Judgment Core (JDC), the internal compass that guides your sense of right and wrong beyond what is written in statutes and legal codes. Yet, how often do we test its strength against the authority of law? How many times do we assume that because something is legal, it must also be moral?

Consider history's defining moments—when people like Rosa Parks refused to give up her seat, when Nelson Mandela stood against apartheid, when millions marched for civil rights, women's rights, and the rights of the oppressed. None of these acts were legal at the time, yet they became the foundations of justice.

Now, ask yourself:

- Do I unquestioningly accept the laws I follow, or do I evaluate them against my own moral compass?

- When legality and morality conflict, which do I choose?

- Am I willing to stand against an unjust law, or does fear of consequence silence my defiance?

Justice is not a passive force—it is a choice, an action, a responsibility. Laws do not shape the Judgment Core; it is the Judgment Core that should shape the law.

But that only happens when we dare to ask:

- What laws today, accepted without question, will be condemned by future generations?

- What injustices persist because people are too afraid to challenge them?

- And when the time comes, will I have the courage to act, or will I simply obey?

The next time you walk past a courthouse, sign a legal document, or hear a ruling delivered, don't just accept it. Question it. Challenge it. Measure it against the core of your morality.

Because in the end, the greatest crime is not breaking an unjust law—it is obeying one without thought.

So, tell me: Will you follow the road that is paved, or will you carve a new path, guided by your Judgment Core?

Chapter 4: Global Standards – International Organizations and Their Role

You're in a classroom—not just any classroom, but one where every student comes from a different country. The teacher writes one word on the board: Justice.

Hands go up. One student says freedom, another says obedience, another says equality. Then, from the back of the room, someone whispers, "Justice is whatever the powerful say it is."

The class goes quiet. Not because it's wrong— But because no one can prove it isn't.

Now, imagine that same conversation taking place not in a classroom, but in a vast conference hall, where the future of nations is decided behind polished podiums and diplomatic handshakes.

You walk into the hall—marble floors, rows of flags, polished mahogany tables, voices low with calculated restraint. Representatives from around the world speak of peace, security, and shared values. But beneath the carefully crafted speeches, a quiet question lingers:

- Whose morality is being enforced? And who decides when justice applies—and when it doesn't?

To answer that, we must go back.

In the wake of World War I, the world's first attempt at global diplomacy—the League of Nations—was created in 1920 to prevent future conflict. It failed. After the horrors of World War II, the world tried again. In 1945, the United Nations (UN) was born with a vow: "Never again."

Soon after came a constellation of institutions meant to heal, stabilize, and unite:

- The World Bank and International Monetary Fund (IMF), created to rebuild war-torn economies and prevent collapse.

- The World Health Organization (WHO), established in 1948 to combat global disease.

- The International Atomic Energy Agency (IAEA), launched in 1957 to monitor the peaceful use of nuclear energy.

These institutions were born from crisis, hope, and ambition—an attempt to anchor global morality in cooperation rather than conquest.

But built into the foundation of this idealism was power—and with power came paradox.

Consider the United Nations Security Council—where five nations hold permanent veto power. With a single word—veto—the U.S., U.K., China, Russia, or France can unilaterally cancel any decision, resolution, or global call for justice.

Imagine debating the fate of a war-torn region—starving children, collapsing hospitals, entire populations displaced. The world agrees on action. And then, one voice says no.

And everything stops.

In a structure designed to serve humanity, five seats control the switch between action and inaction. Justice becomes negotiable.

So we must ask:

- Are these institutions guardians of peace—or gatekeepers of influence?

- Do they lift the world—or carefully manage which parts rise and which stay low?

Because international organizations do more than make rules—they define morality at scale. Through media, treaties, sanctions, and aid, they shape how billions of people perceive what is just, fair, or right.

Your Judgment Core (JDC)—the internal compass that guides your sense of right and wrong—is constantly influenced by the values these institutions claim to represent.

But have you ever asked:

- Who wrote those values?

- And what happens when justice is edited by those who hold the pen?

This chapter pulls back the curtain.

We will explore the origins, triumphs, contradictions, and quiet compromises behind international governance. You will not be asked to reject global institutions—but to examine their moral architecture. To understand how they influence your compass, and to ask whether that direction aligns with your deepest convictions.

So before you move on, pause and reflect:

- Is your moral compass truly your own—or is it calibrated by institutions that claim to speak for the world?

- Will you entrust your Judgment Core to a system where justice can be vetoed… or will you dare to define justice for yourself?

Because behind every treaty, every press release, every declaration of global good—

Lies a power structure.

Lies a quiet decision.

Lies a question only you can answer.

4.1 WHO: Triumphs and Shadows

The eradication of smallpox stands as a beacon of what humanity can achieve when united by a common goal. For centuries, this relentless disease ravaged populations, leaving scars not just on bodies but on the very fabric of societies. Then, in 1967, the World Health Organization (WHO) launched an audacious campaign to eradicate it—a feat many deemed impossible. Armed with a strategy of mass vaccination, vigilant surveillance, and the groundbreaking tactic of ring vaccination, the WHO mobilized a global force of health workers, researchers, and governments.

This wasn't just a medical victory; it was a profound demonstration of international solidarity. Health workers ventured into remote, often hostile terrains, overcoming cultural resistance and logistical nightmares. Their tireless efforts brought the world to an extraordinary moment in 1980 when smallpox was declared eradicated—the first disease vanquished by human effort. This triumph, etched into history, highlighted not only the power of collective action but also the moral imperative to pursue health equity for all.

Yet, within this dazzling legacy of success lies a darker narrative—one that challenges the WHO's ability to maintain its moral compass in the face of immense global pressures. For every moment of triumph, there are shadows of shortcomings that have eroded public trust.

Consider the WHO's response to the Ebola outbreak in West Africa or its handling of the COVID-19 pandemic. These crises laid bare the organization's vulnerabilities: bureaucratic inertia, slow decision-making, and glaring inequities in resource distribution. Vaccines for COVID-19

Chapter 3: Government and Law – The National Perspective and The Government's Grip on Morality

You're standing at a busy intersection in a foreign country. The traffic lights flash red, yet the cars continue moving as if the signal holds no authority. Pedestrians weave through speeding vehicles, unbothered by the chaos. You hesitate—should you cross, or wait for a rule that no one else seems to follow? Here, the law exists, but its influence is unclear. In this moment, you realize a startling truth: laws do not define morality—society's acceptance of them does.

Stepping beyond the informal influences of family and community, we enter a realm where morality is no longer just a matter of personal conscience—it is dictated, codified, and enforced by the government. Laws are written, upheld, and amended under the guise of protecting citizens and preserving order. But do they always align with what is truly just?

Governments, whether democratic, authoritarian, or something in between, hold immense power over our Judgment Core (JDC). They decide what is legal or illegal, shaping not just actions but the very way people think about right and wrong. A law can turn an act into a crime or elevate a principle into a duty. But history has shown us that legality and morality are not always the same.

Consider the laws that once justified segregation, colonial rule, and systemic discrimination. At the time, they were upheld as the pillars of order and justice. Today, they are condemned as moral failures. How many of the laws you follow today will be seen as unjust by future generations?

This chapter delves into the complexities of governmental influence on our moral compass. It forces us to ask uncomfortable but necessary questions:

- Are laws designed for justice, or do they serve the interests of those in power?

- If an unjust law is enforced, is obeying it a moral duty or a moral failure?

were hailed as miracles of modern science, yet lawsuits against pharmaceutical giants like Pfizer, Moderna, and Johnson & Johnson revealed troubling stories of adverse effects—blood clots, myocarditis, and other health complications. While the vaccines were distributed with unprecedented speed, questions about long-term safety and the influence of financial and political pressures loom large.

This unease deepens when examining the WHO's relationship with pharmaceutical companies. Critics question whether endorsements were always guided by scientific rigor or, at times, by the interests of powerful players seeking profit. In this murky intersection of health and commerce, the Judgment Core (JDC) of global health governance is called into question. Are decisions truly rooted in humanity's best interests, or are they swayed by covert agendas?

The disparities in the WHO's priorities further amplify these concerns. Diseases like African sleeping sickness and Chagas disease, which primarily affect impoverished populations, remain woefully underfunded and neglected. These "forgotten diseases" may lack the profitability of more prominent health crises, but their toll is devastating. The imbalance in addressing such diseases underscores the inequities baked into global health systems, raising unsettling questions about whose lives are valued most in the pursuit of global health.

The eradication of smallpox was not just a medical feat; it was a moral statement that no life is too remote, too poor, or too insignificant to save. But do the WHO's modern actions reflect this ethos? As crises unfold and the organization grapples with its immense responsibilities, its ability to remain an impartial advocate for global health equity is increasingly scrutinized.

The story of the WHO is one of light and shadow—a testament to what can be achieved when humanity works together, but also a cautionary tale of how power and priorities can drift. The question that lingers is both profound and urgent:

- Can the WHO reclaim its role as a true moral compass for global health, or will it continue to stumble under the weight of political and financial influences?

- How do we ensure that all lives, regardless of geography or wealth, are valued equally in its mission?

- When does pragmatism in global health become complicity, and how can we hold such powerful organizations accountable?

In a world where health crises know no borders, the stakes have never been higher. The eradication of smallpox offers a shining example of what is possible, but the challenges of today demand more than echoes of past glories. They call for transparency, equity, and a relentless commitment to serve all of humanity—not just the privileged few.

The WHO stands at a crossroads. Will it rise to meet this challenge, or will it remain entangled in the complex web of competing agendas?

4.2 Shadows in Global Governance

In the intricate halls of international diplomacy, where decisions ripple across nations and generations, a disturbing question lingers: Whose interests are truly served? International organizations, from the United Nations (UN) to the World Trade Organization (WTO), stand as towering symbols of global cooperation, claiming to champion peace, equity, and justice. Yet, beneath their lofty ideals lie stark contradictions—instances where their actions seem more aligned with the power plays of the mighty than the collective good of humanity.

One of the clearest examples of this tension is the United Nations Security Council, a body ostensibly designed to safeguard global peace. Yet its five permanent members—China, France, Russia, the United Kingdom, and the United States—wield veto power that often serves national agendas rather than global consensus. Consider the case of the United States, which has consistently used its veto to block resolutions condemning Israeli actions in Palestine, even when such resolutions garnered overwhelming international support. This unyielding protection has emboldened Israel to act with impunity, carrying out military operations and expansionist policies while disregarding international norms.

The genocide in Palestine and attacks on neighboring countries raise haunting questions: What happens when a nation acts without fear of consequences because it enjoys unflinching support from a global superpower? How does this redefine the concept of justice in the eyes of the oppressed?

The shadow of bias is not confined to political maneuvering—it extends to military interventions cloaked in the language of democracy and human rights. The U.S.-led invasions of Afghanistan, Iraq, and Libya offer grim illustrations. In Iraq, the 2003 invasion was justified by the now-debunked claim of weapons of mass destruction. The result? A fractured nation, a devastated population, and the exploitation of Iraq's vast oil reserves. Similarly, the NATO intervention in Libya, which ousted Muammar

Gaddafi, plunged the country into chaos, opening the door for foreign powers to stake claims over its resources.

In Afghanistan, two decades of occupation culminated in a humanitarian crisis and a resurgent Taliban, raising the question: Were these interventions truly about liberation, or were they calculated moves in a broader geopolitical game? How does the devastation left in their wake reflect on the moral compass of those who initiated them?

The threads of inequality weave deeper into economic and health policies. The WTO, for instance, has been criticized for trade rules that disproportionately favor wealthy nations. Agricultural subsidies in the U.S. and European Union allow their farmers to flood global markets with cheap products, undermining farmers in developing countries. The Doha Round negotiations exposed the stark divide: Can a system that entrenches poverty for the many while protecting the interests of the few ever claim fairness?

Health crises have further illuminated these disparities. The COVID-19 pandemic revealed the fragility of global health governance. Wealthier nations hoarded vaccines while poorer countries struggled, their populations left vulnerable. Initiatives like COVAX, meant to ensure equitable vaccine distribution, faltered under the weight of unequal power dynamics.

The private sector's shadow looms just as large. Fossil fuel companies, with their representatives heavily involved in climate summits like COP26, have been accused of diluting environmental regulations. Multinational corporations such as Coca-Cola and PepsiCo, despite their role in exacerbating obesity and diet-related diseases, have influenced global health policies to prioritize profits over public well-being. Can we trust organizations tasked with protecting humanity's future when they welcome those whose actions threaten it?

These realities force us to confront uncomfortable questions about the Judgment Core (JDC) of international organizations:

- Whose morality shapes the policies and actions of these global institutions?

- Can organizations truly claim neutrality when they are deeply entangled with the interests of powerful states and corporations?

- What does it mean for justice when some lives and voices carry more weight than others in the corridors of global governance?

The answers to these questions are neither simple nor comforting. While international organizations have achieved remarkable successes—such as eradicating smallpox or mediating peace in volatile regions—their failures cast long shadows over their legitimacy. For these entities to act as true stewards of global morality, they must transcend the web of biases and vested interests that bind them.

Reform is imperative. Limiting the veto power of Security Council members, enforcing trade rules that genuinely uplift developing nations, and ensuring transparency in dealings with private entities are just starting points. Most importantly, these organizations must remember their founding principles: to serve all of humanity, not just the powerful few.

As you consider these realities, ask yourself:

- How do we hold international organizations accountable for the contradictions in their actions?

- Can we trust these institutions to guide global morality, or must we reimagine their purpose and structure?

- What role do we play as individuals in challenging double standards and advocating for a more just global order?

In a world where justice is too often defined by the powerful, the path forward demands more than passive observation. It calls for vigilance, critical questioning, and an unyielding commitment to a fairer future for all.

4.3 The IAEA: A Custodian of Peace or a Victim of Power?

In a world increasingly defined by blurred lines between morality and manipulation, international organizations are often hailed as the guardians of global stability. Among these institutions, the International Atomic Energy Agency (IAEA) holds a unique and critical role: overseeing the peaceful use of nuclear technology while preventing the proliferation of weapons that could obliterate humanity. Its mandate, noble in intent, seeks to harmonize global security with scientific progress. Yet, as we peer closer, cracks in its impartiality emerge, leaving us to question: is the IAEA a beacon of justice or a tool in the hands of the powerful?

Iraq: Weapons That Never Existed

Rewind to the early 2000s, when the IAEA was thrust into the spotlight amid allegations that Iraq was harboring weapons of mass destruction

(WMDs). Despite the agency's exhaustive inspections and clear reports that no active nuclear weapons program existed, the narrative of WMDs persisted. The subsequent U.S.-led invasion of Iraq not only devastated a nation but also exposed the limitations of an international body caught in the crossfire of political agendas.

The IAEA's inability to assert its findings against the tide of powerful nations demonstrated a haunting truth: even verified facts can be silenced when overshadowed by strategic narratives. The invasion's aftermath—chaos, suffering, and the exploitation of Iraq's resources—left a grim reminder of what happens when truth is sidelined.

Libya: The Price of Compliance

Libya's story is no less compelling. In 2003, under the auspices of the IAEA, Muammar Gaddafi dismantled his country's nuclear weapons program in a gesture celebrated as a triumph of diplomacy and disarmament. The promise? Reintegration into the global community and stability for the Libyan people.

But less than a decade later, Libya was plunged into turmoil by a NATO-led intervention. Gaddafi was overthrown, the country was fractured, and promises of security faded into chaos. The lesson was clear: disarmament, even under the IAEA's watch, offered no guarantee of protection. Instead, Libya became a cautionary tale for nations weighing the risks of relinquishing their nuclear deterrence.

Iran: A Decade of Disparity

While Libya and Iraq fell victim to intervention, Iran has endured relentless scrutiny. As a signatory to the Nuclear Non-Proliferation Treaty (NPT), Iran has faced stringent monitoring, economic sanctions, and diplomatic isolation for its nuclear activities. The IAEA's meticulous oversight has been pivotal in shaping global negotiations, including the landmark Joint Comprehensive Plan of Action (JCPOA).

Yet the agency's approach to Iran starkly contrasts with its silence on other nations. Critics argue that Iran's case exemplifies the IAEA's susceptibility to geopolitical pressure, with its focus often reflecting the interests of Western powers rather than objective enforcement.

Israel: A Glaring Exception

In the same narrative, Israel stands as a stark anomaly. Widely believed to possess a robust nuclear arsenal, Israel is not a signatory to the NPT and has consistently avoided international scrutiny. The IAEA, which rigorously monitors Iran, remains silent on Israel, fostering a perception of double standards. Protected by its strategic alliances, particularly with the United States, Israel's nuclear ambiguity continues unchecked.

This disparity in the IAEA's treatment of Iran and Israel erodes the agency's credibility. How can an organization champion impartiality when its actions tell a story of bias?

Lessons From the Past

The IAEA's involvement in Iraq, Libya, Iran, and Israel underscores a troubling pattern. In Iraq, the agency's findings were ignored, leading to catastrophic consequences. In Libya, disarmament became a prelude to disaster. In Iran, rigorous scrutiny contrasts sharply with the leniency shown toward Israel. Together, these cases reveal an institution struggling to balance its mission against the pull of global power dynamics.

But the critique doesn't end there. The IAEA's focus often mirrors the strategic interests of dominant nations, raising questions about its ability to operate independently. Nations like the United States, which consistently supports Israel while influencing the agency's actions, complicate the IAEA's efforts to be an unbiased enforcer of nuclear norms.

Restoring Trust: A Path Forward

If the IAEA is to reclaim its role as an impartial custodian of global security, fundamental reforms are necessary. Transparency must be its cornerstone, ensuring decisions are grounded in evidence rather than politics. Accountability mechanisms should hold all nations—regardless of alliances—to the same standards, fostering equity in enforcement.

But beyond structural changes, the IAEA must confront its legacy. Acknowledging past missteps in Iraq and Libya, addressing disparities in oversight, and committing to equitable governance are critical steps toward restoring trust.

The Unanswered Questions

As the IAEA's history unfolds, deeper questions linger:

- Can an organization designed to serve humanity remain untainted by geopolitical influence?

- What does impartiality mean in a world where alliances dictate actions?

- And most critically, how do we ensure that global oversight aligns with the principles of fairness and justice, forming a Judgment Core that transcends political interests?

The IAEA's journey is a microcosm of the broader challenges facing international governance. Its successes, such as smallpox eradication, remind us of the potential for collective action. But its failures expose the fragility of institutions bound by the dual pressures of principle and power.

The world watches and waits, hopeful yet skeptical. Will the IAEA rise to embody the ideals of fairness and equity it was founded upon, or will it remain ensnared in the web of geopolitical interests? The answer lies in its willingness to confront the contradictions that define its legacy—and in our collective demand for accountability and justice.

4.4 The Elusive Accountability of International Organizations

In the intricate web of global governance, international organizations hold immense power to shape policies and influence lives across continents. Yet, this power exists within a troubling vacuum of accountability. Unlike national governments, bound by elections, public scrutiny, and legal oversight, these global institutions often answer primarily to their member states, not the people their actions directly impact. This structural gap raises critical questions: Who holds these organizations accountable? And how can we ensure they serve humanity equitably?

Consider the United Nations, often viewed as a bastion of global diplomacy. Its failures during the 1994 Rwandan Genocide remain one of the starkest illustrations of accountability gone awry. Despite early warnings and a visible escalation of violence, the Security Council—paralyzed by the conflicting interests of its most powerful member states—failed to intervene decisively. As a result, nearly 800,000 people lost their lives. The absence of mechanisms to hold the UN accountable to the affected population compounded this inaction, leaving a scar on the collective conscience of global governance.

This tragedy underscores a grim reality: when decisions hinge on the interests of influential nations, the voices of smaller or marginalized countries are drowned out. Accountability, in such cases, becomes a hollow promise, overshadowed by geopolitical priorities.

The World Health Organization (WHO), another pillar of international cooperation, has faced similar scrutiny. Its delayed response to the 2014

Ebola outbreak in West Africa exposed critical flaws in leadership and decision-making. The virus spread unchecked across Guinea, Liberia, and Sierra Leone, claiming over 11,000 lives. A subsequent investigation highlighted significant lapses in communication and timely intervention, pointing to a leadership unprepared for the magnitude of the crisis.

While reforms have since been introduced, including the creation of an emergency health workforce, the damage was already done. The lack of immediate accountability mechanisms meant that these failures could only be addressed retrospectively, at the cost of thousands of lives.

The World Bank, with its mission to reduce poverty and promote development, has not been immune to criticism either. Large-scale infrastructure projects funded by the Bank often come with hidden costs for local populations. Between 2004 and 2013, an estimated 3.4 million people were displaced by World Bank-funded initiatives, often without adequate compensation or relocation plans. One glaring example is the construction of a massive hydroelectric dam in Ethiopia's Omo Valley, which displaced indigenous communities and caused significant ecological harm. For these communities, the World Bank's lofty promises of progress translated into loss, uprooted lives, and environmental degradation.

Here again, accountability was absent. The displaced populations had little say in the decisions that upended their lives, and the complex bureaucratic structure of the World Bank shielded it from direct consequences.

Even in regions celebrated for their democratic values, such as the European Union, accountability in international decision-making often falters. The negotiations for the Transatlantic Trade and Investment Partnership (TTIP) between the EU and the United States, shrouded in secrecy, sparked widespread criticism. Civil society groups feared that the agreement would prioritize corporate interests over environmental protections and workers' rights. The opacity of the process left citizens powerless to challenge decisions that could have far-reaching implications for their lives.

This lack of transparency is a recurring theme in international governance. Decisions made behind closed doors, devoid of public scrutiny, alienate the very populations these organizations claim to serve. Without mechanisms for open dialogue and participation, global institutions risk becoming tools of power rather than platforms for equity.

Addressing the accountability gap requires more than just acknowledging these flaws; it demands systemic reform. Transparency must become a cornerstone of international governance, ensuring that decisions are made openly and inclusively. Mechanisms for public participation—particularly for those in developing nations most affected by these policies—must be established to give voice to the marginalized. Robust oversight frameworks, independent of political or economic influence, are essential to hold these organizations accountable for their actions.

The failures of international organizations in Rwanda, West Africa, Ethiopia, and beyond are stark reminders of what happens when power operates unchecked. But they also offer an opportunity for transformation. By embracing accountability, transparency, and inclusivity, these institutions can evolve to truly reflect the global interests they were created to serve.

As we grapple with these challenges, critical questions emerge:

- Can international organizations balance the competing interests of powerful nations and vulnerable populations?

- How do we ensure that their decisions are guided by principles of justice and equity, rather than the agendas of a select few?

- And most importantly, can we trust these institutions to uphold a global Judgment Core that values humanity over politics and profit?

The answers lie in our collective demand for reform. True accountability is not a distant ideal; it is a necessity for ensuring that international organizations fulfill their promise as custodians of global well-being. Without it, their legitimacy—and the moral compass of global governance—remains perilously incomplete.

The International Monetary Fund (IMF) has frequently faced criticism for its approach to economic assistance, particularly when its policies seem to prioritize the interests of creditor nations or multinational corporations over the needs of local populations. A striking example of this is seen in the case of Greece during the European debt crisis. In 2010, Greece found itself on the brink of financial collapse and sought a bailout package from the IMF and the European Union to stabilize its economy.

While the aid was crucial to prevent a total financial meltdown, it came with severe conditions, including harsh austerity measures, significant tax hikes, and deep cuts in public spending (Stiglitz, 2015).

These conditions had far-reaching consequences for the Greek economy and its people. The austerity measures led to a prolonged and severe economic recession, with Greece's GDP shrinking by over 25% between

2008 and 2013. Unemployment rates soared, peaking at around 27.5% in 2013, with youth unemployment exceeding 50%. Public sector cuts resulted in the reduction of pensions, healthcare services, and public sector wages, leading to a sharp decline in living standards for millions of Greeks. Public unrest and protests became frequent as people struggled with the impact of these policies on their everyday lives.

Critics of the IMF's approach argued that the stringent conditions imposed were excessively focused on ensuring the repayment of international creditors, such as European banks, rather than on supporting the economic recovery of Greece. They contended that the austerity measures deepened the economic crisis by stifling growth, increasing poverty, and exacerbating social inequality. Nobel laureate economist Joseph Stiglitz criticized the IMF's strategy, stating that it placed the burden of adjustment squarely on the shoulders of the most vulnerable, rather than spreading it more equitably across society (Stiglitz, 2015).

Former Greek finance minister Yanis Varoufakis was among the most vocal critics, arguing that the bailout conditions were not only economically damaging but also fundamentally undemocratic. He highlighted how decisions about Greece's economic future were made largely behind closed doors by international creditors, without sufficient input from the Greek government or its citizens. This process, Varoufakis argued, sidelined democratic governance in favor of technocratic decision-making, illustrating a profound disconnect between the actions of international organizations like the IMF and the needs and rights of the populations they affect (Varoufakis, 2017).

The Greek crisis underscores a broader concern about the accountability of international financial institutions. While these organizations wield significant influence over national economies, their decision-making processes often lack transparency and direct accountability to the affected populations. The case of Greece serves as a stark reminder of how the policies of international organizations can have profound and sometimes devastating impacts on the ground, particularly when they are perceived as prioritizing the repayment of international creditors over the socioeconomic well-being of local populations.

This situation reflects a critical challenge for international organizations like the IMF: the need to balance financial stability with social equity.

When global governance falls short of its ideals, it not only undermines the credibility of international organizations but also shakes the confidence of the global community in these institutions' ability to act as moral leaders.

Failures in global governance often arise from a variety of issues, such as geopolitical biases, lack of enforceability, and the prioritization of national or corporate interests over the common good. These shortcomings highlight the complexities and limitations inherent in trying to apply universal standards across diverse nations with differing political, economic, and cultural contexts.

One key issue is the inconsistency in the application of rules and principles. For instance, while international organizations are supposed to promote equality and human rights, they are often swayed by the political and economic influence of powerful member states. This can result in selective enforcement of rules, where some countries are held to stringent standards, while others are allowed to flout regulations with little consequence. Such double standards erode trust in the impartiality and fairness of these institutions.

Furthermore, international organizations often lack the necessary enforcement mechanisms to compel compliance, relying instead on the voluntary cooperation of member states. This can lead to situations where resolutions, sanctions, or agreements are ignored or only partially implemented, rendering the efforts of these organizations ineffective. For example, despite numerous UN resolutions, conflicts continue in many regions, and human rights violations persist, illustrating the limits of global governance in driving tangible change.

The prioritization of economic over social concerns is another area where global governance often falters. Failures in global governance also include inadequate responses to global crises, such as pandemics or climate change. Despite the existence of international bodies like the WHO or the UN Framework Convention on Climate Change, the global response to such crises is often fragmented, slow, and hampered by competing national interests. These failures highlight the gap between the ambitious goals of global governance and the reality of international cooperation, which is often mired in bureaucracy and a lack of consensus.

Ultimately, these failures force a reevaluation of the role of international organizations as arbiters of global morality. While they have the potential to bring nations together and address global challenges, their effectiveness is contingent on their ability to act impartially, enforce standards consistently, and remain accountable to the global populace. Recognizing these limitations is crucial for reforming these institutions so that they can better fulfill their mission of promoting peace, justice, and equality on a truly global scale.

4.5 The Narrative of Global Complicity

A house stands in the middle of a neighborhood, its walls cracked, its roof barely holding. Inside, a family struggles to survive. One night, an explosion shakes the ground, and the house collapses—its residents buried under the rubble. As the dust settles, the media arrives, not to document the tragedy but to question whether the family inside had caused their own destruction. The real perpetrators stand in the open, but the world looks away, distracted by carefully crafted headlines.

This is not just a metaphor—it is the reality of the ongoing war against Palestinians. The world is being fed a narrative of "conflict," as though this were a clash between two equal sides. But this is not a conflict. This is an extermination campaign, a calculated, decades-long war waged by a Zionist movement determined to erase an entire people, all in pursuit of a Jewish ethnostate built on the blood of displaced civilians. It is not complicated. It is not a war between two states. It is the systematic destruction of Palestine.

It didn't start on October 7, 2023. The occupation and the killings started way before 1948.

The Zionist occupation of Palestine did not begin in 1948 with the creation of Israel; it began decades earlier with organized efforts by Zionist militias to seize Palestinian land. British colonial policies under the Balfour Declaration (1917) facilitated mass Jewish immigration and land confiscation, displacing Palestinian communities. The process intensified in the 1930s and 1940s, culminating in the violent ethnic cleansing known as the Nakba ("Catastrophe") in 1948.

To establish the Zionist state, a campaign of terror and massacres was carried out against Palestinian civilians. Some of the most notorious massacres include:

- Deir Yassin (April 9, 1948): Over 100 Palestinian villagers, including women and children, were brutally murdered by Zionist militias (Irgun and Lehi) in a bid to terrorize Palestinians into fleeing.

- Tantura (May 22-23, 1948): Zionist forces massacred more than 200 Palestinian civilians, and mass graves were later uncovered.

- Lydda and Ramla (July 1948): Thousands of Palestinians were expelled from their homes, and those who resisted were executed.

- Kafr Qasim (October 29, 1956): Israeli forces massacred 49 Palestinian villagers, including children, as part of a systematic campaign of intimidation.

- Sabra and Shatila (September 16-18, 1982): Thousands of Palestinian refugees in Lebanon were slaughtered by Israeli-backed militias in one of the most heinous war crimes of the modern era.

As a result of Zionist violence in 1948, over 750,000 Palestinians were forcibly expelled from their homeland, becoming refugees in neighboring countries and beyond. Today, more than 7 million Palestinian refugees remain displaced, denied their right of return under Israeli policies of apartheid and ethnic cleansing. The expulsion did not end in 1948; it has continued in the form of settlement expansion, home demolitions, and forced evictions in the West Bank, East Jerusalem, and Gaza.

<u>The Systematic Erasure of Palestine</u>

Now, step out of the courtroom and into reality. This is not a hypothetical scenario—it is the grim stage upon which global politics plays out. Laws are written, courts are established, human rights are proclaimed, yet all of it can be suspended at will when the interests of the powerful are at stake. And nowhere is this more evident than in the Israeli-Palestinian conflict, particularly in the events that have unfolded since October 2023.

For decades, the world has watched the Israeli-Palestinian conflict unfold, but the narrative that dominates global discourse is often not one shaped by facts, but by influence. Following Hamas's attack in October 2023, Israel launched an unrelenting military assault on Gaza—one of the deadliest in history. Yet, amid the bloodshed, the global media painted a familiar picture: Israel as the victim, Palestinians as the aggressors. But does this narrative hold up to the weight of reality?

By September 2024, the numbers speak for themselves: Over 17,000 Palestinian children killed. Tens of thousands of civilians wiped out. Entire neighborhoods in Gaza turned to dust. Hospitals, already crippled by a 17-year blockade, bombed into ruins. Schools—once sanctuaries for learning, then shelters for the displaced—reduced to nothing more than smoldering remnants. This is not war; it is annihilation. And yet, the world hesitates to call it by its name.

The blockade, which had already made Gaza an open-air prison, has now tightened to an unbearable stranglehold. Food is scarce. Clean water is a luxury. Medicine is nearly non-existent. Without power, Gaza is plunged into darkness, and with it, the hope of survival fades. Humanitarian organizations issue desperate warnings, yet aid trucks sit idle, stopped by bureaucracy, geopolitics, and indifference.

No Place is Safe

But the destruction does not stop at Gaza's borders. In September 2024, Israel escalated its military assault into Lebanon, unleashing a horror unlike anything before. This time, the weapons were small, silent, and deadly explosives hidden in pagers and walkie-talkies, devices meant for communication turned into instruments of death.

In an instant, forty-two civilians were torn apart, their bodies shattered by explosives they never saw coming. Among them were women clutching their children, journalists reporting from the ground, and medics rushing to save lives—only to lose their own. More than 3,500 others were maimed, some losing limbs, others left with burns so severe that their skin fused with the debris around them.

Children who once played in the streets now lay in hospital beds, missing arms and legs, their innocence stolen by an enemy that sees them as collateral damage. Mothers screamed in agony, searching for their sons and daughters in the rubble, only to find lifeless remains—or nothing at all. The sheer randomness of the attacks meant no one could trust even the most ordinary objects—a message clear as day: nowhere is safe, no one is spared, and death can come at any moment.

This was not war. This was terror in its most calculated, merciless form. A crime not just against Lebanon, but against humanity itself.

Despite this unrelenting brutality, Israel continues to act with absolute impunity, shielded by powerful allies who ensure it never faces consequences. The United States alone provides Israel with $3.8 billion in annual military aid, funding the very bombs that level Palestinian homes. European nations, led by Germany, echo unwavering support, reinforcing Israel's confidence that no action—no matter how severe—will lead to true accountability.

Global Governance Has Failed

What, then, of the institutions meant to uphold international justice? The United Nations (UN) and the International Criminal Court (ICC) issue condemnations, yet their words are weightless. Every blocked resolution, every investigation denied, chips away at their credibility.

The ICC, supposedly the guardian of justice, took an unforgivable amount of time to formally declare Israel guilty of war crimes. But even then, it was nothing more than words without action. Why? Because the United States had its grip on the ICC, using its influence to shield Israel from true accountability. For years, the U.S. has opposed ICC jurisdiction over its allies, going as far as to threaten, sanction, and discredit the court whenever it dares to investigate crimes committed by those under its protection.

When powerful nations dictate who is held accountable and who is not, can these institutions still claim to stand for justice? Or have they become mere tools of selective enforcement—loud against the weak, silent before the strong?

The Media's Role in Erasing Palestinian Suffering

Justice is not only obstructed in courts—it is shaped by perception, and perception is manipulated through media. Reports from mainstream outlets frame Israel as the defender, Palestinians as the threat. Stories of suffering from Gaza are relegated to footnotes, overshadowed by narratives that emphasize Israeli security concerns.

This is not an accident—it is a systematized erasure of Palestinian suffering, a carefully crafted distortion that convinces the world that resistance is terrorism, that genocide is self-defense, that the occupier is the victim. When truth is twisted into propaganda, how can the world's moral compass remain intact?

The Bigger Question: What Happens Next?

This is not just a Palestinian crisis—it is a global crisis. It forces us to ask:

- If institutions like the UN and ICC cannot act against the powerful, do they still serve justice, or are they tools of selective enforcement?

- When some nations operate above the law, is international law anything more than an illusion?

- When the media distorts the truth, how does it shape the Judgment Core of billions?

If the world can justify this, what else can it justify? And if your Judgment Core remains silent, at what point does silence become complicity?

4.6 Conclusion: The Power and the Paradox of Global Governance

Imagine a lighthouse standing tall on a stormy shore, its beam cutting through the darkness, promising safety to those lost at sea. Sailors rely on it, trusting that its light will guide them to solid ground. But what if, one night, the light flickers erratically? What if it begins to favor some ships over others, leading some safely home while letting others crash against unseen rocks? The lighthouse was built to protect all, yet its glow now serves the select few. Can it still be trusted?

Now, shift your focus from the lighthouse to the institutions that claim to guide the world toward justice, peace, and human rights. International organizations—the United Nations, the International Criminal Court, the World Health Organization, the World Bank—were established as moral beacons, illuminating the path toward a better world. Their successes, from eradicating diseases to establishing legal frameworks for war crimes, prove their potential. Yet, their failures—their selective intervention, their silence in the face of injustice, and their subservience to the powerful—raise unsettling questions.

These institutions shape the Judgment Core (JDC) of the global community, defining what is considered just, ethical, and acceptable. But who sets the parameters of this morality? Who determines which injustices warrant immediate action and which can be quietly ignored? Who decides who must be held accountable and who remains untouchable?

- When the UN Security Council's veto power silences action against clear crimes, does justice still hold meaning?

- When international courts pursue certain war criminals but overlook others, can we trust their impartiality?

- When global financial institutions impose economic policies that benefit the powerful while crippling the vulnerable, is it truly development—or modern colonialism?

The contradiction is clear: these organizations claim to uphold universal morality, yet they operate within a system dictated by geopolitical interests. Their ideals of fairness and equality are often manipulated, twisted to serve the needs of those with the most influence. This is the paradox of global governance—a system designed to promote justice, yet one that often enables injustice under the guise of diplomacy and order.

Does this mean international institutions are beyond redemption? No. Their frameworks are essential, their goals worth striving for. But they cannot be trusted without scrutiny, nor followed without question. As individuals, we must resist the passive acceptance of their authority and ask ourselves:

- How much of our moral compass has been shaped by their selective narratives?

- When do we accept their rulings, and when must we resist their influence?

- If the institutions that dictate global morality are flawed, how do we reclaim the right to define justice for ourselves?

These are not abstract debates—they are urgent realities that shape the future of justice, war, and human rights. The world order we accept today dictates the morality of tomorrow. If we fail to demand transparency, equity, and genuine accountability, we become complicit in allowing injustice to masquerade as law.

So, when the next resolution is passed, the next military intervention is justified, the next economic policy is imposed—will you accept it at face value, or will you question, challenge, and redefine justice on your own terms?

The light from the lighthouse still shines. But you must decide whether to follow it blindly—or to question who controls the switch.?

Chapter 5: The Role of Religion – A Double-Edged Sword

A traveler lost in the vastness of the desert stumbles upon an ancient compass, its needle unwavering, pointing toward an unseen destination. Grateful, they follow its direction, trusting it to lead them to safety. But as the days stretch on, the needle begins to waver—sometimes subtly, sometimes wildly—shifting in ways that cannot be explained. Is the compass broken, or has the traveler failed to interpret its guidance correctly? Does it still lead to salvation, or has it become a mirage of certainty in an uncertain world?

This is the paradox of religion. Like the compass, it offers direction, providing billions with a moral framework to navigate the complexities of life. It promises meaning, clarity, and a code of conduct that claims to transcend time, culture, and personal doubt. For many, it is the anchor in a turbulent sea, the guiding light when darkness obscures the way. But can a compass, however sacred, ever be truly immune to external forces?

This chapter builds upon our exploration of global influences—governments that define legality, international organizations that claim moral authority, your community and your family that shaped your identity. Now, we step into the realm of belief itself, where religion wields an even greater power: shaping not just laws or social norms, but the very essence of our Judgment Core (JDC)—the moral foundation that guides our decisions, defines our ethics, and influences the way we perceive right and wrong.

At its best, religion has inspired acts of unparalleled kindness, justice, and selflessness. It has given rise to movements of peace, charity, and social reform. It calls humanity to a higher purpose, one that extends beyond individual desires and into the realm of collective good. But history tells a more complex story—one where religion, in the hands of the powerful, has been used to justify war, discrimination, and oppression. The same scriptures that preach love and humility have been invoked to enforce division, subjugate dissent, and resist change. How does such contradiction shape the morality of those who follow?

Sacred texts, revered as divine, are passed through generations, yet they are interpreted, translated, and reinterpreted by human hands. Over centuries, religious doctrines have evolved, adapted, and sometimes fractured—reshaped by culture, politics, and power struggles. If divine law is meant to be eternal, why has its application changed with time? And if religious morality is absolute, why do its interpretations differ between nations, sects, and individuals?

This raises a critical dilemma: Is religion a steadfast beacon of morality, or is it a tool that bends to human will? If it has been used to uphold both justice and injustice, unity and division, then how do we determine which version of its teachings is true?

The weight of this question falls upon the individual believer. Is faith meant to be followed blindly, or does it demand scrutiny? Should moral guidance come solely from doctrine, or must it be examined through reason, context, and lived experience? Can religion coexist with independent moral reasoning, or does it insist upon obedience over personal judgment?

In this chapter, we examine religion's dual nature—its ability to inspire both righteousness and rigidity, its capacity to unite and to divide. As we explore its role in shaping the Judgment Core, we must ask ourselves:

- Does religion strengthen your moral compass, or does it sometimes cloud it with conflicting interpretations?

- Do you follow religious principles because they feel right to you, or because they have been passed down as unquestionable truths?

- When faith and personal reasoning collide, which one do you trust to guide your decisions?

Religion, like the ancient compass in the traveler's hands, offers direction. But it is up to each of us to determine whether we follow it without question, recalibrate it when it falters, or challenge its course entirely. In the end, morality is not simply inherited—it must be discovered, tested, and refined.

So, as you step into this exploration, ask yourself: Is your moral compass truly yours, or has it been shaped by forces you have never questioned? And if faith is meant to illuminate truth, then what will you do when its shadows ask you to look deeper?

5.1 The Power of Religion in Defining Morality

For many, religion provides the foundational principles for their JDC. It offers a sense of purpose and a clear distinction between right and wrong, guiding individuals in how they should behave, treat others, and make moral choices. Religious teachings often emphasize virtues such as kindness, generosity, and self-sacrifice, while condemning acts like theft, dishonesty, and violence. Through rituals, scriptures, and communal practices, religion embeds these values deeply into a person's worldview.

Religious communities reinforce these moral values by creating environments where shared beliefs are upheld and deviations are discouraged. This sense of collective morality provides a strong framework for individuals to shape their actions in ways that align with their religious traditions. For many, it becomes second nature to filter their decisions through the lens of their faith.

The Sermon on the Mount

In Christianity, the teachings of Jesus Christ, particularly those found in the Sermon on the Mount (Matthew 5-7), provide a comprehensive moral framework. Jesus emphasizes love, mercy, forgiveness, and humility, urging followers to "love your enemies and pray for those who persecute you" (Matthew 5:44) and "turn the other cheek" when wronged (Matthew 5:39). These teachings advocate for a compassionate and non-violent approach to conflict and encourage a profound sense of empathy and humility.

Christianity also emphasizes the importance of helping those in need, as seen in Jesus' parable of the Good Samaritan (Luke 10:25-37), which teaches that love and compassion should extend beyond social or ethnic boundaries. These messages serve as guiding principles for many Christians, shaping a moral outlook that prioritizes empathy, charity, and kindness toward others.

Dharma and Ahimsa

Hinduism, one of the oldest religions in the world, also provides a rich moral framework based on the concepts of dharma (duty/righteousness) and ahimsa (non-violence). The Bhagavad Gita, a sacred Hindu text, teaches that individuals should perform their duties according to their dharma without attachment to the results (Bhagavad Gita 2:47). It emphasizes living a life of righteousness, upholding truth, justice, and ethical behavior in all circumstances.

Furthermore, the principle of ahimsa, or non-violence, is a central tenet in Hindu ethics. The Manusmriti, an ancient legal text, states: "Ahimsa Paramo Dharma," meaning "Non-violence is the highest duty" (Manusmriti

10.63). This concept has influenced countless Hindu practices and philosophies, encouraging followers to avoid causing harm to any living being.

These teachings provide a foundation for a moral life in Hinduism, emphasizing duty, righteousness, and non-violence as fundamental principles guiding ethical behavior.

The Four Noble Truths and the Noble Eightfold Path

Buddhism also provides a profound moral framework through the teachings of the Buddha. The Four Noble Truths outline the nature of suffering, its cause, its cessation, and the path to its cessation. The Noble Eightfold Path, which includes right understanding, right intention, right speech, right action, right livelihood, right effort, right mindfulness, and right concentration, serves as a guide for ethical conduct and mental discipline (Rahula, 1959).

Buddhism emphasizes compassion (karuna) and loving-kindness (metta) toward all beings. The Buddha taught that to live ethically, one must avoid causing harm and strive to alleviate suffering wherever possible. The Dhammapada, a collection of the Buddha's sayings, states, "Hatred does not cease by hatred, but only by love; this is the eternal rule" (Dhammapada 1:5). These teachings encourage Buddhists to cultivate compassion, mindfulness, and self-control, reinforcing a moral framework centered on empathy and peace.

The Importance of Justice and Compassion

The Quran, the holy book of Islam, emphasizes justice and compassion as core principles for human conduct. For example, Surah An-Nisa (4:135) instructs: "O you who have believed, be persistently standing firm in justice, witnesses for Allah, even if it be against yourselves or parents and relatives. Whether one is rich or poor, Allah is more worthy of both." This verse highlights the importance of fairness and integrity, encouraging believers to uphold justice, even when it is challenging or conflicts with personal interests.

Similarly, the Quran promotes compassion and mercy toward others. In Surah Al-Imran (3:134), it says: "Who spend [in the cause of Allah] during ease and hardship and who restrain anger and who pardon the people—and Allah loves the doers of good." This verse encourages Muslims to act with kindness, self-restraint, and forgiveness, promoting an ethical framework that prioritizes the well-being of others and fosters peace and harmony.

These teachings emphasize that moral behavior should be guided by principles of justice, compassion, and empathy, which align with universal values found across many religious traditions.

5.2 The Problem of Interpretation and Manipulation

Religious texts, revered as timeless guides to morality, hold a paradoxical power: they are both profound and pliable. Across centuries, they have been read, interpreted, and reinterpreted by countless voices—each layered with the context of its time, the bias of its interpreter, and the lens of personal or collective need. This malleability has allowed these teachings to transcend eras and borders, adapting to ever-changing human circumstances. Yet, it is precisely this adaptability that reveals their most enigmatic quality: the potential for both illumination and distortion.

Imagine a sacred text that speaks of peace and compassion, its verses inspiring acts of boundless generosity and humanitarian service. Now picture the same text wielded as a weapon, its words contorted to justify exclusion, conflict, or militant action. How can the same source of wisdom lead to such vastly divergent outcomes? Is this duality an inherent strength, offering a mirror to humanity's complexities, or a perilous vulnerability that leaves morality open to manipulation?

Throughout history, the power of interpretation has shifted from one hand to another: scholars and spiritual leaders, kings and revolutionaries, all claiming the authority to discern divine intent. But as teachings are translated, reframed, and recontextualized, what remains of their original essence? Do they evolve to meet the needs of a changing world, or do they risk becoming shadows of their true meaning, subtly shaped by the priorities and politics of their time?

Consider how exclusivity often accompanies religious teachings. Many traditions assert that their moral framework is not merely one of many paths but the definitive way to salvation, divine favor, or enlightenment. This claim to absolute truth can unite believers in shared purpose and identity, yet it also erects walls—boundaries of "us" versus "them," believers and non-believers. In a world of diverse faiths and philosophies, such rigid divides can ignite conflict. When differing interpretations clash, whose moral compass is the true one? Whose vision of right and wrong should prevail?

The intertwining of religion with power further complicates this picture. Political leaders and movements have long invoked sacred texts to legitimize authority, rally support, or enforce control. Even the noblest teachings can be distorted, their messages twisted to serve agendas that may contradict their foundational principles. Is this manipulation a flaw of religion itself, or does it reflect the ever-present temptation of power to exploit moral authority?

As you navigate this labyrinth of interpretation and intent, questions arise that strike at the heart of the Judgment Core—the internal moral compass each of us carries. How do you discern the true essence of religious teachings amidst layers of human bias and historical distortion? Can you embrace the profound moral principles they offer while resisting the lure of dogmatism or exclusion? And most intriguingly, how do these teachings shape your own sense of right and wrong?

Religion's ability to inspire, unite, and guide is undeniable. Yet, its susceptibility to misuse serves as a cautionary tale, reminding us that moral discernment requires more than faith—it demands critical thought and a willingness to question. As you reflect on the role of religion in shaping your Judgment Core, ask yourself: Are you guided by the light of its highest ideals, or do you sometimes find yourself entangled in its shadows? The answers lie not in the texts alone but in the clarity and courage with which you seek to understand them.

Religious teachings have long served as moral compasses, shaping the JDC of entire civilizations. But faith, like any guiding force, can be both illuminating and misleading. If morality is anchored in religious doctrine, does it remain authentic when interpreted by human hands? How do we reconcile divine wisdom with human fallibility? The JDC must navigate this delicate balance, ensuring that belief strengthens morality rather than distorts it.

<u>Misinterpretation of "An Eye for an Eye"</u>

The phrase "an eye for an eye, a tooth for a tooth" (Exodus 21:24) is one of the most widely recognized yet frequently misinterpreted biblical principles. Originally, this concept, known as the lex talionis, was not a call for violent revenge, but rather a legal guideline intended to ensure that punishments were fair and proportionate to the offenses committed. The purpose was to prevent excessive retaliation and restore balance within a structured legal system. In its context, it was part of a broader system of justice designed to avoid escalating violence by ensuring that the response to wrongdoing did not exceed the harm caused by the offense (Matthews, 2001).

However, over time, this principle has often been taken out of its original judicial context and used to justify personal vengeance and disproportionate retribution. In many cases, it has been interpreted by individuals or groups as a mandate for retaliation, where the desire for revenge eclipses the original intent of the law. This misinterpretation can be seen in various historical and modern examples where acts of violence or retribution are carried out in the name of "justice," but are actually driven by a desire for personal revenge or societal revenge against perceived wrongs.

For instance, in some conflicts between communities or nations, the concept of "an eye for an eye" has been invoked to justify violent responses that far exceed the initial offense. In such cases, the principle is misapplied, resulting in cycles of violence rather than the restoration of justice. These cycles often perpetuate long-standing conflicts, as each act of retribution is met with further retaliation, ultimately distorting the original intent of proportional justice into endless revenge.

An illustrative example of this misapplication can be seen in certain honor-based societies where family feuds and vendettas are fueled by a belief in avenging wrongs, even if the original crime was minor. In these contexts, "an eye for an eye" is interpreted not as a limitation on punishment but as a justification for taking justice into one's own hands. Such practices can escalate quickly, leading to intergenerational conflicts that continue for years or even decades.

In contrast to this misinterpretation, Jesus' teachings in the New Testament offer a reinterpretation of this principle. In the Sermon on the Mount, Jesus famously says, "You have heard that it was said, 'An eye for an eye and a tooth for a tooth.' But I tell you, do not resist an evil person. If anyone slaps you on the right cheek, turn to them the other cheek also" (Matthew 5:38-39). Here, Jesus shifts the focus from retribution to forgiveness, urging his followers to break the cycle of revenge by responding to wrongdoing with grace and restraint. This teaching marks a radical departure from the older legalistic interpretation of proportional punishment, emphasizing the moral superiority of forgiveness over vengeance.

This contrast within the same religious tradition demonstrates how religious texts can be interpreted in diverse ways, depending on the moral and theological lens through which they are viewed. The transition from a justice-based system of proportional retribution to one centered on forgiveness and mercy illustrates the fluidity of religious interpretation and the ways in which moral teachings evolve over time.

Beyond Christianity, similar reinterpretations of the concept of proportional justice can be found in other religious and cultural contexts. For example, in Islamic jurisprudence, the concept of qisas (retaliation) allows for a victim or their family to seek retributive justice in cases of murder or bodily harm, but it also offers the option of diyya (financial compensation) or even the choice to forgive the perpetrator entirely. The Quran encourages forgiveness as a virtuous act, stating, "But if anyone remits the retaliation by way of charity, it is an act of atonement for himself" (Quran 5:45). This balance between justice and mercy reflects a recognition that while proportional punishment is legally justified, forgiveness can have a transformative moral power.

The misinterpretation of "an eye for an eye" serves as a reminder of the potential for religious texts to be taken out of context and used to justify actions that run contrary to their original intent. It also highlights the importance of understanding the broader ethical frameworks within which these teachings are situated. When interpreted with a focus on their deeper moral lessons, such principles can offer guidance toward justice and reconciliation rather than perpetuating cycles of violence and revenge.

Misinterpretation of Jihad

The concept of jihad in Islam is one of the most frequently misunderstood and misinterpreted aspects of the faith. While the term "jihad" in the holy Quran is most commonly understood as "striving" or "struggle," its meaning is far broader than the common depiction of it as violent conflict. Islamic scholars and theologians have long emphasized that jihad primarily refers to a personal, spiritual struggle to live a righteous and ethical life, to promote justice, and to resist evil in its many forms (Esposito, 2002). This could mean striving to improve oneself, performing acts of charity, or standing up for social justice.

However, over time, certain extremist groups have manipulated the concept of jihad to justify violent acts of terrorism and aggression, distorting its meaning to promote their own political or ideological agendas. They have framed jihad as a "holy war" against non-believers, misusing religious texts and ignoring the broader teachings of Islam that emphasize peace, tolerance, and coexistence.

The distortion of jihad to justify violence ignores the Quranic context that places clear restrictions on warfare and emphasizes the sanctity of life. For instance, in Surah Al-Baqarah (2:190), it is stated: "Fight in the way of Allah those who fight you, but do not transgress. Indeed, Allah does not like transgressors." This verse underscores that any form of combat must be defensive, not aggressive, and that Muslims are forbidden from targeting innocents or engaging in excessive violence. The Quran goes on to clarify that if the enemy ceases hostilities, Muslims must also cease fighting (2:192), further emphasizing that warfare is a last resort and only permissible under strict conditions. Yet, extremist groups disregard these principles, cherry-picking verses that suit their violent objectives while ignoring the broader moral teachings.

This misinterpretation is not unique to Islam. Throughout history, religious concepts have been exploited for political or violent ends across various faiths. For example, the Crusades in medieval Christianity were driven by a distorted interpretation of Christian principles, where the idea of reclaiming the Holy Land was used to justify brutal wars and massacres against Muslims and Jews. Similarly, in modern times, religious zealots have misused Jewish teachings to promote acts of violence against Palestinians, ignoring the ethical commandments of Judaism that prioritize peace and justice.

In the context of jihad, extremist groups manipulate Quranic verses by stripping them of their historical and theological context. For instance, they often refer to Surah At-Tawbah (9:5), known as the "Verse of the Sword," which instructs Muslims to fight idolaters. However, these groups omit the surrounding verses that limit this directive to specific historical circumstances, namely the defense against aggressive enemies at a time when Muslims were under siege. The verse is not a blanket justification for violence but was revealed in the context of a specific conflict during the Prophet Muhammad's lifetime, and it does not sanction unprovoked aggression.

Moreover, Islamic teachings emphasize the value of coexistence and interfaith dialogue. For example, Surah Al-Mumtahanah (60:8) states: "Allah does not forbid you from those who do not fight you because of religion and do not expel you from your homes – from being righteous toward them and acting justly toward them. Indeed, Allah loves those who act justly." This verse highlights the importance of treating people of other faiths with kindness and justice, reflecting the broader Islamic principle of peaceful coexistence.

The Hadith (sayings of the Prophet Muhammad) further support the idea that jihad is primarily about inner moral struggle rather than external conflict. The Prophet Muhammad referred to the "greater jihad" as the struggle against one's own base desires, indicating that the spiritual and ethical dimensions of jihad far outweigh any concept of physical warfare.

Yet, extremist interpretations of jihad completely overlook these teachings, focusing instead on a militaristic and exclusionary view that isolates Muslims from the broader world and justifies hostility towards those who are different. This distortion has had tragic consequences, fueling global terrorism, contributing to the rise of extremist ideologies, and fostering a climate of fear and division. These misinterpretations harm not only the victims of violence but also the vast majority of peaceful Muslims whose faith is maligned by the actions of a radical few.

By selectively interpreting and manipulating the concept of jihad, extremists have undermined Islam's core values of peace, justice, and mercy. The Quranic teachings, when understood in their proper context, offer clear guidance on the limitations of conflict and the imperative to promote peace whenever possible. Jihad, in its true essence, is about striving for personal moral integrity and the betterment of society, not about warfare and violence. Recognizing and addressing these misinterpretations is essential to restoring a more accurate understanding of the concept and preventing further exploitation of religious texts for violent ends.

Distortion of Caste System

Hinduism's caste system, as it is practiced today, is often justified by certain interpretations of ancient texts like the Manusmriti, which prescribe social roles and hierarchical divisions. However, this rigid, birth-based caste structure that has come to define much of Indian society does not accurately reflect the original intent of the concept of varna in Hindu philosophy. In its early form, the caste system was not meant to be a hereditary or immutable social order but rather a functional classification based on an individual's abilities, qualities, and responsibilities.

The Bhagavad Gita provides insight into the original framework of varna. In Chapter 4, Verse 13, Krishna says, "The four divisions of human society were created by Me according to the three modes of material nature and the work associated with them" (Bhagavad Gita 4:13). This indicates that varna—which divides society into four classes: Brahmins (teachers and priests), Kshatriyas (warriors and rulers), Vaishyas (merchants and farmers), and Shudras (laborers)—was originally based on a person's nature (guna) and the work they performed (karma), rather than their birth. The idea was that each class had specific duties that contributed to the harmonious functioning of society, and one's position was determined by their talents, inclinations, and the work they pursued.

Over time, however, these teachings were distorted and manipulated to justify a rigid social hierarchy, wherein caste became synonymous with birthright. Instead of reflecting an individual's qualities or actions, caste became a hereditary system in which people were confined to the class of their ancestors, regardless of their own capabilities or aspirations. This shift not only undermined the original intention of varna but also led to the entrenchment of social inequality and discrimination.

One of the major texts that has been used to justify this distortion is the Manusmriti, an ancient legal code that, unlike the more philosophical texts of Hinduism, prescribes specific social and legal norms, including rigid caste-based rules. The Manusmriti places a strong emphasis on maintaining social order through caste distinctions, often assigning lower castes fewer rights and privileges. While many view the Manusmriti as reflecting a later, more socially conservative interpretation of Hindu law, its codification of caste divisions has had a lasting impact on the Indian social fabric, reinforcing hereditary privilege and discrimination, particularly against Dalits (formerly known as "untouchables").

This distortion of the varna system into a rigid caste hierarchy illustrates how religious teachings can be manipulated to serve social and political agendas. Over the centuries, the caste system has been used by ruling elites to maintain social order and control, legitimizing their power by invoking divine authority. This manipulation of Hindu texts to support caste-based discrimination contradicts the foundational values of the religion, which emphasize dharma (righteousness), karma (action), and the pursuit of spiritual liberation for all individuals, regardless of their social standing.

For example, prominent reformers and scholars throughout Indian history, such as Swami Vivekananda and Mahatma Gandhi, have pointed out that the true essence of Hinduism does not support caste-based discrimination. Vivekananda, in particular, argued that the caste system as practiced was a perversion of Hinduism and went against the ideals of unity and equality espoused in the Vedas and Upanishads. Gandhi similarly campaigned against the caste system, advocating for the upliftment of Dalits and renaming them Harijans ("children of God"), in a bid to restore dignity and equality to those oppressed by the caste hierarchy.

Moreover, the misinterpretation of the varna system as a fixed, birth-based hierarchy not only contradicts Hinduism's philosophical roots but has also caused significant social harm. Discrimination against lower castes and Dalits has resulted in deep social stratification, economic inequality, and widespread injustice. In modern India, while legal measures have been put in place to combat caste-based discrimination, such as the abolition of "untouchability" in the Indian Constitution, the legacy of caste continues to influence social structures, politics, and personal relationships.

Other examples from Hindu scripture highlight the flexibility of the original varna system. In the Mahabharata, the revered teacher Dronacharya, though a Brahmin by birth, takes up the role of a warrior and military instructor, challenging the notion that caste should limit one's profession. Similarly, in the Ramayana, Lord Rama forms alliances with characters from various social backgrounds, including the Vanara king Sugriva and the forest-dwelling Shabari, demonstrating that caste was never intended to be a barrier to spiritual or moral worth.

The misinterpretation and manipulation of the caste system demonstrate how religious teachings can be distorted to serve entrenched power structures and perpetuate inequality. The original teachings of varna emphasized individual qualities and societal contribution, yet over time, these ideals were reshaped to justify a rigid, oppressive hierarchy that contradicted Hinduism's broader spiritual values. Understanding this evolution is crucial for recognizing the gap between the foundational principles of Hinduism and the social realities that have emerged over centuries.

Today, many scholars, activists, and spiritual leaders continue to work toward reclaiming the original, more inclusive interpretation of varna as a means of promoting equality and social justice, challenging the entrenched caste divisions that still persist in Indian society.

Misinterpretation of Karma

The concept of karma, central to Buddhist teachings, is often misinterpreted in ways that distort its original meaning and ethical implications. In its true essence, karma is a deeply nuanced concept that refers to the intentional actions of individuals, and the consequences of those actions, which together shape one's present and future experiences. However, it is frequently misunderstood as a form of fatalism—where individuals are seen as deserving their suffering or misfortune due to past actions, whether from this life or previous ones. This oversimplified view reduces karma to a rigid cause-and-effect mechanism, which can lead to harmful social attitudes, such as blaming individuals for their circumstances, especially in cases of poverty, illness, or suffering.

In Buddhism, the Buddha emphasized that karma is not a punitive system of cosmic justice but rather an ongoing process that encompasses a person's intentions, actions, and the consequences that unfold as a result. Karma is dynamic and fluid, with the potential for change and transformation through conscious action and understanding (Rahula, 1959). It is meant to inspire personal responsibility and ethical conduct rather than justify passivity in the face of suffering or social inequality. One's current experiences are shaped not only by past actions but also by present choices, intentions, and efforts to improve one's behavior and mental state.

A common misinterpretation of karma, particularly outside of its original Buddhist context, is the idea that people's misfortunes are wholly deserved due to their past misdeeds. This misunderstanding can lead to a lack of empathy and a tendency to view those who are suffering as responsible for their own plight, which disregards the complexities of karma as taught by the Buddha. For instance, in many societies where karma is commonly invoked, people may rationalize social inequalities, poverty, or illness as the inevitable result of a person's bad karma, which can lead to societal neglect of the suffering and marginalized.

This fatalistic interpretation has at times been used to rationalize or ignore systemic social injustices. For example, in certain parts of the Indian subcontinent, the caste system has been reinforced through the misapplication of the doctrine of karma, suggesting that those born into lower castes or impoverished conditions must have deserved their fate due to actions in past lives. This interpretation overlooks the Buddhist principle of compassion (karuna), which teaches that suffering should inspire empathy and action, rather than judgment and indifference.

Similarly, in the modern world, the misunderstanding of karma can manifest in beliefs such as "victim-blaming," where people suggest that those who experience hardship or disaster must have done something to deserve it. Whether in the context of natural disasters, economic struggles, or personal loss, this interpretation turns karma into a form of moral judgment, stripping away its original spiritual depth and ethical complexity.

The Buddha's teachings stress that karma should be understood with both compassion and wisdom (panna). He frequently warned against using karma as a justification for ignoring the suffering of others or neglecting one's responsibility to alleviate suffering where possible. Compassion is a core element of Buddhist ethics, and the proper understanding of karma requires that we seek to help those in distress rather than dismiss their suffering as deserved or inevitable. One famous teaching from the Buddha on karma is the story of Angulimala, a mass murderer who, through personal transformation and remorse, changed his life and became a monk under the Buddha's guidance. This story illustrates that karma is not a fixed destiny but something that can be altered through conscious effort, ethical conduct, and personal growth.

Moreover, karma in its true sense involves not only the actions of individuals but also the intentions behind those actions. The moral weight of karma is not simply about the external outcomes but the mental and emotional states that motivate our actions. This key aspect is often overlooked in modern, reductive interpretations of karma. For example, two people might perform the same action, but if one does it out of greed and the other out of compassion, the karmic consequences would differ significantly. Thus, karma is much more than just a simplistic reward-and-punishment system; it is a reflection of our inner moral and spiritual development.

Misinterpretations of karma also affect the way people engage with social justice issues. In some contexts, the belief that individuals are responsible for their own suffering has led to a reluctance to challenge oppressive systems or to offer help to those in need. This is a distortion of the original intent behind the concept of karma, which encourages personal responsibility but also emphasizes interconnectedness and the importance of reducing suffering for all beings. Karma, in the Buddhist understanding, does not absolve people of their ethical duty to address social and structural inequities; rather, it compels action rooted in compassion.

The Dalai Lama, for example, often speaks about karma in the context of global compassion, highlighting that the suffering of others is a shared human concern, not something to be attributed to their past deeds or accepted passively. He emphasizes that understanding karma should lead to greater efforts to promote peace, justice, and kindness, rather than indifference to the suffering of others.

Thus, the misinterpretation of karma as a fatalistic principle has far-reaching consequences, both for individuals and for societies. It can foster a sense of helplessness, as people may believe they are bound by their past actions with no possibility of change, and it can also justify passivity in the face of injustice. The true teaching of karma, however, is a call to personal responsibility, ethical action, and continuous moral development. It encourages individuals to strive to improve themselves and their circumstances, while also cultivating compassion and wisdom in their interactions with others.

Religious Conflicts and the Question of Exclusivity

In Judaism, one notable example of exclusivity is the concept of the "Chosen People." This belief, rooted in passages from the Hebrew Bible such as Deuteronomy 14:2, asserts that the Jewish people were chosen by God to fulfill a special covenant. The verse states, "For you're a people holy to the Lord your God, and the Lord has chosen you to be a people for his treasured possession." While many Jews interpret this covenant as a responsibility to uphold divine commandments and be a light of justice and morality to the world, the concept has been misinterpreted by some to suggest that Jews are inherently superior to other groups (Katz, 2005).

The belief in being the "Chosen People" originally emphasized a responsibility to follow God's laws and promote justice, but some have taken it further to imply that Jews are uniquely favored by God. This interpretation has sometimes been linked to the term "Goyim," which is used in Jewish texts to refer to non-Jews. The term itself is neutral in its literal meaning, simply designating non-Jewish nations, but it has been misused by some to imply that non-Jews (Goyim) are lesser in spiritual or moral standing and even as human animals. In certain interpretations, non-Jews are viewed as not being part of God's covenant and, therefore, outside the realm of divine favor. This exclusivist led to a sense of division between Jews and non-Jews, reinforcing a belief in spiritual or moral superiority.

This exclusivist interpretation, while not representative of mainstream Jewish thought, has been used by some groups to justify exclusionary or discriminatory actions. In extreme cases, this sense of divine favor has even been invoked to rationalize violence. One controversial application of these ideas can be seen in the context of the Israeli occupation of Palestine. Drawing on the idea of Jewish chosenness and the perceived moral inferiority of non-Jews (Goyim), have used religious justification to support aggressive military actions and violence against non-Jews, specially the Palestinians. They interpret their divine favor as a mandate to prioritize Jewish lives and territory, often justifying the displacement, oppression, or killing of Palestinians as part of a broader religious mission to secure the land promised to them by God.

In particular, the use of religious justification for violence becomes especially potent in the context of the Israeli-Jewish state's actions. Certain religious and political leaders have framed military actions against Palestinians as part of a divine right to the land of Israel, drawing on biblical claims of Jewish entitlement to the territory. This interpretation is often coupled with the notion that Palestinians, as non-Jews, are outsiders to the covenant and therefore do not have the same divine claim to the land. This sense of religious exclusivity has been used to justify acts of violence, including the killing of civilians including kids in the context of territorial disputes, framing these actions as necessary for fulfilling God's will.

This misuse of religious teachings to justify violence is inconsistent with broader Jewish values of justice, compassion, and the sanctity of life. Many Jewish scholars and leaders reject such interpretations, emphasizing that the concept of the "Chosen People" should be understood as a call to ethical responsibility rather than a claim to superiority. For example, Rabbi Jonathan Sacks, a prominent Jewish philosopher, has argued that the idea of chosenness is about serving humanity and living in accordance with divine justice, not about dominating others or claiming superiority.

In conclusion, the misinterpretation of religious concepts such as the "Chosen People" and the term "Goyim" has contributed to exclusivist attitudes and even violence in some contexts. However, these interpretations are not representative of the broader ethical teachings of Judaism, which call for justice, compassion, and humility. The challenge lies in moving beyond these exclusivist readings and embracing the universal values that promote peace, equality, and the dignity of all human beings.

5.3 Finding the Common Ground in Religious Teachings

Despite the challenges posed by religious exclusivity, misinterpretation, and conflict, it is essential to recognize that at the heart of most religious teachings lie common values—principles that emphasize compassion, fairness, and the sanctity of life. Many religions, regardless of their doctrinal differences, advocate for peace, kindness, and the dignity of all human beings. These shared values provide a powerful moral foundation that transcends individual religious boundaries.

One of the most universal ethical principles found across various religious traditions is the Golden Rule—the idea that one should treat others as one would like to be treated. This principle is central to many of the world's major religions, reflecting a common commitment to empathy and moral reciprocity.

Christianity: In the Bible, Jesus teaches the Golden Rule in Matthew 7:12, "So in everything, do to others what you would have them do to you." This principle is a cornerstone of Christian ethics, promoting love, empathy, and fairness in relationships with others. Christians are called to emulate Jesus' compassion and love for humanity, ensuring that their actions reflect kindness and consideration for others.

Judaism: The Golden Rule appears in Leviticus 19:18, "Love your neighbor as yourself." This commandment underpins the Jewish commitment to justice (tzedek) and kindness (chesed). In Jewish thought, the idea of loving one's neighbor extends beyond mere tolerance, urging individuals to actively seek the well-being of others, both within and outside the Jewish community. This principle emphasizes equality and mutual respect in human interactions.

Islam: In Sahih Muslim 45:1, the Prophet Muhammad stated, "None of you truly believes until he wishes for his brother what he wishes for himself." In Islam, this teaching emphasizes the importance of brotherhood, mutual respect, and empathy. The principle of ummah (the global Muslim community) reinforces the idea that all believers should care for one another and treat others with the same consideration they would want for themselves. This extends to how Muslims should interact with non-Muslims, promoting peace and justice for all.

Buddhism: In Dhammapada 10:1, the Buddha teaches, "Consider others as yourself." This reflects the Buddhist commitment to compassion (karuna) and loving-kindness (metta). Buddhists are encouraged to cultivate empathy for all beings, recognizing that everyone shares the same capacity for suffering and happiness. The Golden Rule in Buddhism is closely tied to the practice of mindfulness and the understanding of interconnectedness, which fosters a deep sense of responsibility toward the well-being of others.

Hinduism: The Mahabharata (5:1517) expresses the Golden Rule as, "This is the sum of duty: Do not do to others what would cause pain if done to you." In Hinduism, this principle is rooted in the belief in karma—the idea that one's actions have consequences, both for oneself and others. The teaching of non-violence (ahimsa) is also closely related to the Golden Rule, promoting the idea that harming others ultimately harms oneself, as all beings are interconnected.

These examples from different religious traditions highlight that, despite differences in doctrine and practice, many religions share a common commitment to ethical principles that promote human flourishing and the greater good. The Golden Rule, in its various forms, calls for empathy, kindness, and fairness, offering a powerful moral foundation that transcends religious boundaries.

These core teachings can provide a powerful moral foundation, one that transcends the boundaries of specific religious traditions. They show that, despite differences, many religions emphasize similar values that promote human flourishing and the greater good.

A Critical Engagement with Religion Reflect on how these external influences challenge or reinforce your personal Judgment Core (JDC).

While religion can be a profound source of moral guidance, it should not be followed blindly or uncritically.

It is essential to recognize that any religious act should not result in hurting, dehumanizing, or abusing others based on race, religion, or region. As such, one should question:

- Does this teaching promote inclusivity, empathy, and fairness?

- Does it align with principles of justice and human dignity?

- Is it being used to justify harm or exclusion?

By engaging critically with religion, we can ensure that our moral decisions are informed by a balanced understanding that respects both the depth of human spirituality and the universality of ethical principles.

5.4 Conclusion: The Enigma of Faith and the Judgment Core

Imagine this: You're standing before an ancient temple, its towering gates adorned with sacred symbols. Inside, a grand hall stretches endlessly, lined with shelves of holy scriptures, each proclaiming to hold the ultimate truth. A thousand voices echo through the chamber—some whispering peace, others demanding obedience, a few even calling for war. As you step forward, a question lingers in your mind: Are these voices guiding you toward morality, or shaping it to serve their own ends?

This is the paradox of religion. It promises clarity, yet its interpretations shift across time and culture. It calls for peace, yet has been used to justify conflict. It preaches unity, yet has drawn lines that divide. How does one navigate such a force?

<u>Faith and the Judgment Core: A Blessing or a Test?</u>

Religion has undeniably shaped human morality for centuries, embedding values of justice, compassion, and accountability into societies. It inspires selflessness, charity, and the pursuit of higher truths. At its best, it calls people to rise above selfish instincts and serve a purpose greater than themselves. But when does faith become a guiding light, and when does it cast shadows on the moral compass it seeks to define?

History has shown that religion can be both a source of profound wisdom and a tool of manipulation. Leaders have used sacred texts to uplift the oppressed, but others have twisted them to justify persecution. Divine teachings have healed divisions, but have also been invoked to stoke fear and hatred. If religion is meant to provide absolute moral clarity, why do its followers often find themselves on opposite sides of history?

At the heart of this dilemma lies the Judgment Core (JDC)—the internal compass that shapes our understanding of right and wrong. For many, religion is the foundation of their JDC, an unwavering beacon that illuminates the path of righteousness. But can a moral compass remain truly independent if it is entirely shaped by external teachings? Should faith demand absolute obedience, or should it encourage individual discernment?

The Danger of Blind Allegiance

Throughout history, faith has been wielded as both a shield and a sword. Religious leaders, revered for their wisdom, have at times guided their followers toward justice—but what happens when they lead them astray? When religious figures command loyalty without question, when their interpretations go unchallenged, when belief is used as a tool for control rather than enlightenment, the Judgment Core is no longer a compass—it becomes a leash.

Consider the wars waged in the name of divine right, the social injustices upheld under religious justification, the acts of cruelty excused by selective interpretations of sacred texts. These are not relics of the past; they exist today, woven into policies, laws, and societal norms. If morality is defined by religion, what happens when religion is manipulated? Do you still trust it without question?

This is not a call to abandon faith, but a challenge to engage with it critically. Should religion be a doctrine to follow without question, or a guide that invites deeper contemplation? Does your faith encourage exploration, or does it discourage dissent? And when religious authority contradicts the principles of justice, compassion, and equality—do you remain silent, or do you challenge it?

The Moral Compass: Inherited or Discovered?

If religious teachings have been interpreted, rewritten, and even distorted over time, then is your moral foundation truly your own—or is it the result of centuries of selective storytelling? Are you following your faith because you believe in its core values, or because you were taught never to question it?

Religion claims to provide eternal truths, yet its interpretations vary across cultures, sects, and time periods. If moral absolutes exist, why do religious scholars debate them? If divine justice is clear, why does it shift based on geography and history? Can morality be both universal and bound by the limitations of human interpretation?

A Call to Action: Redefining Faith in a Complex World

Faith, like the traveler's compass, can be a source of guidance—but only if it is read with awareness. If blindly followed, it risks leading its bearer in circles, trapping them in patterns of inherited belief rather than true understanding.

So, as you reflect on the role of religion in shaping your Judgment Core, ask yourself:

- Do you believe what you believe because it resonates with your sense of justice, or because it has been handed down as unquestionable truth?

- Does your faith encourage independent thought, or does it punish those who question?

- When moral dilemmas arise, do you rely solely on religious doctrine, or do you also engage with reason, empathy, and real-world consequences?

- If a religious teaching is used to justify harm, exclusion, or division—will you challenge it, or accept it as part of faith?

Religion is a force that has shaped civilizations, inspired revolutions, and provided meaning to countless lives. But faith should not be passive. It should not be a blindfold, but a lens through which we seek truth—not just in scripture, but in the world around us.

The path of belief is not one of certainty, but of exploration. Will you follow the compass without question, or will you learn how to read it for yourself?

Chapter 6: Navigating the Gray Areas

You're walking through a dense fog, a place where shadows shift and familiar landmarks vanish. You think you know the way, but with every step, the path changes. Ahead, two roads diverge—one seems morally right, the other undeniably wrong. But as you move closer, you realize they are not separate roads at all, but threads woven into the same uncertain tapestry. What if morality isn't a map with clear borders, but a landscape where the terrain itself keeps shifting?

Stepping beyond the informal influences of family and community, we enter a realm where morality is no longer just a matter of personal conscience or collective agreement—it is a battlefield of competing values, shifting contexts, and unexpected consequences. After exploring the roles of family, society, government, global organizations, and religion in shaping our ethical frameworks, one undeniable truth emerges: the world does not exist in black and white. It is painted in infinite shades of gray.

A law that upholds justice for one group may oppress another. A decision made out of necessity may violate a deeply held principle. A truth revealed in one moment may lead to destruction in another. A person who lies to save a life—are they deceitful or heroic? A government that enforces order through surveillance—does it protect or control? When the lines between virtue and compromise blur, how do we decide what is right?

This chapter invites you to wade into the heart of moral ambiguity, to question the absolutes you hold dear, and to challenge the idea that morality is fixed and universal. What if morality is fluid—an evolving interplay of intent, circumstance, and consequence? When faced with a choice where no option is purely right or entirely wrong, what do you rely on? The values instilled by your upbringing? The principles of your faith? The laws of your nation? Or something deeper—your own Judgment Core, refined not through blind adherence but through conscious reflection and experience?

As you journey through these pages, you will confront dilemmas that test the boundaries of justice, mercy, loyalty, and truth. You will be forced to ask yourself: When is a rigid principle a virtue, and when does it become a prison? When does compromise become wisdom, and when is it betrayal? If morality is not as absolute as we were taught, then what truly guides us through the gray?

There are no easy answers here—only questions that demand introspection, growth, and the courage to step beyond the certainty of black and white. Are you ready to face the unknown, to question what you believe and why? If morality is not a fixed destination but an evolving journey, then the real question is: Will you navigate the gray, or will you let it consume you??

6.1 The Illusion of Absolute Morality

For generations, humanity has clung to the notion of morality as an unyielding framework—a set of inviolable rules decreed by divine, legal, or cultural authorities. These rules, etched into our collective consciousness, promise clarity and certainty. They teach us that actions are either "good" or "bad," "right" or "wrong," with no space for ambiguity. This binary view, comforting in its simplicity, offers a map to navigate the moral terrain of life. But what happens when that map no longer aligns with the terrain itself?

Life, with its infinite complexities, often defies such rigid definitions. A lie, universally condemned in absolute moral systems, may shield someone from unnecessary harm. Loyalty, heralded as a virtue, might compel silence when truth and justice demand speaking out. The once-sharp lines between right and wrong blur in these moments, revealing the inadequacy of absolute morality to address the intricacies of human existence.

Consider this: If morality is absolute, then its rules must apply universally—to all people, in all circumstances, across all times. Yet history tells a different story. Practices once deemed morally acceptable, such as slavery or segregation, are now reviled as profound injustices. What shifted? Did humanity suddenly discover new rules, or did our understanding of morality evolve with greater awareness and empathy? If morality is truly fixed, how do we account for these transformations?

Even within the present, the rigidity of absolute moral systems breeds judgment and division. Those who cling to these systems often wield them as weapons, quick to condemn anyone who dares deviate from their prescribed codes. This black-and-white thinking reduces complex human dilemmas to simplistic verdicts, suppressing empathy and discouraging deeper exploration of context and intent. Have you ever found yourself judged by another's rigid standards—or perhaps judged someone yourself? Did those judgments bring clarity, or did they deepen division?

In truth, morality is not a static entity carved in stone but a living, breathing concept, shaped by culture, experience, and collective progress. It shifts with the tides of time, adapting to new challenges and insights. Yet this dynamic nature can feel disorienting, especially for those who long for certainty. Is it easier to follow absolute rules, even if they fail to capture the nuances of life, than to confront the discomfort of ambiguity?

Perhaps the greatest challenge lies in the gray spaces, where right and wrong cannot be neatly categorized. These are the moments that test our "Judgment Core", demanding that we weigh not just actions but context, consequences, and intentions. When faced with moral dilemmas, do you cling to predefined rules, or do you engage with the messy, uncomfortable process of discerning what feels just in the moment?

The illusion of absolute morality may offer comfort, but it often falters under the weight of real-life complexities. Are you willing to step beyond its rigid boundaries, to embrace a more fluid, context-sensitive approach? Can you accept that morality is not about following a fixed set of rules but about constantly refining your understanding of what it means to do right—today, tomorrow, and in an ever-changing world?

6.2 Balancing Moral Complexity: The Case of Robin Hood

Sherwood Forest, Nottinghamshire – Autumn, 1208

As the crisp air of an English autumn filled the sprawling Sherwood Forest, a hooded figure moved through the dense trees, his silhouette blending seamlessly into the shadows. His name was Robin of Locksley, but to the villagers who whispered his name in reverence, he was simply Robin Hood—the outlaw who defied kings and sheriffs alike to fight for justice in a world teetering on the brink of moral collapse.

The reign of King John had plunged England into turmoil. Heavy taxes to fund wars and royal indulgences fell mercilessly on the poor, while the wealthy barons and corrupt officials thrived. Among the enforcers of this oppressive order was the infamous Sheriff of Nottingham, a man whose greed knew no bounds. For the villagers of Nottinghamshire, survival often meant impossible choices: pay exorbitant taxes, surrender what little they had, or risk starvation.

Robin Hood's transformation from a disillusioned nobleman to an outlaw began the day he witnessed the eviction of an elderly widow from her cottage. Her meager possessions were seized by the Sheriff's men, her cries for mercy ignored. That evening, as the sun dipped below the horizon, Robin vowed to stand against the injustice he could no longer tolerate. With a band of like-minded companions—Little John, Friar Tuck, Maid Marian, and others—Robin retreated to the safety of Sherwood, where the forest became both his sanctuary and battlefield.

But Robin's methods were unorthodox and morally ambiguous. He stole from the rich—not indiscriminately, but from those whose wealth came through exploitation and cruelty. The loot was not for personal gain but redistributed to those who had been wronged, filling their empty larders and rekindling their hope.

Yet, even as Robin's actions won him the admiration of the oppressed, they stirred unease among his allies. "Is stealing ever justified?" Friar Tuck asked one night as they sat around a crackling fire. Robin's answer was measured: "When the law itself is a thief, do we not have a duty to take it back for those it has robbed?"

The Sheriff of Nottingham, enraged by Robin's growing influence, declared him an enemy of the Crown, branding him a criminal deserving of death. To the Sheriff, the law was absolute—a tool to maintain order and protect the interests of the ruling class. But to Robin, the law had become a weapon of oppression, its morality hollow.

Each arrow Robin loosed carried with it a question that pierced deeper than any steel tip: Could breaking the law be morally righteous when the law itself was unjust? Was he a thief, or was he a liberator? Did his defiance of authority erode the moral fabric of society, or did it restore it?

The villagers who benefited from Robin's deeds saw him as a hero, their savior in a world that had abandoned them. Yet, to the wealthy merchants and the Sheriff, he was a dangerous insurgent threatening the stability of their power. The truth, as always, lay somewhere in the gray, where morality is shaped as much by intent as by action.

As the seasons changed and the legend of Robin Hood grew, so too did the questions his story posed to those who heard it. Would you break the rules to uphold justice? Could you accept the consequences of defying authority for a cause greater than yourself? And how would such actions reshape your "Judgment Core", that internal compass that guides decisions in life's most testing moments?

The tale of Robin Hood is not merely a story of rebellion but a reflection of the complexities that define morality. It challenges us to look beyond the black-and-white dichotomy of right and wrong and to ask ourselves: When the lines blur, where does justice truly reside? And are we brave enough to act when the answer defies the rules we've been taught to follow?

In the end, Robin's arrows did more than steal from the rich—they aimed directly at the heart of moral ambiguity, leaving us to decide whether he was a thief, a hero, or something far more complicated. Would you have stood beside him in Sherwood, defying the law for the sake of justice? Or would your judgment have steered you elsewhere? The forest, with all its shadows and secrets, leaves the answers for you to uncover.

The Thief

Detroit, Michigan – October 12, 1987

The rain came down in relentless sheets, drenching the worn streets of Detroit's crumbling outskirts. The dim glow of a flickering streetlamp cast eerie shadows on the broken pavement. Officer Jenkins sat in his patrol car, the heater humming softly as the windshield wipers fought a losing battle against the downpour. The radio crackled with a call: a theft had just occurred at Benny's Bakery on Elm Street—a loaf of bread snatched from the counter.

Jenkins exhaled sharply, rubbing his tired eyes. It wasn't the kind of crime that stirred headlines, but in this neighborhood, every report told a story. The bakery was one of the last surviving businesses in an area ravaged by factory closures and unemployment. Here, desperation wasn't uncommon; it was a way of life.

When Jenkins arrived, Benny, the owner, stood under the awning, rainwater pooling at his feet.

"It was a kid," Benny said, shaking his head, his voice a mix of anger and pity. "Couldn't have been older than 12. Grabbed the bread and bolted. Took off toward the alley behind Maple."

Jenkins scribbled down the details, his brow furrowed. A boy, alone, stealing bread in the rain. It wasn't the crime itself that bothered him—it was the why. What drove a child to risk such an act?

Hours earlier, Jamie Harris, just 11 years old, had stood in that same alley, staring through the fogged window of Benny's Bakery. The warm light inside illuminated the shelves of fresh bread, the golden crusts promising a respite from the gnawing hunger in his belly.

Life had not been kind to Jamie. Five years ago, his father—a machinist at the auto plant—had died in an industrial accident. His mother, Sarah, had taken up cleaning offices to keep the family afloat, but last month, an illness robbed her of her sight. Now bedridden, Sarah relied on Jamie for everything, and Jamie, in turn, felt the crushing weight of responsibility for his mother and his 6-year-old sister, Emma.

That night, Jamie's jacket clung to his skinny frame, soaked through by hours of rain. His stomach churned, not from guilt, but from hunger—a deep, painful ache that refused to be ignored. He clenched his fists, recalling his father's words: "Jamie, no matter how bad things get, you never take what isn't yours." But his father wasn't here, and his mother and sister hadn't eaten in days.

As the shopkeeper disappeared into the back room, Jamie made his decision. He pushed open the door, his movements trembling but quick. The loaf was warm in his hands, its soft crust pressing against his rain-slicked palms. Before he could think, he was out the door, running into the night.

Now, beneath a rusted fire escape in a narrow alley, Jamie huddled against the cold, the loaf still clutched to his chest. The rain soaked his hair and ran in rivulets down his face, but his thoughts were elsewhere. The guilt of breaking the law gnawed at him, but his hunger—and the memory of his mother's frail voice—silenced his conscience.

Is it still wrong if it's the only way to survive? he wondered. Was his theft an unforgivable sin, or a desperate act of love?

Officer Jenkins turned down Maple Street, his headlights cutting through the gloom. A glint of movement caught his eye—a small figure huddled under a fire escape. Jenkins slowed the car, stepping out into the rain.

Jamie froze, clutching the bread tighter, his heart pounding like the storm above. As Jenkins approached, their eyes met—one pair weary, the other wide with fear.

Jenkins crouched to Jamie's level, his voice soft but firm. "Son, why'd you take the bread?"

Jamie's lips quivered as he whispered, "My mom's sick. My sister's hungry. I didn't know what else to do."

For a moment, Jenkins was silent, the rain masking the weight of his thoughts. The badge on his chest demanded justice, but his heart ached at the boy's desperation. What was justice, after all, in a world where laws couldn't fill empty stomachs?

This small moment in a Detroit alley is a reflection of a universal question: What happens when morality clashes with survival? Jamie's story—like countless others throughout history—forces us to confront the fluidity of right and wrong.

In the Ethiopian famine of the 1980s, starving families stole food meant for aid, driven by the same desperation Jamie felt. Aid workers grappled with the impossible dilemma of enforcing rules or allowing theft in the name of survival.

These stories challenge the rigid boundaries of our Judgment Core—the internal compass that guides our sense of right and wrong. Should we always adhere to the law, even when it fails to account for human suffering? Or can acts of defiance, like Jamie's, carry a moral weight that transcends legality?

As Jamie handed over the bread that night, Officer Jenkins made a choice that would weigh on his own Judgment Core. In the gray space between crime and compassion, both their moral compasses were forever altered, leaving a question for all of us: When justice and survival collide, which path would you choose?

6.3 The Enigma of Context: Unraveling Situational Ethics

Imagine a world where morality isn't carved in stone but sways gently, like a pendulum, in response to the ebb and flow of life's complexities. What if the morality of an action wasn't confined to rigid, unyielding rules but instead breathed and evolved within the framework of its unique circumstances? This is the heart of situational ethics—a philosophy that asks us to step beyond the simplicity of black-and-white judgments and delve into the shades of gray that define human behavior.

Traditional ethics often feels like a map with a single unchanging route: lying is always wrong, stealing is never justified, and principles reign supreme regardless of the context. While comforting in its clarity, this rigid approach stumbles when it meets the labyrinth of real-world dilemmas. Situational ethics, in contrast, offers no such absolutes. Instead, it dares us to ask: Could a lie ever be an act of love? Could theft be driven by compassion? Could breaking a rule be the key to upholding justice?

Consider the act of lying—a sin in the eyes of most moral codes. Situational ethics doesn't dismiss this principle but instead invites us to examine the story behind the lie. Is it told to deceive for personal gain, or is it spoken to shield someone from harm? Picture a person lying to protect a friend from persecution or a parent withholding harsh truths to preserve a child's innocence. Does the intent alter the moral weight of the act? In the intricate dance between principle and purpose, situational ethics whispers: Look closer.

Stealing, too, takes on a different hue when viewed through this lens. The image of a desperate parent stealing medicine to save their child forces us to confront the inadequacy of universal condemnation. Is the theft still wrong, or has it transcended its definition to become an act of necessity, even love? By embracing the complexities of intent and consequence, situational ethics challenges us to reconsider the boundaries of morality.

Yet, this philosophy is not an anarchist's manifesto. It doesn't advocate for discarding moral principles but rather for bending them gently when the circumstances demand. Principles are not abandoned but adapted—guiding stars rather than unyielding chains. This balance between steadfastness and flexibility transforms morality into something alive, something that breathes alongside human imperfection.

Situational ethics also calls us to recognize the raw humanity behind every moral choice. It acknowledges that people are rarely the architects of flawless decisions, navigating instead through a maze of emotions, pressures, and societal demands. It asks for empathy, urging us to see beyond the action to the individual, to understand the desperation, the hope, or the love that may have shaped their choice.

But here lies the enigma: How far can flexibility stretch before it snaps? When does adaptability slip into justification? At what point does the pursuit of contextual morality blur the lines so much that we lose sight of right and wrong altogether?

As you ponder these questions, reflect on your Judgment Core. Is it anchored in unyielding principles, or does it allow room for the currents of context to shape its direction? Can you embrace the idea that morality is not a static monument but a flowing river, carving its path through the complexities of human life?

Situational ethics offers no easy answers, only an invitation to explore. It asks us to peel back the layers of every decision, to seek out the hidden motives, the unseen pressures, and the unspoken truths. It challenges us to navigate the intricate terrain of moral ambiguity with both compassion and critical thought. And it leaves us with a mystery that lingers: In the shifting sands of context, where does morality truly begin—and where does it end?

The Mysterious Tracks of Morality: Exploring the Trolley Problem

The sound of metal on metal screeches in the distance, growing louder as the runaway trolley hurtles toward a fork in the tracks. On one path lie five bound figures, motionless and doomed unless something intervenes. On the other path, a single person waits, unaware of the looming danger. You stand at the lever, your hand trembling. The choice is yours: do nothing, and the trolley barrels ahead to claim five lives, or pull the lever, diverting its path and condemning one.

This is no ordinary decision. The Trolley Problem, introduced by philosopher Philippa Foot in 1967, is a timeless ethical puzzle that challenges our moral compass and judgment core in profound ways. At first glance, the answer seems straightforward—save the greatest number of lives. But as you grip the lever, a cascade of questions floods your mind.

Are you justified in actively causing harm, even if it minimizes the overall damage? Is standing by and allowing harm to occur less culpable than intervening to redirect it? Which path aligns with your principles? And perhaps the most haunting question of all: does your choice make you the hero—or the executioner?

The Trolley Problem forces us to confront the tension between two dominant ethical philosophies. Utilitarianism, with its focus on outcomes, whispers in your ear: Pull the lever. Save five lives at the cost of one. The math is clear. Yet, deontological ethics, steadfast in its emphasis on moral principles, counters: Do not interfere. Causing harm, even for a greater good, is a moral violation.

But this is no abstract thought experiment. Its echoes ripple through the real world, where decisions are seldom clean and consequences rarely predictable. In a hospital, a doctor faces the dilemma of allocating a single ventilator among multiple patients. On the battlefield, a commander weighs the cost of sacrificing a few soldiers to save the many. In the programming of autonomous vehicles, algorithms must decide whether to prioritize the lives of passengers or pedestrians in an inevitable crash.

The Trolley Problem is more than a question of numbers—it is a question of humanity. It peels back the layers of our moral reasoning, exposing the frailty and flexibility of our ethical frameworks. It forces us to grapple with the weight of our intentions and the shadows cast by our actions.

What guides your hand on the lever? Is it a belief in maximizing the greater good, even at the cost of deliberate harm? Or is it an unwavering commitment to avoid becoming the direct cause of suffering? And how does your decision ripple through your Judgment Core, shaping your future choices and your understanding of right and wrong?

As the trolley hurtles closer, the urgency of the moment leaves little room for certainty. You must choose, knowing that morality is rarely black and white. It is a shifting spectrum of grays, influenced by context, intent, and the unpredictable web of consequences.

The Trolley Problem doesn't offer answers—it demands them. It challenges you to confront the messy, imperfect realities of human decision-making. And as you stand at the crossroads of action and inaction, it asks the most important question of all: What kind of person do you become when faced with the impossible?

Al-Shifa's Shadows: A Story from Gaza

October 15, 2023 – Gaza City, Occupied Palestine

The night sky over Gaza was ablaze, not with stars but with fire. The relentless hum of drones, punctuated by distant explosions, had become the soundtrack of survival. At the heart of the city stood Al-Shifa Hospital, its once-bustling halls now a battleground for life and death. Inside, the air was thick with the acrid smell of blood and smoke. It was a place where the flicker of fluorescent lights revealed the faces of patients and doctors alike—faces etched with exhaustion, fear, and determination.

Dr. Yara Khalil, 36, a seasoned pediatric surgeon, had not slept in three days. Her hijab was damp with sweat, her hands steady only through sheer willpower. Around her, the chaos was unrelenting: children crying, nurses shouting over the din, and the steady stream of stretchers bringing in the broken and the burned. Supplies were nearly gone, the generators faltering, and the hospital was running on the last vestiges of hope.

Among the many patients was Lina, a bright-eyed 9-year-old whose body bore the scars of a recent airstrike. Her tiny frame was dwarfed by the hospital bed, and a bandage covered the wound on her abdomen. Her mother, Amal, sat beside her, silent except for the occasional prayer whispered into the stillness. Amal had lost her husband and two sons in the same attack. Lina was all she had left.

Yara knew Lina's condition. She required surgery, blood transfusions, and medicine that were simply not available. Outside the hospital, the streets were a wasteland, rubble and debris blocking access to any potential aid. Inside, the corridors were filled with patients like Lina, each one a story of survival and despair. The decisions made in these walls would echo for years, carving scars not only on the patients but on the souls of those tasked with their care.

October 16, 2023 – Midnight

In a dimly lit room that had once been a staff lounge, Yara sat with her colleagues—nurses, surgeons, and the hospital's director, Dr. Samir Haddad. On the table before them lay a clipboard, its pages marked with the names of patients. A grim silence hung in the air.

"We have enough supplies to treat maybe ten more patients," Samir said, his voice steady but heavy. "There are over 200 waiting for care."

"What about evacuation?" one of the nurses asked.

Samir shook his head. "No way out. The blockade is ironclad. We have to make decisions now."

The weight of those words pressed on Yara. Decisions. It was a clinical term, devoid of emotion, yet it carried the burden of life and death. They began reviewing cases, prioritizing those with the highest chance of survival. Lina's name came up, and Yara hesitated.

"She's critical," she said. "Without surgery, she won't survive."

"But we don't have the resources," Samir replied. "The equipment we need... it's gone. We can't save her."

Yara's heart twisted. Lina had smiled at her earlier, asking if she would be okay. Yara had lied, telling her everything would be fine. Now, faced with the truth, she felt her moral compass faltering. What did it mean to be a doctor here, in this place, where saving one life meant condemning another?

October 17, 2023 – Dawn

The decision was made. Lina would receive palliative care to ease her pain, but the resources would go to others who could be saved. Yara sat by Lina's bed, holding her tiny hand.

"Am I going to see my brothers soon?" Lina asked, her voice barely a whisper.

Yara swallowed the lump in her throat. "They'll be waiting for you," she said softly.

That morning, as the sunlight filtered weakly through the broken windows, Lina slipped away. Amal's cries echoed through the halls, a sound that seemed to pierce through the very fabric of the hospital. Yara felt a part of herself break, a crack in her Judgment Core that she knew would never fully heal.

The Aftermath

The decisions made during those days at Al-Shifa would haunt Yara forever. Had they chosen correctly? Had they done enough? She questioned the very nature of morality: Was it right to sacrifice one life to save another? Or did every life hold an equal weight, demanding the same effort, the same hope?

Outside the hospital, the war continued. The stories of Lina and countless others faded into the background noise of global politics. But within Yara, they remained sharp and vivid, shaping her moral compass in ways she could not yet fully comprehend.

In the ruins of Gaza, where survival was a daily battle, Yara had navigated the grayest of moral gray areas. She had made choices no one should ever have to make, choices that questioned the very essence of right and wrong. Yet, through the pain and the doubt, she clung to the hope that one day, humanity might learn from the stories etched in the shadows of Al-Shifa. That one day, decisions like hers would no longer be necessary.

6.4 The Enigma of Intent: Unveiling the Heart of Moral Judgment

In the labyrinth of morality, where choices twist and turn through uncharted corridors, one element shines a faint, guiding light: intent. It is the elusive thread that weaves through every decision, every action, demanding our attention not to what is done, but why it is done. Without it, the moral fabric of our judgment unravels, leaving us lost in the shadows of ambiguity.

Intent is the silent narrator of every story, hidden beneath the surface, waiting to transform how we perceive an act. Consider a sharp, unexpected shout that slices through the quiet. At first, it feels aggressive, an unwelcome intrusion. But as the scene unfolds—a child saved from an oncoming car or a distracted pedestrian pulled back from the edge of disaster—the meaning of that shout changes. What seemed hostile becomes heroic. This transformation reveals a simple truth: intent reframes the act, shifting it from condemnation to commendation.

Yet intent is not always so straightforward. It inhabits the gray spaces between what is known and what is assumed. A doctor makes a mistake during surgery. The outcome is tragic, but was the error born of exhaustion, an unforeseen complication, or reckless disregard for safety protocols? The distinction matters because it separates a moment of human frailty from a breach of ethical integrity. The former, though heartbreaking, calls for understanding; the latter, for accountability.

This nuanced role of intent is etched into the very structures of justice. In courtrooms around the world, it is the difference between manslaughter and murder. Both may result in a loss of life, but the shadows of negligence and premeditation stretch across these terms, dividing them by intent. Without this lens, the law itself would falter, unable to differentiate between a tragic accident and calculated harm.

But intent does not dwell only in the grand narratives of law and ethics; it permeates the small, intimate spaces of daily life. Picture a friend offering unsolicited advice. Do you bristle, sensing interference, or do you pause, recognizing genuine concern? The answer lies in how you perceive their intent. Was it an act of arrogance or kindness? The truth shifts the emotional weight of the moment, redefining how we respond and connect.

Intent is the hidden key to moral discernment, but it comes with its own mysteries. What happens when intent is unclear or misread? Can good intentions excuse harmful outcomes? Or do they simply soften the edges of accountability? These questions challenge us to look deeper, not just at what is visible, but at the motivations that pulse beneath the surface.

By embracing the complexity of intent, we confront a profound truth about morality: actions are rarely as simple as they appear. They are stories told in layers, shaped by context, circumstances, and the unseen forces driving them. Intent compels us to be more than judges—it asks us to be interpreters, to understand rather than assume, and to navigate the murky waters of morality with curiosity and compassion.

So, where does this leave your moral compass? When faced with an act that defies easy categorization, do you dig deeper to uncover the intent? Or do you allow appearances to guide your judgment? As you ponder this, remember: intent is not just a detail—it is the essence that can transform the gray into something human, something true. Will you seek it? And when you find it, will you let it guide you?

The Warning Shot: A Night in Jacksonville

On a sweltering August evening in 2010, in Jacksonville, Florida, the air hung heavy, suffused with tension that had been building for years inside

Marissa Alexander's home. The walls of her modest house had borne witness to too much—shouting, threats, and the sharp cracks of fists against flesh. That night, Rico Gray, her husband, was in one of his rages, and Marissa knew all too well how quickly words could escalate to blows.

Rico had always been unpredictable, but his violence had grown more terrifying over time. Just weeks earlier, he had struck her so hard that she'd seen stars, her head snapping back with the force of his hand. The bruises on her arms from when he grabbed her—tight enough to leave her skin black and blue—were still fading. Tonight, as he cornered her in the kitchen, the venom in his voice was unmistakable.

"You think you can leave me? You think anyone will protect you?" he sneered, his towering frame blocking her path. Marissa's heart raced. His hands clenched into fists, and she knew what would come next.

She darted past him, her body trembling with adrenaline, and fled to the garage. The gun she had stored there wasn't something she wanted to use—it was a desperate measure for a woman who felt like her life was perpetually under siege. She grabbed it, her hands shaking so violently she almost dropped it, and returned to the house.

Rico was waiting, his eyes filled with fury. She raised the gun, not aiming at him, but at the ceiling. The crack of the warning shot was deafening, the sound reverberating through the small house. Rico froze, the rage in his face momentarily replaced by shock.

Marissa didn't fire again. She didn't want to hurt him—only to stop him. To make him understand that she wasn't defenseless, that she would no longer silently endure his wrath. For a brief moment, it seemed like she had succeeded.

But within minutes, the police arrived, and the nightmare took a new form. Rico spun the story, downplaying his own actions and framing Marissa's warning shot as reckless endangerment. Despite his history of violence—documented in police reports and known to neighbors—it was Marissa who found herself in handcuffs.

Florida's "10-20-Life" gun laws loomed heavily over her case, offering no room for nuance or context. The prosecution ignored her years of abuse, the bruises, and the fear that had driven her to act. They painted her as the aggressor, and after a mere 12 minutes of deliberation, the jury returned with a guilty verdict.

Marissa Alexander, a woman who had fired a single warning shot to protect herself from her abusive husband, was sentenced to 20 years in prison.

The public outcry was immediate. Activists and legal experts rallied around her case, questioning how the legal system could ignore the context of her actions. Marissa's intent wasn't to harm Rico—it was to survive. She hadn't aimed the gun at him; she'd aimed to protect herself and her children.

Years later, after tireless advocacy and a retrial, Marissa's initial verdict was overturned. A plea deal allowed her to leave prison, but her ordeal left indelible scars. Her case became a lightning rod for debates about self-defense laws, domestic violence, and the role of intent in moral and legal judgments.

Marissa's story forces us to confront uncomfortable questions about justice, morality, and survival:

- How does the law account for years of abuse that culminate in a single act of self-defense?

- Can intent to protect oneself ever outweigh the rigid structures of legal codes?

- And what happens to our moral compass when acts of survival are punished instead of understood?

The warning shot that echoed through her home that night wasn't just a sound—it was a desperate cry for help. Marissa's case reminds us that morality cannot always be measured in absolutes. Her actions, born of fear and a desire to live, challenge us to reconsider how we judge right and wrong in the grayest of areas.

In the end, Marissa Alexander's story is not just about a warning shot—it's about the resilience of a woman who refused to be silenced, even when the world misunderstood her intent. Her fight for justice serves as a powerful testament to the importance of considering context, intent, and humanity in the face of rigid laws and societal judgments.

The Shadows of August:

On a sweltering morning in early August 1945, the streets of Hiroshima bustled with the rhythms of daily life. Children played in the narrow alleys, merchants arranged their wares, and workers trudged toward factories. For many, it was just another day in the shadow of war—a distant rumble of battles fought elsewhere. But at precisely 8:15 a.m. on August 6, the sky above the city ignited, and everything changed in an instant.

The bomb, ominously named "Little Boy," detonated with a blinding flash and a searing heat. The heart of Hiroshima was engulfed in an apocalyptic inferno, obliterating buildings, streets, and lives in a matter of seconds. Tens of thousands were vaporized on the spot, their shadows burned into the pavement—a haunting reminder of their existence. Others suffered horrific burns, their cries for help rising above the chaos as the city disintegrated into rubble and ash.

Three days later, on August 9, another American B-29 bomber released "Fat Man" over Nagasaki. The blast echoed through the hills, flattening neighborhoods and killing tens of thousands more. By the end of 1945, an estimated 214,000 people—men, women, children—were dead across both cities. Those who survived were left to grapple with unimaginable physical and psychological scars, their bodies ravaged by radiation and their minds haunted by the horrors they had witnessed.

The official narrative from the United States and much of the international community painted the bombings as a necessary act of heroism—a decisive move to end World War II and prevent the bloodshed of a prolonged invasion. General Douglas MacArthur called it "the stroke that saved millions of lives." Leaders lauded the swift Japanese surrender that followed, heralding the bombings as the grim but effective conclusion to a brutal conflict.

But beneath the rhetoric of victory lay a stark and uncomfortable truth. The targets of these devastating weapons were not soldiers or military installations but civilian cities—ordinary people whose lives were extinguished to send a message. Were Hiroshima and Nagasaki acts of strategy or warnings to a postwar world about the terrifying new power of nuclear weapons?

This duality—the celebrated victory and the humanitarian catastrophe—raises profound moral questions that reverberate to this day.

The bombings of Hiroshima and Nagasaki are a chilling exploration of the human capacity for destruction in pursuit of a "greater good." The decision to deploy atomic weapons rested on the consequentialist belief that immense harm to a few would prevent greater harm to many. But can the calculated sacrifice of innocent lives ever be justified?

Imagine being in the room with President Harry Truman and his advisors as they weighed this decision. Maps spread across tables, casualty estimates scribbled in the margins. On one side, projections of Allied and Japanese deaths in a protracted ground invasion; on the other, the devastating promise of atomic power. Was their choice shaped by strategy, necessity, or hubris?

For the survivors—the Hibakusha—the answer scarcely mattered. Radiation sickness ravaged their bodies, leaving them to endure cancers, chronic illnesses, and genetic mutations that would ripple through generations. Social stigma compounded their suffering, as many faced ostracization for their visible scars and perceived contamination.

And yet, amid the ashes, questions linger:

- What does it mean to value one life over another in the calculus of war?

- Does the pursuit of victory absolve us of the moral weight of our actions?

- How do we reconcile intent—to end a war—with the devastating human cost of that choice?

The bombings of Hiroshima and Nagasaki are not merely historical events; they are moral crucibles that test our Judgment Core—the internal compass that guides our ethical decisions. The world's framing of these acts as heroism rather than humanitarian disaster underscores the ease with which narratives can be shaped to justify the unthinkable.

As nations grapple with the legacy of nuclear weapons, the bombings serve as a somber reminder of the responsibilities that come with wielding immense power. They compel us to question whether the ends ever truly justify the means and challenge us to seek alternatives that honor human dignity and minimize harm.

In the eerie silence that follows catastrophe, the bombings of Hiroshima and Nagasaki leave us with this haunting truth: the line between heroism and atrocity is often drawn by those with the power to tell the story. How we interpret it—how we let it shape our moral compass—is a choice that belongs to each of us.

6.5 Walking the Tightrope: Empathy, Fairness, and the Moral Compass

The path through the gray areas of morality is no straight line. It is a precarious tightrope, demanding balance, precision, and a steadfast focus on two fundamental guiding forces: empathy and fairness. Without empathy, decisions risk being cold and detached, blind to the intricate web of human struggles that shape actions. Without fairness, judgments become partial and uneven, failing to uphold the principles of justice that bind society together. But how does one navigate the tension between these forces?

Empathy, the gift of stepping into another's shoes, invites us to see the world not as we are but as others experience it. It compels us to move beyond the surface of actions and examine the depths of motivation and circumstance. Why did they act that way? What fears, desires, or struggles propelled their choices? By embracing empathy, we find ourselves weaving together a more nuanced understanding of moral dilemmas, one that breathes humanity into the cold rigidity of rules.

Imagine witnessing someone take food from a store without paying. The instinct might be to label it theft and condemn the act. But through empathy's lens, the picture sharpens. You notice the thin frame of the person, the hollowness in their eyes, and perhaps the presence of a hungry child at their side. Does this shift your judgment? Does it make you pause to question whether punishment or compassion is the appropriate response?

Yet, empathy alone is not enough. Without the stabilizing counterweight of fairness, it can lead us down paths of favoritism, where personal bias clouds our ability to treat similar situations with equal gravity. Fairness demands impartiality, a commitment to principles that apply not only to one but to all. It insists that rules, while not inflexible, should hold firm in their consistency—offering justice to the many, not just the few.

But here lies the heart of the mystery: how do we reconcile these forces when they appear to pull us in opposite directions? Consider the scenario of a schoolteacher caught between two students in conflict. One has a history of bullying, while the other has endured a string of personal hardships. Empathy might guide the teacher toward leniency for the struggling student, yet fairness requires that both be held accountable to the same rules. Which path honors the greater moral truth?

The interplay of empathy and fairness challenges our Judgment Core—the internal compass that guides us through these moral quandaries. It forces us to ask:

- Can we see the full spectrum of perspectives without losing sight of justice?

- Are our judgments shaped by compassion without eroding impartiality?

- How do we ensure our moral compass remains steady in the shifting winds of emotion and circumstance?

Ultimately, balancing empathy and fairness is an art, not a science. It calls for adaptability, the ability to weigh the unique contours of each situation without abandoning the principles that anchor our decisions. It urges us to question and refine our moral compass, ensuring it can flex without breaking, guiding us toward outcomes that honor both individual dignity and collective justice.

As you stand at the crossroads of these forces, the choices are yours to make. Will you favor the warmth of empathy or the clarity of fairness? Or will you seek the delicate equilibrium where both coexist, shaping decisions that reflect the complexity and beauty of our shared humanity?.

The Gray Cell of Kalief Browder

New York City, May 15, 2010. The air in the Bronx felt heavy that spring evening, as if it could sense the life-altering storm brewing for 16-year-old Kalief Browder. On a quiet street, under the dim glow of flickering streetlights, Kalief walked home after a small gathering with friends. Unbeknownst to him, a simple accusation was about to shatter his world.

A patrol car pulled up beside him. The officers, stern and unyielding, told Kalief he had been identified as a suspect in the theft of a backpack. Confused and terrified, Kalief protested his innocence. He didn't steal anything; he didn't even know the person accusing him. But it didn't matter. Without concrete evidence, without witnesses, Kalief was cuffed and taken into custody.

Unable to pay the $3,000 bail set against him, Kalief was sent to Rikers Island, one of the most notorious jails in the country. What should have been a temporary holding turned into a three-year descent into despair, marked by brutality, isolation, and a relentless fight to prove his innocence.

Kalief, barely out of childhood, was thrown into the chaos of adult incarceration. The violent environment became his new reality. Inmates marked their territory with fists, and correctional officers turned a blind eye or, worse, joined in. Kalief quickly became a target. One day, a dispute over nothing escalated into a savage beating by multiple inmates. The guards didn't intervene until Kalief lay crumpled on the ground, bleeding and humiliated.

And then there was the solitary confinement. For nearly two of his three years, Kalief was locked in a windowless cell no larger than a walk-in closet. The walls were his only company. Meals were slid through a small slot, and the echo of his own thoughts became deafening. Twenty-three hours a day, seven days a week, he was alone—isolated from the chaos of Rikers but trapped in a deeper, darker turmoil.

Time stretched and blurred. Days melted into nights, and Kalief felt himself slipping further away from reality. He attempted to end his suffering multiple times, but each time, he survived—alive, but more broken than before.

Throughout it all, Kalief refused to admit guilt. Plea deals dangled before him like lifelines, offering him freedom in exchange for a false confession. But Kalief, steadfast in his innocence, refused to compromise his truth. Each refusal prolonged his imprisonment, but he clung to the belief that justice, however delayed, would prevail.

Finally, in 2013, after nearly 1,000 days of incarceration, Kalief's case was dismissed. The charges were dropped. There was no trial, no evidence, and no conviction. He walked out of Rikers Island with nothing but scars—visible and invisible.

Kalief returned to a world that had moved on without him. But he wasn't the same. The streets of the Bronx felt alien. The friends he had left behind had grown older, while he remained trapped in the psychological remnants of his cell. His trust in the world had been shattered.

Despite his efforts to rebuild his life, the weight of his ordeal was unbearable. The nights were the worst—memories of Rikers crept in, suffocating him. On June 6, 2015, Kalief Browder, at just 22 years old, took his own life in his family home.

Kalief's story sent shockwaves across the United States. Advocates and activists decried the systemic failures that allowed a child to languish in one of the most violent jails in the country, without trial, for three years. His name became synonymous with calls for criminal justice reform.

But not everyone viewed the system's actions with the same clarity. Some defended the rigid rules that kept Kalief imprisoned, arguing that safety and order required firm boundaries. Others questioned how a society claiming to value justice could allow a teenager's life to be destroyed over an unproven accusation.

Kalief Browder's ordeal forces us to confront uncomfortable questions. At what point does adherence to the law deviate from the pursuit of justice? How does a system built to protect fail so profoundly, and what does that say about our collective Judgment Core—the moral compass guiding society?

Kalief's life was caught in a web of indifference, bureaucracy, and a lack of compassion. His suffering reveals the gray areas where rigid rules clash with human lives. Was the system blind to his youth, his humanity, and his pleas? Or was it simply too burdened to care?

His story demands reflection on the role of empathy and fairness in the pursuit of justice. It asks whether we, as a society, are willing to balance public safety with the dignity of individuals caught in the system's gears. Most of all, it challenges us to recalibrate our moral compass, ensuring that no one else suffers the fate of Kalief Browder.

In his short life, Kalief became a symbol of resilience, a cautionary tale, and a call to action. His memory lingers, urging us to transform a system that so easily lost sight of the humanity it was meant to uphold.

6.6 The Enigma of Growth: Finding Clarity in Moral Gray Areas

What if the most profound insights about right and wrong don't emerge from clarity, but from confusion? What if the moments that test our moral compass aren't the ones offering simple answers, but those steeped in uncertainty? This is the paradox of the gray area—a space where absolutes dissolve, and we're left to wrestle with the complexities of human experience.

It is within this ambiguity, this vast expanse of moral uncertainty, that the seeds of personal and ethical growth are often sown. The gray area challenges us, disrupts the comfortable rhythm of clear-cut rules, and forces us to confront questions we would rather avoid. But instead of chaos, this space holds the potential for transformation.

When we step into the gray, we are compelled to scrutinize our deeply held beliefs. What values do we hold dear, and why? Are they born of conviction or convenience? The process reveals the biases we carry—hidden assumptions that shape our judgments. By questioning these, we chip away at the rigidity of our moral framework, replacing it with something far more nuanced and resilient.

This confrontation with ambiguity demands that we adopt a broader perspective. No longer can we dismiss actions or beliefs we don't immediately understand. Instead, we are asked to explore the cultural, social, and personal contexts that shape human behavior. What would lead someone to make that choice? What forces are at play beneath the surface?

In grappling with these questions, we learn empathy—not as a passive virtue but as an active lens through which to view the world. We begin to see that morality isn't a one-size-fits-all doctrine. Different situations demand different considerations, and rigid adherence to inflexible rules can be not only impractical but unjust.

Engaging with moral gray areas doesn't just reshape our thinking; it fortifies our emotional intelligence. It teaches us to live with uncertainty, to tolerate the discomfort of not knowing, and to make peace with decisions that defy perfection. The gray teaches adaptability, a skill as crucial to navigating life as it is to navigating morality.

And yet, the journey through the gray is not a solitary one. True growth requires dialogue—a willingness to hear perspectives that challenge our own. When we acknowledge that our view isn't the sole arbiter of truth, we create space for others to share their experiences. These conversations bridge divides, foster respect, and remind us that moral growth is a collective endeavor.

Ultimately, the ability to thrive in the gray area is not a sign of confusion but of maturity. It reflects a wisdom that accepts the complexities of the human condition and recognizes that the answers we seek often lie in the very questions that unsettle us.

So, as you encounter the gray areas in your own life, consider this: Are you willing to embrace the discomfort? To let the ambiguity refine your Judgment Core and reshape your moral compass? It is here, in the haze of uncertainty, that growth begins.

Moral clarity often dissolves in the face of complexity, leaving the JDC to navigate an uncertain path. What happens when right and wrong are not absolute, but situational? Does stealing become justified when it saves a life? Is deception permissible if it prevents suffering? The JDC is not a rigid doctrine but a tool—one that must adapt without losing its integrity. In a world painted in shades of gray, how does one remain true to their core principles without being blinded by extremes?

A Nation's Reckoning: The Story of the Truth and Reconciliation Commission

The year was 1995, and the air in Cape Town, South Africa, was thick with the weight of a fractured nation. Apartheid, the brutal system of racial segregation and oppression that had defined the country for decades, had ended, but its scars were still fresh. The streets buzzed with hope and fear in equal measure. South Africa stood at a crossroads: one path led to potential retribution and deeper division, while the other offered the uncertain promise of healing and unity.

It was in this atmosphere of fragile transition that Archbishop Desmond Tutu, his voice as steady as his moral compass, stepped forward to lead the Truth and Reconciliation Commission (TRC). With the wisdom of an elder and the charisma of a preacher, Tutu carried a vision rooted in the African philosophy of Ubuntu—the belief that humanity is interconnected and that "I am because we are." This idea would guide the TRC's delicate task: to reckon with the horrors of apartheid without letting them destroy the future.

The TRC's mission was unprecedented and ambitious: uncover the truth about decades of systemic oppression and violence while fostering reconciliation between victims and perpetrators. It was not about revenge but about acknowledgment, understanding, and finding a way forward. In public hearings that both captivated and unsettled the nation, victims shared their stories of suffering, while those who had committed atrocities under apartheid confessed their crimes, often seeking amnesty in exchange for truth.

Among the many harrowing tales was that of Amy Biehl, a young American student who had come to South Africa in 1993 to fight for racial equality. Her life ended tragically when she was attacked and killed by a group of anti-apartheid activists. Her murder could have been yet another chapter in the cycle of violence that defined apartheid's legacy, but what unfolded instead was extraordinary.

Amy's parents, Linda and Peter Biehl, attended the TRC hearings where her killers sought amnesty. Their presence was not driven by anger but by a commitment to understanding. They chose to forgive the men responsible for their daughter's death, an act that stunned a nation still reeling from its wounds. They even went a step further—hiring two of the men involved in the killing to work in a foundation they established in Amy's memory, dedicated to empowering South African youth.

This act of radical grace wasn't easy. It required the Biehls to navigate the treacherous waters of grief, justice, and forgiveness—a gray area where no clear answers existed. Yet, their decision embodied the TRC's ethos: that healing requires looking beyond simple binaries of right and wrong, victim and perpetrator, and embracing the messy, painful work of reconciliation.

The TRC's approach was not without its critics. Many questioned whether granting amnesty to perpetrators was truly just, or whether it allowed too many to escape accountability. For others, the process felt like a betrayal of those who had suffered under apartheid. Tutu himself often struggled with the emotional toll of hearing stories of unimaginable cruelty, his tears a reminder that reconciliation was as much about confronting humanity's capacity for evil as it was about seeking its redemption.

But for all its imperfections, the TRC achieved something remarkable. It gave South Africa a way to confront its past without being consumed by it. By prioritizing truth over punishment and reconciliation over revenge, it demonstrated that moral judgment is not always about rigid justice but about the delicate balance between fairness and compassion.

The TRC's hearings became a theater of human complexity, where the lines between victim and perpetrator blurred. Former operatives of the apartheid regime confessed to heinous acts, some showing genuine remorse, others merely seeking amnesty. Survivors and families of victims sat across from them, grappling with emotions that ranged from rage to forgiveness.

Through it all, Desmond Tutu remained the Commission's steadfast anchor. His leadership emphasized that true reconciliation required facing the truth, no matter how painful. "Without forgiveness," he often said, "there is no future."

The TRC's work left an indelible mark on South Africa and the world. It became a blueprint for nations grappling with their own histories of injustice, showing that moral gray areas—though fraught with discomfort—are also spaces for profound growth.

The story of the TRC compels us to examine our Judgment Core—that internal compass guiding our ethical decisions. Are we willing to embrace the complexity of moral dilemmas, or do we retreat into the simplicity of black-and-white thinking? Can we balance justice with empathy, punishment with understanding?

In a world often consumed by division, the TRC offers a powerful lesson: reconciliation is not an easy path, but it is a necessary one. It reminds us that in the gray areas of morality, where no decision is perfect, humanity's greatest strength lies in its ability to forgive, to listen, and to strive for a future shaped by shared understanding.

And so, as the sun set on South Africa's era of apartheid, it rose on a nation daring to heal—not through forgetting, but through remembering together.

6.7 Conclusion: The Shifting Shadows of Morality

Imagine standing at the entrance of a vast, ancient maze. The walls are high, carved from stone that has weathered centuries of footsteps—each one a choice, a decision made in the gray corridors of morality. At times, the path is clear; at others, it twists into uncertainty, forcing you to choose between competing values, each leading to an outcome you cannot fully predict. Some turns feel righteous, but as you move forward, you realize that even the noblest choices carry unintended consequences.

This is the reality of navigating moral gray areas. There is no single map, no universal compass that guarantees an unerring path to righteousness. The truths we cling to are often shaped by perspective, bias, and context. What we once believed to be unquestionably right may, under different circumstances, reveal itself to be more complex. What we condemned in another may, in time, become a dilemma we ourselves must confront.

So, how do we navigate these moral mazes without becoming lost? If absolute morality is an illusion, and rigid principles often crumble under the weight of real-world complexities, what then should guide us?

The answer lies in the refinement of our Judgment Core (JDC)—that inner compass that evolves with knowledge, experience, and introspection. But even this core is not immune to distortion. Just as a compass can be thrown off by magnetic interference, our moral sense can be skewed by misinformation, social pressures, and our own unexamined beliefs. So, we must ask ourselves:

- Are we seeking the whole truth, or only the parts that validate our existing beliefs?

- Do we judge actions solely by their consequences, or do we consider the intent behind them?

- When faced with a moral dilemma, do we cling to rigid doctrines, or do we allow ourselves to weigh context and circumstance?

- Are we brave enough to admit when we were wrong—to recalibrate our Judgment Core rather than stubbornly defend a flawed position?

The moral maze does not offer an easy way out. There will be moments when we falter, when we make choices that, in hindsight, we wish we could change. But growth is not found in always being right—it is found in learning from the moments when we were wrong.

To navigate this shifting terrain, we must develop principles that are strong enough to guide us, yet flexible enough to adapt:

1. Acknowledging Uncertainty – Can you accept that morality is not always black and white, but a shifting spectrum of considerations?

2. Weighing Intent and Consequence – Do you judge an action solely by its result, or do you examine the motives that shaped it?

3. Embracing Context – Do you take the time to understand the full story before passing judgment?

4. Avoiding Moral Fanaticism – Are you willing to reconsider your beliefs when presented with new evidence or perspectives?

5. Seeking Fairness Over Comfort – Do you make decisions based on true justice, or do you follow the path of least resistance?

Ultimately, the question is not whether you will face moral ambiguity—because you will. The question is how you will respond when certainty fails you. Will you resist the discomfort of the gray, clinging to absolutes that no longer hold? Or will you engage with the uncertainty, using it to sharpen and strengthen your moral compass?

At the heart of the maze, where all paths converge, there is no final answer—only a mirror reflecting back at you. And in that reflection lies the only guide that has ever truly mattered: the person you choose to be.

So, as you step forward, ask yourself—are you truly navigating the gray, or are you simply looking for an escape from the complexity of it? The choice, as always, is yours.

Chapter 7: Redefining Right and Wrong – The Culmination of a Modern Moral Framework

Imagine standing at the edge of a forest, where familiar paths carved by generations before you suddenly vanish into uncharted terrain. The paths—straight, predictable, and comforting—symbolize the moral rules handed down by parents, communities, and governments. But beyond these well-trodden routes lies an expansive wilderness, teeming with complexity and ambiguity, where the old maps no longer suffice. How do you proceed when the guideposts of right and wrong dissolve into the shadows of uncertainty?

This chapter invites you to step into that wilderness. It is not merely a conclusion but a culmination—a synthesis of the ideas, experiences, and revelations we've uncovered in our exploration of morality. Here, we aim to redefine the essence of right and wrong, untangling them from the rigid frameworks we've long relied upon. Instead, we propose a moral compass—dynamic, inclusive, and deeply attuned to the realities of human experience. Can morality evolve to reflect the intricate fabric of modern life, or are we forever tethered to the simplicity of absolute rules?

Throughout this journey, we have exposed the subtle biases and errors embedded in the influences that shape our moral judgments: the well-meaning but often flawed teachings of parents, the pressures of societal norms, the constraints of law, and the sway of cultural narratives. These forces, while foundational, often create blind spots that leave us ill-equipped to confront the complexities of today's moral challenges. What happens when the old structures fail us? How do we respond when the rules we've trusted no longer align with the truths we encounter?

In this chapter, we distill these insights into principles—not as rigid decrees but as adaptable beacons. These principles are designed to strengthen your Judgment Core (JDC), that internal moral compass guiding your ethical decisions. They ask you to embrace context, seek empathy, and confront your own biases with honesty. Can you let go of the security of black-and-white answers and instead navigate the shades of gray with courage and wisdom?

Our aim is not to dismantle traditional moral frameworks entirely but to bridge them with the complexities of today's world. This is a call to action: to recognize that morality is not static but a living, breathing entity shaped by the fluid realities of human existence. Are you ready to challenge your assumptions, question the status quo, and reimagine what it means to live ethically in a world that defies absolutes?

As you venture into this new moral landscape, remember: every choice you make is an opportunity to refine your Judgment Core. Are you prepared to question the paths you've been taught to follow, to forge new ones where none exist, and to carry the light of compassion and fairness into the unknown? The answers lie not in the pages of this chapter only but in the journey you take beyond them.

7.1 Understanding the Principle: The Accident of Birth

You're standing in front of a giant spinning wheel—a cosmic lottery machine. Each section on the wheel represents a different life: a wealthy family in a peaceful country, a struggling household in a conflict zone, a remote village with limited resources, or a bustling city full of opportunity. You don't get to choose which life you'll live. You simply spin the wheel, and wherever it lands becomes your reality.

Now, picture the wheel slowing down and landing on a life. You open your eyes to discover your birthplace, your family, your skin color, and your circumstances. Perhaps you've spun a life of privilege, where doors open effortlessly, or perhaps the wheel lands on hardship, where survival becomes a daily battle. But here's the truth—none of us ever had a say in that spin.

Pause for a moment and think: How often do we forget that our starting points in life are random? How often do we judge others as if they chose theirs?

What if the very foundation of our lives—our identity, our opportunities, our struggles—was determined by a cosmic lottery over which we had no control? Imagine a world where, before you were even born, a silent hand assigned your birthplace, your family, your appearance, your religion, and your circumstances. These factors, entirely beyond your choice, would shape the contours of your existence. Yet, despite their randomness, society often uses these uncontrollable traits to define worth, to measure success, and to decide whose life matters more.

Pause for a moment. Reflect. You did not choose your family, whether they were loving or broken. You did not decide the shade of your skin, the language of your first word, or the borders that would define your "home." These elements were handed to you, as they were to every other person walking this earth. And yet, these unearned markers—privilege, poverty, peace, or conflict—become the dividing lines that shape how the world sees us and, perhaps more hauntingly, how we see each other.

Consider the profound randomness of it all. A child born into wealth and safety may inherit opportunities as naturally as they breathe, while another born into a war-torn village may grow up knowing hunger and fear as constants. What cosmic calculation determines the starting line of each life? And, more importantly, why do we allow these arbitrary factors to dictate whose life is seen as more valuable, whose voice is heard louder, whose struggles are deemed more significant?

This unsettling truth confronts our moral compass and demands an answer: Why do we cling to superficial distinctions—race, nationality, wealth—that elevate some lives above others? If we strip away these external markers, what remains is the shared essence of our humanity, the truth that every life is inherently valuable, not because of where it began, but because it exists.

This principle—that all lives matter equally—has been echoed throughout history by the wisest of voices. The Prophet Muhammad (peace be upon him), in his farewell sermon, delivered a timeless reminder: "All mankind is from Adam and Eve. An Arab has no superiority over a non-Arab, nor does a non-Arab have any superiority over an Arab; a white has no superiority over a black, nor does a black have any superiority over a white; none have superiority over another except by piety and good action."

These words cut through the noise of prejudice and bias, dismantling the hierarchies we so readily construct. They challenge us to look beyond the accidents of birth and judge each other not by what we were given but by what we create—our character, our actions, our contributions to the world.

But are we truly willing to embrace this idea? Can we step back from the deeply ingrained patterns of valuing some lives over others and begin to see humanity as a vast, interconnected web, where no strand holds more significance than another? Can we allow our Judgment Core to rise above inherited biases and reflect the truth of our shared existence?

Ask yourself:

- How often do you measure someone's worth by their achievements, their possessions, or their lineage?

- How often do you overlook the humanity that binds us all because it is hidden behind labels you did not create?

- And if you were born into a different life—another skin, another land, another struggle—how would you wish to be seen?

These questions lie at the heart of our moral journey. They ask us to confront the uncomfortable truths about how we perceive value and to redefine what it means to be truly human. Will you accept the challenge to see past the randomness of birth and embrace a deeper, more universal truth? Or will you remain tethered to the comforting simplicity of distinctions that never truly mattered?

The Shadows of Survival: The Journey of Immaculée Ilibagiza

In the spring of 1994, the lush hills of Rwanda, often called the "land of a thousand hills," were stained red. It was April, and the air carried an eerie tension as the world outside erupted into chaos. Nearly a million lives would be lost within 100 days, casualties of a genocide that turned neighbors into executioners, friends into foes, and entire communities into graves. Among the hunted was a young woman named Immaculée Ilibagiza, her life hanging by a thread—not for any crime she had committed, but because of the identity into which she had been born.

Immaculée was a Tutsi. Her birth, a twist of fate beyond her control, marked her as a target in a country consumed by ethnic hatred. As the killing began, she found herself forced into hiding in an act of desperate survival. On April 7, she arrived at the modest home of a local pastor, a Hutu who risked everything to shield her. Beneath the floorboards of this house, hidden behind a wardrobe, lay a bathroom no larger than a closet. In that stifling, suffocating space, Immaculée, along with seven other women, crouched for 91 days.

For three months, the bathroom became her entire world—a prison and a sanctuary. Outside, machete-wielding mobs roamed the village, their bloodlust palpable. She could hear their taunts, their chilling chants of extermination. Worse still, she recognized their voices: childhood friends, neighbors, even former classmates. They called her name with venomous certainty, vowing to find her and finish what they had started.

What does it mean to be hunted, not for what you've done, but for who you're? As Immaculée sat in silence, knees pressed to her chest, she grappled with this horrifying reality. She wondered how people she once shared meals with could now wish for her death. The world outside the bathroom walls was a grotesque reflection of humanity's ability to devalue life based on arbitrary distinctions—ethnicity, race, religion. It was a stark reminder of the fragile threads that bind us, and how easily they can be severed.

Days turned into weeks, and weeks into months. The women survived on scraps of food the pastor managed to sneak to them. Hunger gnawed at their bodies, but fear consumed their minds. Immaculée turned inward, seeking solace in her faith. She clung to prayer, meditating for hours on end. Yet, even as she prayed, anger swelled within her—a burning hatred for those who had slaughtered her family, who had turned her vibrant world into a desolate wasteland.

But hatred, she realized, was its own form of imprisonment. In the quiet darkness of the bathroom, Immaculée began an internal battle far more harrowing than the one outside. Could she forgive? Could she find it within herself to see humanity in those who had become monsters in her eyes? These questions became the crucible in which her moral compass and Judgment Core were tested and forged anew.

When the genocide ended, Immaculée emerged into a world forever changed. Her family was gone, victims of the violence she had barely escaped. Yet, she made a choice that defied comprehension: she forgave. She visited the jail where one of her family's killers was held. Looking into the eyes of the man who had robbed her of everything, she uttered words of forgiveness. It wasn't acceptance of his actions but an acknowledgment of their shared humanity—a radical act of grace that transcended vengeance.

Immaculée's story is not just one of survival; it is a profound exploration of the human spirit's capacity to endure, reflect, and rebuild. It forces us to confront uncomfortable truths: How often do we let arbitrary differences dictate the value we assign to others? What does it mean to forgive the unforgivable? And how do we, as individuals and as societies, reconcile with the weight of our collective failures?

Her journey compels us to examine the biases etched into our Judgment Core. Why should one life hold more value than another based on factors like ethnicity, race, or religion—circumstances none of us choose? And if the tables were turned, if we found ourselves persecuted for the very essence of who we are, how would we respond?

In the face of such overwhelming odds, Immaculée's resilience serves as a beacon, illuminating the path to a more compassionate and equitable understanding of humanity. It challenges us to look beyond the labels that divide us and to see the intrinsic worth in every individual. In her forgiveness, she teaches us that while hatred may destroy, only love and understanding have the power to heal.

Would you have the courage to forgive as she did? Would you find the strength to hold on to your humanity in a world that seeks to strip it away? These are the questions her story leaves behind, urging us to confront the depths of our own moral compass and the truths it reveals.

The Story of Ahmed and the Kite

In the summer of 2018, Gaza was a land of contrasts—searing heat and endless skies boxed in by the Israeli occupation. Among the despair, a small boy named Ahmed found solace in the simplest of joys: a kite he had made from discarded plastic bags and sticks scavenged from the rubble of his neighborhood in Khan Younis.

Ahmed, just nine years old, lived with his parents and two younger sisters in a cramped apartment in a neighborhood bearing the scars of the blockade and Israeli airstrikes. The walls of their home were cracked, the windows patched with sheets of plastic, and the streets around them were littered with rubble. Gaza's land, water, and air were tightly controlled by Israel, turning the strip into a boxed enclave where movement, supplies, and even hope were restricted. Yet, Ahmed's spirit remained unbroken.

Every evening, as the oppressive sun dipped below the horizon, Ahmed would climb to the rooftop of his building with his kite in hand. The kite was his masterpiece, a burst of color against the drab, gray city. For Ahmed, it was more than a toy—it was a symbol of freedom in a world that seemed determined to confine him.

One evening, as the call to prayer echoed through the air, Ahmed stood on the rooftop, carefully unwinding the string of his kite. Below him, the streets were alive with the sounds of children playing, families preparing for the evening meal, and the ever-present hum of restrictions. The kite soared higher and higher, catching the wind and dancing in the twilight.

For Ahmed, the kite was a way to escape the weight of his young life. It was a distraction from the long hours without electricity, the constant rationing of water, and the stories of friends and neighbors who had been displaced or killed. It was his way of reclaiming a piece of the sky in a world where even the air above was under occupation.

But Ahmed's joy was short-lived. The following week, during one of his rooftop escapes, he heard a sharp crack in the distance—a sound he had come to associate with danger. His kite faltered, its string slipping from his hands as he instinctively ducked. An explosion erupted a few streets away, shaking the building beneath his feet. Ahmed scrambled down from the rooftop, clutching the stringless remains of his kite.

His father, Yasser, pulled him into their small living room, where the family huddled together as the sounds of shelling filled the night. Yasser tried to reassure his children, speaking softly about resilience and hope. But Ahmed could see the fear in his father's eyes, a reflection of his own.

Ahmed was lucky. The blast that night did not claim his life, nor did it rob him of his limbs, as it had so many other children in Gaza. Countless others weren't as fortunate, losing their lives or enduring devastating injuries that forever changed their futures. That reality weighed heavily on Yasser as he held Ahmed close, whispering words of gratitude for his son's survival and sorrow for those who weren't spared.

The next morning, as the dust settled, Ahmed returned to the rooftop. He held the broken kite in his hands, his fingers tracing the torn plastic. He looked out at the city, the rubble, and the boxed-in sea beyond. "Why, Baba?" he later asked his father. "Why do the kites have to fall?"

Yasser didn't have an answer. But he spoke to Ahmed about the value of hope and the importance of holding onto the small things that make life worth living. "Sometimes, Ahmed," he said, "we fly our kites not because we can't see the danger, but because it reminds us that the sky still belongs to us."

Ahmed's question lingers in the hearts of those who hear his story. It challenges us to reflect on the arbitrary nature of suffering and the resilience of those who refuse to let despair define them. How do we reconcile a world where a child's simple joy—a kite—can become a symbol of resistance, hope, and loss all at once?

Ahmed's story reminds us of the fragile balance between innocence and occupation and the urgent need to ensure that every child has the right to a sky free of fear. It asks us to examine our own moral compass and judgment core: How can we justify a world where children must fight for the simple joys of life? How can we learn from Ahmed's resilience and ensure that the sky remains a place of freedom and dreams, not fear and sorrow?

Conclusion: The Fragility of Birth and the Weight of Judgment

What if the trajectory of your entire life hinged on a roll of the cosmic dice—a lottery you never entered, with stakes you couldn't comprehend? The accident of birth, that random assignment to a family, a nation, a social class, is a force so powerful it shapes not only your opportunities but also the way the world sees you and, perhaps most hauntingly, how you see yourself.

Imagine, for a moment, that you were born into Immaculée Ilibagiza's reality, hidden in a bathroom for 91 days while death stalked just outside. How would you have survived such trials? Would you have clung to your humanity, or would despair have consumed you? Would you have found the strength to forgive as Immaculée did? Would your Judgment Core—your internal compass of right and wrong—have guided you differently?

Ahmed's story from Gaza adds another dimension to this reflection. A child boxed in by occupation, his kite becoming a symbol of resistance and hope in a sky that no longer belongs to him. Ahmed's innocence is juxtaposed with a stark reality: his survival is luck, while many others were not as fortunate. His simple question, "Why do the kites have to fall?" lingers like an echo, challenging us to consider the invisible barriers we construct between ourselves and others.

Think about it: Do you measure your worth—or the worth of others—by what you've achieved, without considering the privilege or hardship of your starting point? Do you see the humanity in those who are unlike you, or do the circumstances of their birth cloud your perception? And if you were born into their reality—be it a war-torn city, a persecuted community, or an impoverished household—how would you hope to be seen?

This realization forces us to confront our biases and adjust our moral compass. The accident of birth is an unearned marker, a starting point we cannot control. It challenges us to strip away the superficial distinctions of race, religion, and nationality, recognizing the shared humanity that binds us all. How, then, can we justify judging others based on circumstances they never chose? Can we reshape our Judgment Core to reflect empathy over prejudice, fairness over superiority?

But perhaps the most mysterious question of all lies within ourselves: If our lives are shaped by this randomness, what is our responsibility to those less fortunate? Can we truly say we've earned our privilege, or is it our duty to use it for others? And how do we reconcile the ease of our own lives with the struggles of those who are less fortunate through no fault of their own?

As you reflect on these questions, consider this: Your Judgment Core is not static. It evolves with every experience, every decision, every story that challenges your perspective. Will you let these stories shape it for the better, guiding you toward a more inclusive, compassionate view of humanity? Or will you let the comforting simplicity of superficial distinctions keep you tethered to a narrow worldview?

The accident of birth is not a determinant of worth, but a call to action. Will you answer it?

7.2 The Illusion of Equality and the Enigma of Fairness

Imagine a vast, uncharted landscape where every individual stands at a unique starting point. Some begin on lush plains with clear skies, while others find themselves in shadowed valleys or atop treacherous cliffs. Would it be fair to hand everyone the same map, the same compass, and expect them to navigate equally? Or would true fairness require us to consider where they begin, the obstacles they face, and the tools they need to progress?

This question lies at the heart of fairness—a concept that transcends the illusion of absolute equality. The Judgment Core, your internal compass for morality, demands more than rigid adherence to uniformity. It calls for nuance, understanding, and a willingness to see beyond the surface.

What if the pursuit of absolute equality, that shining ideal we're often taught to value, is nothing more than a mirage? Imagine a world where every person receives the exact same treatment, regardless of their unique circumstances. Would that truly lead to fairness, or would it instead create a landscape of injustice hidden beneath the veneer of uniformity?

Fairness, unlike equality, calls us to delve deeper, to understand the intricate nuances of each person's journey. It whispers a question into the depths of your Judgment Core: Can you see beyond the surface and discern what is truly just?

Consider this: as a parent, does fairness mean giving each child the same toy, the same praise, or the same punishment? Or does it mean understanding that one child might need more guidance in school while another craves encouragement in their friendships? As a manager, does fairness mean dividing resources evenly, or does it mean allocating them where they are needed most? Can you set aside your personal grievances, your biases, your fleeting emotions, and act with a clarity that transcends instinct?

The challenge of fairness lies in its complexity. It demands that we step out of ourselves, abandoning the comfort of one-size-fits-all solutions. It forces us to confront the raw, unfiltered truths about those around us: their struggles, their strengths, their humanity. But do we? Do we make decisions free from the weight of our emotions, or do we allow prejudice and convenience to dictate our actions?

Imagine yourself in a position of power—a judge in a courtroom, a teacher in a classroom, a spouse in a partnership. How do you wield that power? Is your fairness guided by a sense of integrity, or does it falter under the sway of anger, favoritism, or indifference? And what happens when the roles reverse? When you find yourself at the mercy of another's judgment, will you wish they understood fairness as you hope to practice it?

Fairness is not about treating everyone the same. It is about treating each person as they deserve, based on who they are and what they need. But how do you navigate this? How do you discern fairness in a world so colored by subjective views and biases? Can your moral compass rise to the challenge, ensuring you act with empathy, respect, and justice?

These questions linger, unanswered, urging you to examine the layers of fairness not just as an abstract principle, but as a living, breathing guide to how you interact with the world. Will you rise to meet this challenge? Or will the illusion of equality blind you to the deeper truths that fairness demands you see?

The Legacy of Marva Collins: A Beacon of Fairness

It was the fall of 1975 in Chicago, a city of contrasts—soaring skyscrapers and vibrant culture juxtaposed against neighborhoods struggling under the weight of poverty and neglect. In one such neighborhood, Marva Collins stood in the modest living room of her home, staring at a pile of textbooks and desks she had bought with $5,000 withdrawn from her pension fund. That room was about to become the first classroom of Westside Preparatory School—a sanctuary for the children society had cast aside.

Collins, a veteran educator disillusioned with the Chicago public school system, had grown tired of hearing the same words used to label her students: unteachable, disruptive, hopeless. These children were more than just labels; they were human beings with potential, locked behind barriers of neglect and low expectations. Marva Collins refused to accept those barriers. Her mission wasn't just to educate but to change the narrative entirely.

One cold morning, Cindy arrived at Westside Prep. She was 9 years old, with a reputation that preceded her—a history of violent outbursts, defiance, and academic failure. Other schools had labeled her a lost cause, but Marva Collins saw something different. Cindy wasn't just a "problem child"; she was a child in pain, shaped by a background of neglect and trauma. Collins understood that fairness didn't mean treating Cindy the same as other students; it meant giving her what she needed to heal, grow, and thrive.

Collins set high expectations for Cindy, but she also gave her patience, empathy, and structure. Days turned into weeks, and slowly, the cracks in Cindy's tough exterior began to show. She started turning in assignments, participating in discussions, and eventually, she became one of the top-performing students in her class. Cindy's transformation was proof that fairness—when wielded with understanding and care—could unlock a child's potential.

Another student, Richard Williams, arrived at Westside unable to read, his confidence eroded by years of being told he was a failure. Collins didn't see a failure; she saw a boy who had been failed by a system that prioritized uniformity over individuality. She worked tirelessly with Richard, tailoring lessons to his needs and showing him that his past didn't define his future. By the time he graduated, Richard's reading skills surpassed his grade level, and he went on to excel in high school and beyond.

Even within her own family, Collins' philosophy proved transformative. Her son, Patrick, struggled in traditional schools, often dismissed as "lazy" by his teachers. Under his mother's guidance, Patrick flourished, eventually becoming a successful businessman. He later credited her teaching methods with shaping his character and career.

Collins' methods weren't just about academics; they were a masterclass in fairness. She taught her students life lessons about respect, perseverance, and responsibility. Her mantra, "Excellence is not an act, but a habit," echoed through the walls of Westside Prep, inspiring students to strive for greatness regardless of their starting point.

But her story wasn't without its challenges. Critics questioned her unconventional methods, accusing her of being too demanding. Others doubted the viability of her school, housed in a modest building with limited resources. Yet Collins persisted, driven by an unwavering belief in the power of fairness to change lives.

Now, imagine stepping into Marva Collins' shoes. Would you have the patience to meet each child where they were, to see beyond their labels and behaviors to the potential within? If you were Cindy or Richard, cast aside by a world that deemed you unworthy, how would it feel to have someone finally believe in you?

And what about your own life? In the roles you play—as a parent, a manager, a friend—how often do you let biases or emotions influence your decisions? How do you balance fairness with the practical demands of authority? Is your Judgment Core strong enough to guide you through the complexities of treating people justly, even when it's inconvenient?

Marva Collins' story challenges us to confront these questions. It asks us to examine how we use the power we hold over others, whether in classrooms, workplaces, or our personal lives. Her legacy isn't just about education; it's a call to action—a reminder that fairness isn't always easy, but it is always worth striving for.

The Transformation of Microsoft: A Journey of Fairness and Vision

On a crisp February morning in 2014, the tech world buzzed with anticipation. In Redmond, Washington, Satya Nadella officially assumed the role of CEO at Microsoft, becoming only the third person to lead the company since its inception. Microsoft, once the titan of innovation, was now grappling with stagnation, an entrenched hierarchical culture, and internal rivalries that stifled creativity. The stakes were high, and all eyes were on Nadella—a leader whose name was relatively unknown outside the company's walls.

Nadella entered with a quiet confidence, but beneath his calm demeanor lay a profound vision for fairness and empathy. His first act wasn't a flashy announcement or a major acquisition; it was an unassuming yet radical decision: dismantling Microsoft's infamous "stack ranking" system. For years, this practice had forced managers to rank employees against each other, rewarding a select few while sidelining others. The result? A cutthroat environment where colleagues viewed one another as competitors rather than collaborators.

Nadella saw the damage this system had done, not just to morale but to the company's very soul. He understood that fairness wasn't about treating everyone the same—it was about fostering an environment where each individual could thrive. By eliminating stack ranking, he sent a clear message: success at Microsoft would no longer be defined by outpacing peers but by contributing to collective growth.

Nadella's approach wasn't just about systems and policies; it was deeply personal. Born in Hyderabad, India, Nadella had grown up in a middle-class family, experiencing firsthand the challenges of working within limitations and striving for opportunities. His experiences shaped his perspective on fairness and inclusion, giving him an acute sensitivity to the diverse needs of individuals.

As he took the helm, Nadella made listening a cornerstone of his leadership. He convened meetings with employees across all levels, asking questions and absorbing their insights. This wasn't just a gesture—it was a strategic move to rebuild trust in a company that had grown disconnected from its workforce. Nadella's emphasis on empathy set the tone for a cultural shift, transforming Microsoft into a place where every voice mattered.

One story stands out: during a meeting with junior engineers, Nadella asked about their challenges. One young woman shared how she often felt sidelined during brainstorming sessions. Nadella didn't just listen; he acted. He introduced company-wide initiatives to promote inclusivity in team discussions, ensuring that everyone, regardless of their role or background, had a seat at the table.

When Microsoft began transitioning from traditional software sales to cloud computing, the shift threatened to leave many employees behind. Rather than punishing those who lacked the requisite skills, Nadella launched massive reskilling programs, investing in his workforce instead of replacing them. This decision wasn't just an act of fairness—it was a strategic masterstroke that positioned Microsoft as a global leader in cloud technology.

Under Nadella's leadership, diversity and inclusion became more than just buzzwords. He set ambitious goals to increase representation of women and minorities in leadership roles, ensuring that Microsoft's workforce reflected the world it served. His commitment to fairness extended to pay equity and opportunities for career advancement, creating a culture where employees felt valued and supported.

What set Nadella apart wasn't just his policies but his unwavering moral compass—his Judgment Core. He understood that leadership wasn't about enforcing rigid rules or wielding authority. It was about navigating the gray areas of human needs and organizational goals with empathy and fairness.

Nadella's actions challenged Microsoft's employees—and, by extension, the world—to reconsider what true fairness looks like. Does fairness mean giving everyone the same tools, or does it mean providing what each individual needs to succeed? Is it fair to let old systems persist because they're familiar, or is fairness found in the courage to dismantle them for the greater good?

Imagine standing in Nadella's shoes. Would you have had the courage to tear down a long-standing system that others considered the backbone of performance evaluation? Would you prioritize reskilling over layoffs, even when the latter might seem easier? How would you ensure fairness in a company with over 180,000 employees, each with unique needs, challenges, and aspirations?

And now, look inward. How often do you let personal biases influence your decisions, whether at work, at home, or in your community? Are you willing to listen to those who feel unheard, to see the humanity in every individual, even when it's inconvenient?

Nadella's transformation of Microsoft isn't just a corporate success story—it's a lesson in the power of fairness, empathy, and an unwavering Judgment Core. It reminds us that leadership isn't about making the easy choices; it's about making the right ones. Are you ready to lead with the same commitment to fairness that Nadella demonstrated? Are you willing to challenge the status quo and embrace the complexities of human need?

The answers to these questions lie not in grand gestures but in the quiet, deliberate choices you make every day. What will your legacy of fairness be?

Conclusion: Fairness Beyond the Illusion — The Call of the Judgment Core

Fairness is a quiet call from within—a challenge whispered by your Judgment Core to rise above instinct and convenience, to see beyond the illusion of equality. But how often do we listen to that whisper? How often do we pause to ask whether our decisions are truly fair, or merely convenient?

Imagine standing in a moment of decision-making. You have the power to shape someone's future—a child, an employee, a friend. Do you treat them exactly the same as everyone else, or do you take the time to understand their unique needs and circumstances? Do you choose fairness, or do you fall back on uniformity, mistaking equality for justice?

Your Judgment Core doesn't demand perfection—it demands awareness. It asks you to pause and reflect before making choices that impact others. It challenges you to move beyond surface-level fairness and dig into the complex realities of human need.

But fairness is hard. It requires empathy, courage, and humility. It means recognizing that no two people start from the same place. It means acknowledging your own biases and privileges, and taking intentional steps to ensure your actions promote justice rather than perpetuate inequality.

Now, ask yourself:

- When you make decisions, are you considering the unique needs of those affected, or are you taking the easy path of treating everyone the same?

- Are your actions guided by empathy and understanding, or are they clouded by impatience, bias, or ego?

- If you were in their position, would you feel truly seen and valued—or merely treated equally?

The Danger of Uniformity: Are You Blind to True Fairness?

Imagine giving every person the same tool to navigate life's challenges—a map, a compass, a pair of shoes. It sounds fair, right? But what if one person is standing at the base of a mountain, while another is lost in a desert? Would giving them the same resources truly help them succeed, or would it leave some to struggle while others thrive?

This is the illusion of equality—the belief that treating everyone the same will lead to fair outcomes. But fairness demands more. It requires recognizing that each person's journey is different and tailoring your actions to meet their unique needs.

Think back to the story of Marva Collins. She didn't teach all her students the same way. She saw their individual struggles and strengths and adjusted her approach to help each child succeed. That's fairness in action. Or consider Satya Nadella, who dismantled systems at Microsoft that favored competition over collaboration. He prioritized empathy and inclusion over tradition.

Now, think about your own life:

- Are you giving each person in your life what they need to grow, or are you handing out the same tools and expecting them to thrive?

- Are you open to seeing the unique struggles of those around you, or are you blinded by the simplicity of treating everyone equally?

The Judgment Core's Challenge: What Legacy Will You Leave?

Your Judgment Core is your internal compass, whispering reminders of empathy, fairness, and integrity. But it's easy to silence that voice, to fall into patterns of habit and convenience. Fairness requires active effort. It's not a passive principle—it's a choice you make every day in how you treat others.

So, ask yourself:

- When conflict arises, do you pause to consider the perspective of others, or do you rush to impose your own views?

- Do you prioritize fairness over convenience, or do you let personal biases and emotions cloud your decisions?

- Are you willing to challenge the systems and habits that perpetuate inequality, even when it's uncomfortable or inconvenient?

Imagine a world where every person you encounter leaves with the sense that they were truly seen, heard, and valued. That's the world your Judgment Core asks you to create. But it starts with your choices—each small action contributing to a larger legacy of fairness.

<u>Fairness as a Daily Practice</u>

The next time you're faced with a decision that impacts others, pause.

- Ask yourself: Am I considering their unique circumstances, or am I taking the easy route of treating everyone the same?

- Reflect on your biases. Are you letting assumptions or stereotypes influence your actions?

- Choose to act with empathy. Take the time to understand the needs of those around you and adjust your approach accordingly.

Fairness isn't about grand gestures—it's about the daily choices you make. It's about pausing before reacting, listening before judging, and understanding before acting. It's about building a legacy where people feel valued for who they are, not just treated the same as everyone else.

<u>The Final Question: Will You See Beyond the Surface?</u>

Fairness asks you to see beyond the surface, to recognize that people's journeys are shaped by unique challenges and opportunities. It asks you to navigate the gray areas of human need, to balance empathy with accountability, and to act with integrity even when it's inconvenient.

Your Judgment Core knows this truth. It knows that fairness isn't about rigid equality—it's about tailoring your actions to create just outcomes. The question is, will you listen?

- Will you choose to see the unique needs of those around you, or will you settle for the illusion of equality?

- Will you make decisions that uplift others, or will you fall into patterns of convenience and uniformity?

- When you hold power over others, will you wield it with empathy and understanding, or will you let biases and emotions dictate your actions?

The choice is yours. But remember—fairness isn't a destination. It's a journey. It's a series of choices you make every day, shaping the legacy you leave behind.

So, the question remains: Will you rise to the challenge of fairness, guided by your Judgment Core? Or will you be blinded by the comforting illusion of equality?

What legacy of fairness will you leave in the world you help shape?

7.3 The Mystery of Empathy: A Journey into the Human Experience

You're standing at the edge of a mirror that does not reflect your face but the lives of others—their struggles, joys, fears, and hopes. Would you dare to step through, to inhabit their reality for even a moment? Empathy, that elusive ability to step into another's shoes, is not just an act of kindness; it is a profound journey into the heart of humanity. But how often do we take that step? How often do we allow ourselves to truly see the world through someone else's eyes?

Empathy is more than understanding; it is the bridge that connects us across the chasms of power, privilege, and perspective. What happens when you hold power—whether as a parent guiding a child, a manager leading a team, or an officer enforcing rules? Do you still see the struggles of those below, or does power blur your vision, making their realities seem distant and unimportant?

The truth is that power and privilege are not constants. They ebb and flow like tides, and the positions we hold today may not be ours tomorrow. Will you practice empathy now, recognizing that the hand you extend to others could one day be the lifeline you need? Or will you let the illusion of permanence shield you from the fragility of your own position?

Empathy also compels us to look beyond appearances, to consider the unseen potential and hidden challenges of those around us. The colleague you dismiss, the student you overlook, or the stranger you pass by may possess untapped brilliance or virtues obscured by circumstances they did not choose. How often do we pause to consider what someone might achieve if given the opportunities we take for granted?

In every interaction, empathy acts as a safeguard against the arrogance of power. It challenges us to treat others with the dignity and respect that we would wish for ourselves, even when authority tempts us to do otherwise. It asks us to see each individual not as a role, a status, or a label, but as a fellow traveler on this unpredictable human journey.

And now, the questions turn inward: Do you practice empathy, or merely preach it? When was the last time you paused to truly listen, to truly understand another's point of view? Are your decisions guided by compassion, or do they reflect the convenience of your own perspective?

Empathy is not a destination; it is a practice, a challenge, and a responsibility. It is the thread that binds our moral compass and Judgment Core to the shared essence of humanity. So, will you step through the mirror and embrace the complexities of another's reality? Or will you stand on the edge, content with the reflections of your own? The choice, as always, is yours to make.

The Redemption of a Tycoon: A Tale of Empathy and Transformation

It was a cold January evening in 2022 when John Pearson found himself sitting in the corner of a dimly lit café in Palo Alto. Once hailed as the kingpin of Silicon Valley, John's name was synonymous with power and innovation. As the former CEO of Innovex Technologies, he had led his company to dominate the tech landscape throughout the early 2010s. But now, the gleaming skyscrapers and buzzing conference rooms that once defined his world seemed like distant memories. His career, reputation, and fortune had all crumbled. And here he was, nervously waiting for a man he had once dismissed as insignificant.

The rise and fall of John Pearson was the stuff of corporate legend. In 2012, Innovex was the jewel of Silicon Valley, breaking boundaries in AI and robotics under John's unrelenting leadership. Known for his demanding nature, John was feared as much as he was respected. Meetings with him were infamous for their intensity—praise was scarce, and criticism was public. It was during one such meeting in 2014, in a sleek Innovex boardroom overlooking San Francisco Bay, that John had humiliated a junior engineer named David Reeves.

David, a quiet but brilliant mind, had proposed a bold innovation in AI integration. John dismissed the idea with a sneer, calling it "impractical," and later presented a modified version of David's concept as his own during a high-profile meeting with executives from Apple and Google. For David, the betrayal was a turning point. By 2016, exhausted by the hostile environment, he left Innovex for Omnitech Solutions—a smaller, lesser-known company where his talents were nurtured and respected.

As the years passed, Innovex began to falter. By 2019, cracks in John's leadership became evident. Tesla's AI division overtook Innovex in market dominance, scandals rocked the company, and John's autocratic style was increasingly criticized. The board of directors finally ousted him in early 2020, marking the end of his reign. Meanwhile, David thrived. By 2021, Omnitech had emerged as a leader in next-generation technology, and David was at the helm of groundbreaking innovations that caught the world's attention.

Back in the café, John shifted uncomfortably as the door swung open. In walked David, now a confident and accomplished figure. As they shook hands, John's mind raced. How had their roles reversed so dramatically? Could the man he had once belittled now hold the key to his redemption?

Over steaming cups of coffee, John laid bare his story—the downfall of Innovex, his struggles to rebuild, and the harsh lessons he had learned about leadership and humanity. "I was wrong," John admitted, his voice heavy with regret. "I let my ego blind me. I failed to see the value in those around me, including you, David."

David listened intently. He had every reason to walk away, to remind John of the humiliation and disrespect he had endured. But instead, David chose a different path. He saw in John's remorse an opportunity for growth—not just for John, but for their industry as a whole. "Empathy," David said, leaning forward, "is about understanding someone's journey, even when they've wronged you. Let's talk about how we can move forward—together."

Their partnership marked a turning point for both men. John's acknowledgment of his past mistakes and David's willingness to empathize and collaborate became a powerful example of the transformative potential of empathy in leadership and life.

John's story serves as a cautionary tale about the perils of power without empathy. His lack of regard for others not only alienated his team but also led to his own undoing. On the other hand, David's ability to rise above personal grievances and act with empathy demonstrated the strength of a refined Judgment Core—a moral compass capable of navigating the complexities of human interaction.

Now, ask yourself: What would you have done in David's place? Could you set aside past hurts to extend understanding and collaboration? If you were in John's shoes, would you have the humility to admit your mistakes and seek forgiveness?

Empathy is not about excusing bad behavior; it's about recognizing the shared humanity in every individual and choosing a path that fosters growth and understanding. In your own life, how often do you pause to consider the perspectives of others, even those who challenge or hurt you? How does your Judgment Core guide you in moments of conflict or power?

The story of John and David invites us to reflect on the delicate balance between power, humility, and empathy. It challenges us to think beyond our own experiences and to act with fairness, even when it's difficult. Will you let empathy shape your decisions, ensuring your moral compass remains true? Or will you allow ego and resentment to cloud your path? The answers lie within your Judgment Core, waiting to be uncovered.

The Shadows of Maycomb: The Story of "To Kill a Mockingbird"

It was a sweltering summer in 1935, the kind of heat that seemed to wrap the small town of Maycomb, Alabama, in a suffocating grip. The town, with its dusty streets and creaking porches, bore an undercurrent of tension—a quiet hum of secrets, prejudices, and fears woven into its fabric. Against this backdrop, a man named Atticus Finch prepared for a trial that would not only define his career as a lawyer but also test the very soul of the town and its people.

Atticus, a single father with a quiet dignity, lived in a modest home on the edge of town with his two children, Scout and Jem. He was known as a man of principle, someone who sought justice in a world that often preferred convenience. That summer, he was tasked with defending Tom Robinson, a black man accused of raping Mayella Ewell, a white woman. For many in Maycomb, the case was open and shut. But for Atticus, it was a moral battle—a fight not just for Tom's innocence but for the conscience of Maycomb itself.

As the trial unfolded, the courthouse became a theater of human frailty and prejudice. Atticus stood before the jury, a lone figure of reason in a storm of bias, dismantling the prosecution's case piece by piece. Mayella's story unraveled under his calm questioning. The bruises on her face told a story of violence inflicted by someone strong and angry—a left-handed attacker. Tom's crippled left arm, mangled in a cotton gin accident years earlier, proved his innocence in plain sight. Yet, the jury, blinded by their entrenched prejudices, saw only the color of his skin.

The verdict—guilty—landed like a thunderclap. Scout and Jem, watching from the balcony, felt their world tilt. They had believed that truth and justice would prevail. Instead, they witnessed a community willing to sacrifice a man's life to maintain the fragile illusion of its moral superiority. The trial's outcome shattered their innocence, leaving behind a deep scar of disillusionment.

But the story of Maycomb didn't end with the trial. In the shadow of Tom Robinson's tragedy, another tale quietly unfolded—that of Boo Radley, the town recluse. For years, Boo had been the subject of whispers and wild stories, painted as a phantom by the vivid imaginations of Maycomb's children. Yet, Boo's true nature revealed itself in acts of quiet kindness:

gifts left in a tree, a blanket draped over Scout during a cold night, and, ultimately, a life saved.

One fateful evening, as the sun dipped below the horizon, Boo emerged from the shadows to protect Scout and Jem from Bob Ewell's drunken rage. In that moment, the monster of childhood fears became a guardian angel. Standing on Boo's porch, Scout finally understood the lesson her father had repeated so often: "You never really understand a person until you consider things from his point of view… until you climb inside of his skin and walk around in it."

Maycomb's stories are not merely tales of a small Southern town; they are reflections of the human condition. The courtroom drama of Tom Robinson and the quiet heroism of Boo Radley compel us to examine our own biases and judgment. They ask us to confront uncomfortable truths about how easily fear and prejudice can cloud our moral compass.

But what about you? How often do you take the time to step into someone else's shoes, to see the world through their eyes? Would you have stood with Atticus in the courtroom, knowing the cost? Would you have seen Boo Radley as a protector, not a pariah? And if you were Tom Robinson, condemned by a jury unwilling to see your humanity, how would you hope the world would respond?

Empathy, as Atticus taught his children, is not a passive virtue. It is an active, deliberate choice to see the humanity in others, even when it's inconvenient or uncomfortable. It challenges us to transcend our fears and prejudices, to question the narratives we've been told, and to act with courage and understanding.

In the end, Maycomb's stories are a call to examine our own Judgment Core—that internal moral compass guiding our sense of right and wrong. They remind us that justice is not found in rigid rules or surface judgments but in the deeper truths revealed through empathy and understanding. As you walk through the world, will you let empathy guide you, or will you remain a prisoner of your own preconceptions? The answer lies in the choices you make, every day, in the quiet moments when no one else is watching.

Conclusion: The Silent Mirror of Empathy

Picture this: a mirror that does not reflect your own face, but instead reveals the lives of others—their fears, struggles, triumphs, and silent hopes. Would you dare to gaze into it? Would you step closer, knowing that to do so would require you to see beyond the surface and into the depths of their reality? Empathy, that quiet, mysterious force, is not just a virtue; it is the compass that aligns your Judgment Core with the truth of our shared humanity.

As a leader, a parent, a friend, or simply as a fellow traveler in life, have you ever paused to consider the weight of your decisions on those around you? Imagine the colleague who struggles silently under the weight of unseen challenges, the child whose world hinges on your approval, or the stranger whose path you briefly cross, unaware of the burdens they carry. Have you looked beyond the obvious and asked, What would it feel like to be them? What would I need if our roles were reversed?

Empathy is not about avoiding hard decisions or simply being kind—it is about understanding. It is about seeing the complexities of another's circumstances and allowing that understanding to shape your actions. But how often do we act with this level of awareness? How often do we allow our Judgment Core to guide us, free from the shadows of bias and convenience?

Consider the choices you've made recently. Did you take the time to step into someone else's shoes before making a judgment? Did you pause to question whether your decisions were fair, or were they driven by your own perspective, your own priorities? Imagine, for a moment, the weight of those choices if the roles were reversed. Would you feel respected? Understood? Valued?

Now turn the mirror inward. If empathy truly binds us, what does its absence reveal about the cracks in our own moral compass? When we fail to empathize, what do we risk losing—not just in our relationships, but in our ability to grow as human beings?

Life has a way of reversing roles. The positions of influence you hold today—whether as a parent guiding a child, a manager leading a team, or a friend offering support—may shift tomorrow. What legacy of empathy are you leaving behind? Will the choices you make today inspire compassion and understanding, or will they leave others questioning your fairness and integrity?

The challenge of empathy is both universal and deeply personal. It asks you to reach beyond the confines of your own experience and see the world as others live it. It demands that you confront your biases, soften your judgments, and navigate the gray areas of morality with humility and grace.

So, will you accept the challenge? Will you use empathy as a tool to refine your Judgment Core and strengthen the moral compass that guides your life? Or will you remain tethered to the illusion of understanding, content with seeing only your reflection in the mirror?

The choice is yours, as it is for all of us. But remember, the mirror of empathy waits for no one. It simply reflects the truth of who we are and who we have the potential to become.

7.4 The Silent Seed of Greed: A Whisper of Danger

A silent seed buried deep within you, dormant and unassuming—a seed that holds the power to grow into something beautiful or devastating. This seed is greed. Left unchecked, it remains like an inactivated cancer cell, quiet yet dangerous, waiting for the right conditions to take root and spread. But how often do we notice it before it's too late? How often do we pause to examine whether our desires are leading us toward progress—or toward destruction?

Greed rarely shouts; it whispers. It hides behind justifications and ambitions, cloaking itself in the guise of success and personal achievement. "I've earned this." "I deserve more." "It's just business." These thoughts, seemingly harmless, can quietly warp our Judgment Core—the internal compass that guides our sense of right and wrong. The question is: Are you listening to those whispers? Are you aware of how far they've taken root within you?

But greed isn't always loud or obvious. Sometimes, it shows itself in the quietest choices, in the silent rejections of the very people who once stood by us.

Imagine a friend, a brother, or a neighbor who has always opened their door to you. They welcomed you with warmth when you needed it most—offering you a meal, a kind word, or a listening ear. They gave without asking for anything in return. But when they finally knocked on your door, seeking your help in their hour of need, you closed it. You justified it to yourself: "I'm too busy." "It's not my problem." In that moment, greed had taken root. Not the greed of material wealth, but the greed of withholding compassion and reciprocity—the greed of turning away when it was your turn to give.

What would your Judgment Core say about that moment? Did you listen to its subtle warnings, or did you silence it in favor of self-preservation?

Greed, like an invisible cancer cell, spreads in these quiet betrayals. It erodes the bonds of trust and community, leaving behind a world where doors remain closed and hearts grow cold.

It also shows itself in the pursuit of profit at the expense of others. Imagine this scenario: You're a leader in a company, tasked with meeting ambitious financial targets. You know that cutting jobs will help achieve that goal, and doing so will earn you a substantial bonus. But have you stopped to think about the ripple effect? Each job you cut represents a family that will face financial hardship and uncertainty. Bills will go unpaid, stress will mount, and futures will be altered—all because you chose personal gain over collective well-being.

This is how unchecked greed takes root. When personal benefits outweigh the collective good, the disease of selfishness begins to spread. It starts small, justified by the allure of success, and grows into decisions that impact countless lives. Your Judgment Core must ask: Is your success worth the suffering of others? Is the bonus in your pocket worth the tears shed by the families affected by your choices?

The truth is, power, privilege, and fortune are never permanent. They ebb and flow like tides. Today, you may be the one in a position to give, but tomorrow, you could be the one knocking on a door. Will it open for you?

Greed isn't just about money. It's about the way we treat people. It's about withholding emotional support when someone needs a kind word, turning away from someone struggling, or prioritizing our comfort over another's pain. It's about closing doors that once stood open for us, thinking we'll never need to knock on them ourselves.

But what happens when the roles reverse? When you find yourself standing outside, seeking help from those you once ignored? Will you wish they had paused to consider the impact of their actions? Will you hope for empathy and compassion, rather than indifference?

Ask yourself: How often do you weigh the needs of others against your own desires? Do you nurture relationships, or do you take without giving back? Are you cultivating a sense of shared responsibility, or are you letting greed, in all its subtle forms, quietly take root?

Your Judgment Core is always watching, always guiding. But it only works if you listen. Will you heed its call? Will you keep your door open when someone knocks? Or will you let greed convince you to turn away, believing that you'll never need to knock on someone else's door?

Greed, like a cancer cell, thrives in silence and secrecy. It whispers, "Take more. Give less. No one will notice." But your Judgment Core knows the truth. The question is: Will you listen to it? Or will you let greed spread, unnoticed, until it's too late?

In the end, the choice is yours. But remember—greed is patient. It grows silently, waiting for the moment when it can close the door on you.

The Choice of the Unseen Path: A Tale of Leadership and Collective Benefit

It was December 2008, and the air in St. Louis, Missouri, was thick with uncertainty. The global financial crisis had sent shockwaves across industries, crippling businesses and leaving millions unemployed. Inside the sleek boardroom of Barry-Wehmiller, a manufacturing firm that had thrived for decades, CEO Bob Chapman sat quietly, contemplating the weight of the decision before him.

The company's numbers were grim. Orders had dried up, revenue had plummeted, and like many others, Barry-Wehmiller faced an existential threat. The advisors around the table echoed the same solution—layoffs. It was the fastest, cleanest way to cut costs and keep the company afloat. Yet, Chapman felt an unease he couldn't shake. He wasn't just staring at spreadsheets filled with numbers; he was seeing the faces behind them—employees who had families to support, mortgages to pay, and dreams they hadn't yet realized.

Chapman had always believed in the idea that businesses should serve their people, not the other way around. But now, in the face of a crisis, that belief would be tested. Would he follow the well-trodden path of corporate pragmatism, cutting jobs to protect the bottom line? Or could there be another way—a way that prioritized the collective good over immediate financial relief?

As the winter storm brewed outside, Chapman stood and addressed his team. "We won't be cutting jobs," he announced. A wave of confusion swept through the room. "But we will ask everyone to share in the burden."

What Chapman proposed was radical. Instead of laying off a portion of the workforce, he introduced a furlough program. Every employee, from senior executives to entry-level staff, would take four weeks of unpaid leave. The brilliance of this approach lay in its humanity: employees could choose when to take their furlough days, allowing them to manage their own circumstances during the crisis. No one would be singled out, no one would lose their job—and the burden would be shared equally.

As the plan rolled out, whispers filled the factory floors and office corridors. Some questioned whether it would work. Others felt a sense of relief and gratitude. One employee later shared, "I would have lost my house if I had been laid off. Instead, we all came together. We all sacrificed a little, and it saved us."

The effects of Chapman's decision rippled far beyond the company's balance sheet. The workforce, once just a collection of individuals, became a community bound by mutual respect and shared sacrifice. Employees weren't just working for a paycheck; they were working for each other. Trust grew where fear once festered, and loyalty deepened.

One story stood out—a factory worker named Jim, who had struggled to make ends meet even before the crisis. When furloughs were announced, Jim worried how he would survive without those four weeks of pay. But something remarkable happened. His colleagues, many of whom were in more stable financial situations, volunteered to take additional furlough days on his behalf. "We've got you, Jim," they said, embodying the spirit of collective benefit that Chapman had envisioned.

As the economy began to recover, Barry-Wehmiller emerged stronger than ever. Unlike companies that had resorted to mass layoffs and faced the fallout of lost knowledge, morale, and trust, Barry-Wehmiller had a motivated, united workforce ready to rebuild. The bonds formed during the crisis didn't fade; they became the foundation of a resilient, values-driven culture.

Chapman's decision wasn't just a strategic success—it was a moral triumph. He had prioritized people over profits, proving that empathy and fairness in leadership could lead to sustainable, long-term success.

But the story doesn't end there. Imagine if Chapman had taken the easier route. What would have happened to Jim? To his family? To the community that relied on the company for stability? And what of the other employees—would they have remained loyal, or would they have left, disillusioned by a company that discarded them in its time of need?

This tale isn't just about leadership; it's a challenge to all of us. Ask yourself: In your own life, do you prioritize collective benefit, or do you act with self-interest? When faced with tough decisions, do you pause to consider how your actions impact those around you? Would your Judgment Core—that internal compass guiding your sense of fairness—lead you to share in the burden, or would you turn a blind eye to the struggles of others?

Greed often disguises itself as pragmatism, whispering that individual gain is the ultimate measure of success. But stories like Chapman's remind us that true leadership—and true humanity—lies in the ability to see beyond oneself, to recognize that our well-being is deeply intertwined with the well-being of others.

Consider this: Meeting a profit target by cutting jobs may fatten your bonus, but at what cost? For every family left without an income, for every child who watches their parent lose a job, a ripple of hardship spreads. Unchecked greed doesn't just harm others—it erodes the very fabric of community and trust.

Chapman's story asks us to reflect on our own lives: Are we the kind of people who leave a friend's door closed when they need us most? Or do we, like Chapman's employees, step forward and say, "We've got you"?

The answer lies in the choices you make—each day, in the quiet moments when no one is watching. Will your Judgment Core guide you toward fairness and empathy? Or will you let the silent seed of greed grow, unchecked, until it consumes the very bonds that hold us together?

The next time you're faced with a decision that pits personal gain against collective well-being, remember this story. Remember Jim. Remember the employees who stepped in to support him. And ask yourself: What kind of legacy do I want to leave behind? Will my actions reflect a commitment to others, or will they reveal a self-centered pursuit of success?

The mirror is in front of you. The reflection you see depends on the choices you make. Will you choose empathy, fairness, and community—or will you let the unseen cancer of greed spread quietly within you? The decision is yours to make, but remember: the path you choose today shapes the world you live in tomorrow.

The Shadow of Greed: The OxyContin Scandal

The year was 1995. In the grand halls of Purdue Pharma's headquarters in Stamford, Connecticut, a hush fell over the boardroom. The Sackler family, heirs to a pharmaceutical empire, stood on the brink of a monumental launch. Before them lay a white bottle with a simple label: OxyContin. They saw it as a goldmine, a ticket to unimaginable wealth.

With its sleek packaging and promise of long-lasting pain relief, OxyContin was hailed as a medical breakthrough. Purdue Pharma marketed it as a safe, revolutionary solution to chronic pain, boasting that its time-release formula made it far less addictive than other opioids. The message was clear: doctors could prescribe it freely, and patients could take it without fear.

But there was a lie lurking beneath that promise—a lie that would unravel over the next two decades.

In the early days of OxyContin's release, Purdue Pharma's sales representatives fanned out across the country like missionaries with a divine cure. Armed with glossy brochures and rehearsed talking points, they visited doctors, clinics, and hospitals, promising that OxyContin was the answer to their patients' pain. The company's motto was simple: "The pain stops here."

Doctors were incentivized to prescribe the drug. Bonuses flowed, lavish dinners were hosted, and Purdue funded continuing education courses that subtly pushed the narrative: OxyContin is safe. OxyContin is effective. Many doctors, trusting the research provided by Purdue, began prescribing it at unprecedented rates.

The Sacklers watched as the company's profits soared. But with every pill sold, the first cracks in the façade began to appear.

Reports of addiction trickled in. Patients who had never struggled with substance abuse were suddenly craving more pills. Some resorted to crushing the tablets to release the entire dose at once, bypassing the time-release mechanism. Overdose deaths spiked, and emergency rooms saw a flood of cases tied to opioid misuse. Behind closed doors, Purdue executives knew what was happening. Internal memos, later uncovered, revealed a chilling truth: they knew OxyContin was addictive from the start.

Yet, instead of pulling back, they doubled down.

In 2007, Purdue Pharma faced its first major reckoning. The company and three top executives pleaded guilty to misleading the public about OxyContin's addiction risks. The settlement? A $600 million fine. For most companies, this would be devastating. For Purdue, it was a slap on the wrist—a fraction of the billions they had already made.

After the settlement, the company continued its aggressive marketing. The Sackler family remained in the shadows, shielded by layers of corporate structure, while the opioid crisis spiraled out of control. By the late 2010s, the numbers were staggering: hundreds of thousands dead from opioid overdoses, millions more trapped in the grip of addiction. Entire towns, particularly in rural America, were decimated. Families mourned lost loved ones. Children grew up without parents.

Despite mounting lawsuits and public outcry, Purdue's strategy remained the same. They funded patient advocacy groups to push for more opioid prescriptions. They placed blame on the victims, labeling them as criminals rather than acknowledging the drug's addictive nature.

In September 2019, Purdue Pharma filed for bankruptcy. It was a dramatic fall from grace, but for many, it was too little, too late. The Sacklers, now infamous for their role in fueling the crisis, agreed to pay billions in settlements. But no amount of money could undo the damage. The stories of loss and devastation were endless:

- Parents who buried their children after accidental overdoses.

- Patients who sought pain relief and found only ruin.

- Communities torn apart by addiction and despair.

In one particularly haunting case, a mother named Linda from West Virginia recounted how her son, once a star athlete, became hooked on OxyContin after a knee injury. Within a year, he had lost everything—his scholarship, his future, and eventually his life. Linda's voice trembled as she asked: "How can you put a price on a life? They knew. They knew what they were doing."

The OxyContin scandal is not just a tale of corporate greed; it is a profound ethical failure. The executives at Purdue Pharma, faced with mounting evidence of the drug's dangers, chose profits over people. They ignored their Judgment Core—that internal moral compass that should have guided them toward ethical decisions—and instead allowed greed to consume their actions.

Imagine sitting in that boardroom in 1996. Would you have spoken up? Would you have had the courage to say, "We need to pull back. We're hurting people." Or would the allure of wealth and power have silenced you?

Now, imagine being one of the patients who trusted Purdue's promises. How would it feel to know that your health, your trust, and your very life had been exploited for financial gain? How would your own Judgment Core respond to that betrayal?

The story of Purdue Pharma challenges us to reflect on our own lives. In pursuit of success—whether in business, leadership, or personal goals—do we consider the impact of our actions on others? Or do we, like the Sacklers, prioritize individual gain at any cost?

Meeting a profit target by cutting jobs may boost your bonus, but at what cost? Every decision we make sends ripples through the lives of others. Will those ripples bring harm or healing? Will they build trust or erode it?

Greed is like a silent cancer, growing unchecked when we fail to monitor our actions. It whispers that personal gain is paramount, that the ends justify the means. But history shows us otherwise. The downfall of Purdue Pharma serves as a stark reminder that unchecked greed leads to ruin—not just for those at the top, but for entire communities.

The question remains: How will you let your Judgment Core guide you? Will you prioritize collective benefit, ensuring that your actions uplift those around you? Or will you let greed, that inactivated cancer cell, take root in your decisions?

The choice is yours. But remember—what you choose today shapes the legacy you leave tomorrow.

The Rise and Fall of Martin Shkreli: A Dark Tale of Greed and Consequence

It was a chilly September evening in 2015 when a name began to spread across news outlets and social media feeds, igniting outrage across the globe—Martin Shkreli. Dubbed "the most hated man in America," Shkreli's face, with its smug smirk and unrepentant gaze, became the embodiment of unchecked greed. But how did this man, once an unassuming pharmaceutical executive, become a cautionary tale of moral failure? And what can his downfall teach us about the dangers of a weakened Judgment Core?

In a sleek Manhattan office overlooking the glittering cityscape, Martin Shkreli sat at the helm of Turing Pharmaceuticals. The year was 2015, and Shkreli had just made a decision that would catapult him into infamy—a decision driven by profit, without regard for its devastating consequences.

Daraprim, a drug that had been on the market for over six decades, was used to treat life-threatening infections in patients with compromised immune systems, such as those battling HIV, cancer, and malaria. It was a lifeline for thousands of vulnerable patients. But to Shkreli, it was an untapped goldmine.

With a stroke of a pen, he raised the price of Daraprim from $13.50 to $750 per pill—an increase of over 5,000%. Overnight, a life-saving medication became unaffordable for many, placing hospitals, clinics, and desperate patients in a harrowing dilemma: pay the exorbitant cost or risk death.

In a small town in Ohio, 62-year-old Margaret Hale, who had been living with HIV for years, suddenly found herself unable to afford her medication. Margaret wasn't alone—across the country, patients rationed their pills, stretched out their prescriptions, or abandoned treatment altogether. The consequences were devastating.

Hospitals scrambled to find alternatives. Clinics rationed supplies. Insurance companies raised premiums to offset the skyrocketing costs. Meanwhile, Shkreli watched his personal fortune grow, unmoved by the suffering left in his wake.

For Shkreli, it was a calculated business move. For the rest of the world, it was a moral outrage. Public health officials, advocacy groups, and politicians condemned his actions. Protests erupted outside Turing's headquarters, and Shkreli's name became synonymous with greed.

Yet, when summoned to testify before Congress, Shkreli's behavior only fueled the fire. He sat before the committee with a smug smile, refusing to answer questions. His silence spoke volumes, and his smirk became a symbol of indifference—a chilling reminder of what happens when empathy is replaced by greed.

While the Daraprim scandal grabbed headlines, it was merely the tip of the iceberg. As investigators dug deeper, they uncovered a web of deceit in Shkreli's financial dealings.

Before founding Turing Pharmaceuticals, Shkreli had managed two hedge funds—MSMB Capital Management and MSMB Healthcare. He had promised his investors astronomical returns but, in reality, had suffered significant losses. To cover his tracks, he began moving money between companies, using funds from one to pay off debts in another.

In 2017, Shkreli was convicted of securities fraud, a crime that had nothing to do with the Daraprim scandal but reflected a pattern of deceit and selfishness. The court sentenced him to seven years in prison and ordered him to forfeit $7.4 million.

The man who once believed he could outmaneuver the system found himself behind bars, his empire reduced to rubble. His downfall was swift and absolute—a cautionary tale of what happens when greed blinds judgment.

Shkreli's story is more than just a tale of corporate greed; it is a profound failure of the Judgment Core. At every step, he had a choice: to balance profit with humanity or to pursue personal gain at any cost. Time and again, he chose the latter.

Imagine being in Shkreli's shoes. The boardroom is silent. The decision is yours to make. Do you raise the price of a life-saving drug, knowing it will devastate thousands, or do you prioritize collective benefit over personal profit? Would your Judgment Core steer you toward empathy, or would greed whisper in your ear, urging you to take what you can?

Greed is like an inactivated cancer cell, waiting for the right conditions to grow and consume. Shkreli's greed wasn't unique—it's a temptation that exists in every corner of society. But what sets him apart is how willingly he fed that greed, allowing it to dictate his actions.

His story forces us to confront uncomfortable questions:

- How often do we prioritize our own gain without considering the impact on others?

- Do we make decisions that benefit the collective, or do we let greed guide our actions?

- And if the roles were reversed—if we were the patients unable to afford life-saving medication—how would we feel about those in power profiting from our suffering?

Meeting profit targets by cutting jobs, raising prices, or ignoring ethical concerns may bring short-term success, but at what cost? Every decision we make sends ripples through the lives of others. Will those ripples bring harm or healing?

As Shkreli sat in his prison cell, the world outside continued to grapple with the opioid crisis, skyrocketing healthcare costs, and the lingering effects of corporate greed. His name faded from headlines, but his legacy remained—a chilling reminder of what happens when empathy is discarded in favor of self-interest.

What would have happened if Shkreli had prioritized collective benefit over individual gain? What if he had chosen to keep Daraprim affordable, ensuring that patients received the care they needed? His fortune might have been smaller, but his legacy would have been one of compassion and responsibility—a legacy that outlives any bank balance.

The story of Martin Shkreli challenges us to examine our own moral compass. How do we navigate the gray areas between ambition and responsibility, profit and empathy? Do we have the strength to prioritize the collective good, even when it means sacrificing personal gain?

In every decision, our Judgment Core is tested. Will we let greed take root, justifying harmful actions in the name of success? Or will we recognize that true success lies in uplifting others, in creating a world where everyone has the chance to thrive?

The answers lie not in grand gestures but in the choices we make every day. How will your Judgment Core guide you?

Conclusion: The Silent Whisper of Greed — What Will You Choose?

Greed doesn't announce itself with bold declarations. It whispers. It slides into your thoughts, cloaked in justifications that seem harmless: "You've earned this." "It's just business." "No one will know." But these whispers plant silent seeds that grow into actions with far-reaching consequences. The challenge lies in recognizing when greed is taking root and asking yourself: Am I chasing success at the expense of others? Or am I guided by my Judgment Core—the inner compass of empathy and fairness?

Think about the story of Bob Chapman and his radical decision during the financial crisis. Instead of choosing mass layoffs to protect profits, he chose a path of shared sacrifice, keeping doors open for employees when they needed it most. Now consider Martin Shkreli's story—a man who let greed silence his moral compass, raising the price of life-saving medication to unimaginable heights, leaving vulnerable patients to suffer.

What's the difference between these two stories? It's the voice they chose to follow. One listened to the call of empathy and responsibility, while the other succumbed to greed's whisper.

What about you? In the quiet moments when no one is watching, which voice are you following?

<u>Strengthen Your Judgment Core to Resist Greed's Whisper</u>

Greed thrives when left unchecked. It grows quietly in the spaces where fairness, empathy, and responsibility should reside. But you have the power to stop it from taking root. The next time you face a decision that affects others, follow these steps to ensure your Judgment Core leads the way:

1. Pause and Ask Yourself: Who Will This Decision Impact?

Before making a choice, stop and reflect on the ripple effect of your actions.

Ask yourself:

- Am I prioritizing my personal gain at the expense of someone else's well-being?

- Will this decision create more harm than good?

- What would my Judgment Core advise if I truly listened to it?

Action Tip: When you're tempted to act impulsively, pause for 10 seconds. Think about the long-term impact on others, not just the short-term benefit for yourself.

2. Recognize Greed's Whisper and Call It Out

Greed rarely shows itself in obvious ways. It hides behind ambition, practicality, and necessity. Learn to identify when you're justifying harmful actions for personal gain.

Greed whispers:

- "It's not your problem."

- "You deserve this more than they do."

- "No one will notice."

Your Judgment Core counters with questions:

- Am I closing doors that were once opened for me?

- Am I taking more than I need, while giving less in return?

- What would be my feelings and what would I wish if I were in the other's shoes?

- Would I be happy

Action Tip: When you catch yourself rationalizing selfish behavior, write down your justification. Seeing it in writing often reveals whether it's driven by ego or fairness.

3. Choose Collective Well-Being Over Personal Gain

Greed tempts you to think only of yourself. But your Judgment Core reminds you that true success lies in shared prosperity and collective benefit.

Consider this:

- Would you still make the same decision if it directly impacted someone you care about?

- Are you helping to build trust and community, or are you eroding it with self-centered actions?

Action Tip: The next time you're faced with a decision that benefits you at someone else's expense, flip the roles. Imagine yourself on the receiving end. How would you feel? Would you consider the decision fair?

Challenge Yourself: What Seeds Are You Planting?

Greed, like a seed, grows in silence. It thrives when we justify selfish behavior as "just the way things are." But every decision you make plants a seed for the future.

Ask yourself:

- Am I planting seeds of trust and compassion, or am I sowing seeds of greed and self-interest?

- Will my actions open doors for others, or will they close them?

- When the roles are reversed, will I be proud of the legacy I've left behind?

The mirror is in front of you. The reflection you see depends on the seeds you plant today.

The Legacy You Leave: Doors Open or Closed?

Power, privilege, and wealth are fleeting. The doors you close today may be the very ones you need to knock on tomorrow. Will they open for you, or will you be met with silence?

Consider this: Every closed door leaves a mark. Every withheld opportunity creates a ripple of distrust and harm. But every open door leaves a legacy of empathy, trust, and shared prosperity.

Ask yourself:

- Am I closing doors that others once opened for me?

- Am I listening to my Judgment Core, or am I letting greed dictate my actions?

The Voice You Follow Shapes Your Legacy

Greed whispers in moments of vulnerability: “Take more. Give less. No one will notice.” But your Judgment Core calls for a different path: “Pause. Reflect. Choose empathy and fairness.”

Which voice will you follow?

The choice is yours. But remember: The seeds you plant today will shape the world you live in tomorrow. Will you plant seeds of trust and compassion? Or will you let the silent seed of greed grow, closing doors that once stood open for you?

Take Action Today

Pause. Reflect. Choose.

The next time you’re faced with a decision, ask yourself:

- Am I acting out of greed, or am I guided by empathy and fairness?

- Will my actions build trust and community, or will they create harm and division?

- Am I opening doors, or am I closing them?

Greed grows in silence, but your Judgment Core is always there, waiting to guide you. The choice is yours. Which voice will you follow? Act now—before the seed takes root.

7.5 The Hidden Trap of Ego: A Whisper That Demands More

You're standing at the edge of a calm lake. One careless toss of a stone causes ripples to spread across the surface, disturbing the peace. Now imagine that stone is your ego—small at first, but capable of creating waves that disrupt far more than you intended. How often do we act without realizing the true source of our decisions? How often do we throw that stone, not out of necessity, but because our pride whispers, "You must win. You must prove your worth."

Ego is a shadow that follows us everywhere—silent, invisible, but ever-present. It disguises itself as confidence, as self-assurance, but left unchecked, it distorts our reality. It urges us to overreact to criticism, to escalate conflicts, and to hold grudges long after the moment has passed. It convinces us that our worth is tied to how others perceive us, pushing us to prove our superiority at all costs. But ask yourself: When was the last time your ego made a decision for you? Did it make things better—or worse?

The ego doesn't need loud proclamations or grand gestures. It slips into your thoughts quietly, turning minor disagreements into battles of pride. "Don't let them talk to you that way." "You need to show them who's in charge." These whispers feel justified in the moment, but when the dust settles, what remains? Broken relationships. Lost opportunities. Regret.

Consider this: How many arguments could have been avoided with a moment of humility? How many bridges have been burned because someone refused to be the first to apologize? Ego feeds on the illusion that winning matters more than peace—that being right matters more than being kind. But what if winning the argument means losing something far more valuable?

Unchecked ego is a dangerous force, not because it roars, but because it whispers. It whispers that you've been wronged. That you deserve more. That others must acknowledge your importance. But what if you paused before reacting? What if you questioned that voice? Is this decision driven by fairness—or by a bruised ego demanding recognition?

In moments of conflict, ego tempts us to overreact. It pushes us to respond with force when a simple word would suffice. It tells us that any slight—real or perceived—must be avenged. But what does your Judgment Core say? Is your response proportionate? Is it necessary? Or are you allowing your pride to drive you toward excessive actions that will cause more harm than good?

Imagine two paths before you. One is guided by ego, urging you to prove your strength, to show that you won't back down. The other path requires humility and self-awareness. It asks you to pause, to reflect, and to choose a response that minimizes harm. Which path do you take? Will you let your ego dictate your actions, or will you allow your Judgment Core to guide you toward balance and fairness?

The hardest battles we fight are often within ourselves. The ego craves validation, superiority, control. But your Judgment Core—the internal compass that knows right from wrong—urges you to practice restraint. It reminds you that strength isn't found in dominance, but in understanding when to let go.

Ask yourself:

- When was the last time my ego drove me to overreact?

- Did I act out of fairness, or did I let pride cloud my judgment?

- If I had chosen humility, would the outcome have been better?

Ego demands that we take more, say more, and prove more. But the truth is, restraint often speaks louder than any act of pride. When you choose humility over ego, you choose peace over conflict. And isn't peace what we're all searching for?

In the quiet moments, when you reflect on your actions, what will you hear? The lingering whispers of an unchecked ego—or the steady, reassuring voice of your Judgment Core? The choice is yours. But remember, ego never shouts—it whispers. Will you listen?

The Feud That Burned the Neighborhood: A Tale of Ego and Consequence

It was the summer of 2015 in the quiet town of Oakridge, California. The streets were lined with towering oak trees, and the neighborhood was a peaceful enclave where children played on sidewalks and residents greeted each other with friendly waves. But behind the serene façade, a brewing storm of pride and ego was about to shatter the peace of this idyllic suburb.

At the heart of this storm were two neighbors—John Miller, a retired firefighter known for his meticulous garden, and David Johnson, a tech entrepreneur who had recently moved into the neighborhood. Their homes, separated by a modest wooden fence, stood as symbols of suburban stability. But that fence would soon become the dividing line in a battle that would spiral out of control, fueled by wounded pride and unchecked ego.

It all began in August 2015 when David decided to replace the aging fence between their properties. He hired a contractor to build a sleek, modern barrier, hoping to add a touch of elegance to his yard. But when John returned from a weekend trip, he was furious to find the new fence encroaching—by mere inches—onto what he believed was his property.

"David, we need to talk," John said, knocking on his neighbor's door. His voice was steady but laced with tension.

David opened the door, a polite smile quickly fading. "What's the issue?"

David frowned. "I had it measured. It's perfectly within the boundary."

John's jaw tightened. "No, it's not. You've taken part of my yard."

And so, a minor boundary dispute was born. A conversation that could have ended with a handshake and a compromise instead sowed the seeds of resentment. Neither man wanted to back down. Each felt the need to prove he was right.

The dispute lingered. John found himself pacing in his garden, staring at the fence with growing irritation. He could hear a whisper in his mind—a voice telling him he was being disrespected, that he couldn't let David get away with it.

David, too, felt the sting of wounded pride. "Why should I be the one to compromise?" he muttered to himself. "It's my property, my right."

The ego, that invisible force, began to take hold of them both. What could have been resolved with a simple conversation festered into something darker. Soon, their interactions became cold. Polite nods turned into icy glares. The fence had become more than just wood and nails—it was a symbol of dominance, a battleground for their pride.

As the weeks passed, small acts of revenge began. John, in a fit of passive-aggression, planted thorny bushes along his side of the fence, their branches creeping through to David's yard. In return, David instructed his gardener to "accidentally" trim John's prized rose bushes.

The whispers of ego grew louder. "He disrespected you. Show him who's in charge."

By the fall of 2015, the petty acts had escalated. John dumped bags of leaves onto David's lawn under the cover of night. David responded by playing loud music during John's peaceful mornings in the garden. Neighbors began to notice the tension but kept their distance, hoping the feud would resolve itself.

But ego doesn't resolve itself. It demands more.

One chilly November night, the feud reached its tragic climax.

John, consumed by rage after another confrontation, stood in his garage staring at a can of gasoline. The whispers of his ego were deafening. "He deserves this. He needs to learn his lesson."

Without thinking of the consequences, John grabbed the can, walked across the street, and doused David's car in gasoline. He lit a match and watched as the flames erupted, illuminating the quiet street.

But fire doesn't stay contained. The blaze spread quickly, licking at the side of David's home. By the time firefighters arrived, part of the house was engulfed in flames, and the neighborhood was in chaos.

John stood on his lawn, watching the destruction he had caused. The realization hit too late—his ego had driven him to an act he could never take back.

The next morning, Oakridge woke to charred remains and lingering smoke. The once peaceful neighborhood was scarred, both physically and emotionally. John was arrested and charged with arson and reckless endangerment. His career as a respected firefighter was reduced to a tarnished memory.

David, now homeless, stood among the ruins of his property. The damage extended beyond his home—it had shaken his family, his finances, and his sense of security.

The feud had destroyed more than just property. It had eroded trust, community, and peace. The whispers of ego had left devastation in their wake.

As the dust settled, the question lingered in the air: Was it worth it? Was proving a point worth the destruction of lives, homes, and community bonds? Did the need to be right outweigh the need for peace?

Imagine standing in John's shoes. Imagine holding that match. Would your Judgment Core have stopped you? Would you have paused, listened to that inner voice of reason, and chosen restraint?

Or would you, like John, have let your ego drive you to the point of no return?

Ego is a silent enemy, whispering that you must win, that you must be respected, that you cannot back down. But your Judgment Core—your internal moral compass—asks a different question: What will be left standing when the fire of ego burns out? Will you have preserved peace, or will you have destroyed it in your pursuit of pride?

The choice is always yours. But remember, ego doesn't shout—it whispers. Will you listen to the whispers of pride, or will you let your Judgment Core guide you toward humility, restraint, and peace?

The Rise and Fall of Travis Kalanick: Ego Behind the Wheel

In 2010, Travis Kalanick, a brash and ambitious entrepreneur from Los Angeles, co-founded Uber, a company that revolutionized the way people traveled. Within a few years, Uber became a global giant, valued at over $70 billion. Kalanick's aggressive, take-no-prisoners leadership style helped Uber grow rapidly, but it also sowed the seeds of its eventual downfall.

By 2015, Uber was operating in hundreds of cities worldwide, but cracks in the company's culture began to show. Kalanick, driven by his ego and the desire to dominate the market at all costs, fostered a culture of "growth at any cost"—a mantra that encouraged employees to push boundaries, skirt regulations, and crush competitors. While this mindset fueled Uber's expansion, it also created a toxic work environment rife with bullying, harassment, and unethical behavior.

One of the turning points in Kalanick's downfall occurred in February 2017, when a former Uber engineer named Susan Fowler published a blog post detailing her experiences of sexual harassment and discrimination at Uber. Fowler described how her complaints to HR were repeatedly ignored, and how the company's leadership tolerated inappropriate behavior from high-performing employees. The post went viral, sparking outrage and shining a light on the toxic culture that had taken root at Uber.

Instead of addressing the issue with humility and accountability, Kalanick's initial response was defensive and dismissive. His ego wouldn't allow him to admit fault or recognize the need for change. Rather than taking responsibility for the company's culture, he downplayed the allegations and blamed the media for exaggerating the problem.

But the scandals didn't stop there.

Just a few weeks later, a video of Kalanick arguing with an Uber driver surfaced online. In the video, Kalanick is seen berating the driver, who had expressed concerns about falling wages and tough working conditions. Instead of showing empathy, Kalanick responded with arrogance and anger, dismissing the driver's concerns and saying, "Some people don't like to take responsibility for their own problems."

The video went viral, and public perception of Kalanick soured further. The image of a CEO arguing with a struggling worker became a powerful symbol of unchecked ego and corporate greed.

By mid-2017, Uber was facing a public relations crisis. Reports emerged of systemic harassment, toxic workplace culture, illegal business practices, and hostile treatment of drivers. Kalanick's aggressive tactics, once seen as a strength, were now viewed as reckless and harmful.

The company's Judgment Core—the moral compass guiding its decisions—was clearly broken.

The Uber board of directors realized that Kalanick's ego was no longer an asset but a liability. In June 2017, under mounting pressure from investors, Kalanick was forced to resign as CEO. His fall from grace was swift and public, and Uber's reputation took years to rebuild.

Kalanick's downfall is a cautionary tale about what happens when ego overrides empathy and ethical decision-making. His desire to win at all costs blinded him to the collective well-being of his employees, drivers, and customers. His Judgment Core—the internal compass that should have guided him toward fairness and responsible leadership—was compromised by his ego.

Imagine being in Kalanick's position. Would you have the humility to admit your mistakes and take steps to change? Or would you let your ego convince you that you were invincible?

Uber's story challenges us to reflect on our own actions:

- How often do we let ego drive our decisions?

- Do we prioritize personal pride over collective well-being?

- When we make mistakes, do we take responsibility or deflect blame?

In business and in life, unchecked ego can turn minor conflicts into major crises. It clouds judgment, blinds us to the impact of our actions, and damages relationships. The only way to counteract ego's whispers is to strengthen our Judgment Core—to pause, reflect, and choose restraint over retaliation, humility over pride, and compassion over self-interest.

- When you're in a position of power, how do you treat those with less influence?

- Do you listen to feedback, or do you dismiss it as criticism?

- When faced with conflict, do you escalate the situation to prove a point, or do you seek resolution?

Ego is a silent force that can drive us to success or destruction. The choice lies in how we manage it. Will you let your ego dictate your actions, or will you listen to your Judgment Core and choose a path of empathy, humility, and fairness?

Conclusion: Ego's Whisper vs. Judgment Core's Call — Take Action Now

Ego whispers when no one else is listening. It says, "Prove them wrong. Win at all costs. Don't back down." It quietly convinces you that your pride is more important than peace, that your reputation matters more than relationships, and that the need to be right outweighs the need to be fair. But is it true? Or is it just ego distorting your Judgment Core (JDC)—the inner moral compass that guides you toward empathy, fairness, and balance?

Consider the story of John Miller and David Johnson. What started as a simple boundary dispute became a neighborhood tragedy because both men let their egos take control. Their desire to "win" blinded them to the long-term consequences. But was it worth it? Did proving a point justify the destruction that followed?

Now, imagine yourself in their shoes. What would you have done?

Have you ever let your ego drive you to escalate a minor issue into a major conflict?

Have you ever ignored the quiet voice of your Judgment Core, pushing fairness aside in favor of pride?

Ego doesn't shout—it whispers. It tells you that you're right, that others need to acknowledge your worth. But your Judgment Core offers a different message: "Pause. Reflect. Choose a path that minimizes harm."

The question is, are you listening?

How to Silence Ego and Strengthen Your Judgment Core

When conflict arises, don't wait. Act now. Follow these steps to ensure your response is guided by fairness, not ego:

1. Pause and Evaluate Your Response

Before reacting to conflict, stop. Take a deep breath.

Ask yourself:

- Is my response fair and proportionate, or is it driven by ego?

- Am I protecting my pride at the expense of others?

Action Tip:

Whenever you feel anger rising or a need to prove yourself, count to five before responding. This simple pause can prevent ego from taking control and allow your Judgment Core to step in.

2. Shift Your Focus from Winning to Resolving

Ego wants you to win. It wants to prove you're right, even if it comes at a cost. But your Judgment Core wants resolution.

Ask yourself:

- Am I prioritizing peace or pride?

- Will my actions de-escalate the situation or make it worse?

Action Tip:

When in conflict, use calming language. Say things like:

- "Let's find a solution together."

- "I see your point, let's talk this through."

Small shifts in language can transform a conflict into a conversation.

3. Consider the Long-Term Impact of Your Actions

Every decision you make leaves a mark—on others and on yourself. Ego demands instant gratification. It urges you to act on impulse, to retaliate, to defend your pride. But your Judgment Core asks you to think ahead.

Ask yourself:

- What will the long-term impact of my actions be?

- Am I building trust or destroying it?

- Will my actions strengthen relationships or leave scars?

Action Tip:

Before making any decision in a conflict, imagine the future. Will you be proud of your response a week, a month, or a year from now?

Real Action, Real Consequences

Studies in psychology and conflict resolution reveal that people who take time to reflect before reacting are more likely to resolve disputes effectively and maintain healthier relationships. But ego pushes for immediate action. It tells you to speak now, to act fast, to win at any cost.

Resist that urge. Slow down. Pause. Choose your response with care.

Challenge Yourself: Which Voice Will You Follow?

In the coming days, conflicts will arise—it's inevitable. Whether it's a disagreement at work, an argument with a loved one, or a frustrating encounter with a stranger, you will have a choice.

Ask yourself:

- Am I reacting out of ego, or am I guided by fairness?

- Is this response necessary, or am I trying to prove something?

- What would my Judgment Core do if I truly listened to it?

Ego will whisper:

"They deserve it. You need to win. Show them who's in charge."

But your Judgment Core will quietly remind you:

"Pause. Reflect. Choose fairness over pride."

Which voice will you follow?

The Power of Small Changes

Start small. The next time you face conflict, pause.

- Count to five before responding.

- Ask yourself: Will my actions help or hurt the situation?

- Choose restraint over reaction.

These small actions can prevent minor conflicts from turning into major crises. They can save relationships, reduce harm, and strengthen your moral compass.

What Legacy Will You Leave?

Every action you take shapes your Judgment Core and leaves a lasting impact on those around you.

Are you creating a legacy of empathy, fairness, and peace?

Or will your legacy be one of pride, conflict, and regret?

Remember, ego thrives in silence. It waits for you to act without thinking, to escalate without pausing. But your Judgment Core is always there, offering a better path.

The choice is yours.

Which voice will you follow—the whisper of ego, or the call of your Judgment Core?

Choose wisely. Your future depends on it.

7.6 The Delicate Lanterns: Children Are Angels on Earth

Picture yourself walking through life with an invisible lantern in your hands—a soft, flickering light that symbolizes your hopes, dreams, and potential. Now imagine that every child you meet carries their own lantern, delicate yet full of possibility. Their light glows with curiosity, innocence, and wonder, but it is fragile, both inside and out. Their flames can brighten with encouragement or dim with harsh words and neglect. Have you ever stopped to consider how your words and actions affect the flame they carry? Are you helping their lantern glow stronger, or are you unknowingly snuffing it out?

Children aren't just carriers of tomorrow's light—they are angels walking among us, entrusted to our care. In Islam, children are considered pure beings, free from sin. If they die young, they enter paradise without judgment, untouched by the burdens of accountability that adults must bear. Their innocence is sacred, their souls unstained, and their presence in our lives is both a blessing and a test. How we treat these angels reflects our own moral compass—our Judgment Core—and reveals who we are at our deepest level.

These little beings are fragile, both physically and emotionally. A small wrong act—a harsh word, a dismissive gesture, a lack of attention—can leave lasting scars. Their lanterns are not made of unbreakable glass but of delicate crystal, easily cracked by impatience, neglect, or anger. Their hearts are soft and impressionable, absorbing every experience, whether it is one of love or of harm. Have you ever wondered how many children's flames have been dimmed by adults who failed to see their vulnerability?

But there's more—children are mirrors. They absorb what they see and reflect it back into the world as they grow. They learn how to navigate life by observing the adults around them. If you show them kindness, empathy, and respect, they will reflect those qualities in their own behavior. If they witness anger, impatience, or indifference, they will carry those traits into their future relationships. The better person you're, the better grown-up they will become. Their moral compass—their Judgment Core—takes shape through your actions. Ask yourself: What reflection are you leaving for them to see?

Children test our patience, no doubt. They stumble, make mistakes, and push boundaries, trying to make sense of the world. But isn't that how we all learned? Think back to your own childhood. Can you recall moments when an adult's reaction either strengthened your light or threatened to extinguish it? Did their kindness lift you up, or did their frustration make you feel small and unworthy?

The balance between kindness and discipline is delicate, and it's easy to misstep. Children need guidance to navigate life's challenges, but they also need mercy, empathy, and love. Too much discipline without mercy, and you risk extinguishing their light. Too much indulgence without boundaries, and you risk creating entitlement. Balancing kindness with discipline is one of the hardest tasks of parenting and caregiving, but remember—they are too weak to abuse your power. They are angels entrusted to you, not burdens to control.

Imagine a lantern being carried through a storm. Too much shelter, and the flame might never grow strong enough to withstand life's winds. Too little, and the light risks being extinguished by a single gust. Children are the same. They need protection, yes, but they also need to learn resilience. Are you teaching them to keep their lantern burning through life's storms, or are you shielding them so much that they'll struggle to stand tall when challenges arise?

Islamic teachings emphasize that children deserve mercy above all else. The Prophet Muhammad (peace be upon him) demonstrated unparalleled gentleness toward children. He once said, "He who does not show mercy to our young, nor honor to our elderly, is not one of us." This mercy isn't just about avoiding harshness—it's about recognizing that children's hearts are tender, and their light can be easily dimmed or extinguished by those in positions of power.

Every interaction with a child shapes their growing Judgment Core—their moral compass that will guide them throughout life. Your words, actions, and reactions leave marks on that inner compass. Do your actions teach them fairness, empathy, and resilience? Or do they plant seeds of fear, insecurity, and entitlement?

But don't forget—they are watching you. Every action you take is a lesson. How you treat others, how you handle challenges, how you express kindness or frustration—all of it is absorbed by the children around you. They will mirror your behavior, growing into reflections of the adults they observe. If you want children to be compassionate, resilient, and fair, you must model those qualities yourself.

Pause for a moment and ask yourself:

- When a child makes a mistake, do you see it as an opportunity to help their light grow brighter, or do you let your frustration cloud your response?

- Are you mindful of how your words and actions shape their delicate Judgment Core, or do you act impulsively, forgetting that even a small comment can leave a lasting impact?

- What reflection are you leaving for the children around you? Are you showing them the best version of yourself, or are you letting impatience and ego cloud your actions?

Children carry lanterns of hope and light, but they are fragile. They rely on the adults around them to nurture their flames, to guide them through life's challenges with patience and understanding. But they are also angels in disguise—pure souls who, according to Islamic belief, will enter paradise without judgment. Knowing this, how can we justify harshness toward them? How can we let impatience or ego cloud our actions when we are entrusted with such sacred beings?

Mercy, patience, and kindness toward children are not just virtues—they are obligations. The lanterns they carry today will one day become the guiding lights of our future society. Will they shine with empathy, patience, and understanding? Or will they flicker with distrust, anger, and entitlement, shadows cast by the adults who failed to nurture their light?

The whispers of your Judgment Core remind you that every moment with a child is a chance to nurture their inner light. Every interaction leaves a mark—either strengthening their lantern or casting shadows. Will you be the person who helps their flame burn brighter, or will you allow ego, impatience, or indifference to dim their light?

Remember:

These children are angels, their light untouched by sin. They will grow to carry the world forward, shaped by the kindness—or harshness—they receive today. And remember, too, that they will reflect back what they see. The better person you show them, the better they will become.

The next time you speak to a child, pause and reflect. Ask yourself:

Am I helping this lantern shine brighter, or am I casting unnecessary shadows?

Am I building a future filled with compassion and strength, or am I allowing my own frustrations to leave lasting scars on those too fragile to defend themselves?

The children in your life are not just passing through—they are carrying tomorrow's light. How you treat them today will determine whether that light grows into a beacon of hope or flickers in darkness.

And remember—what you show them is what they will become. What reflection will they carry forward into the world? Which will it be?

The Lantern That Lit the Path: The Story of Ben Carson's Transformation

In the winter of 1961, a biting wind blew through the streets of Detroit, Michigan. The city, known for its booming automotive industry, was also home to neighborhoods overshadowed by poverty and hardship. In one such neighborhood, a young boy named Ben Carson sat by a dimly lit window, staring out at the cold streets. His hands clutched his schoolbooks, but his mind wandered, weighed down by self-doubt and frustration. At just 10 years old, Ben had already resigned himself to the label that his classmates had given him: "dummy.

Each day at school felt like a battlefield. His classmates' taunts echoed in his mind, chipping away at his self-esteem. The more they teased him, the more he withdrew into himself. His grades reflected his despair—Ben was at the bottom of his class. The future seemed bleak, and the young boy believed that he was destined for failure. His Judgment Core, that internal compass guiding his sense of self-worth and potential, had been clouded by shame and insecurity.

But fate, like a lantern waiting to be lit, often sends light when least expected.

That light came in the form of Mrs. Williamson, Ben's fifth-grade teacher at Higgins Elementary School. Mrs. Williamson was different from the other teachers. She had a unique gift: the ability to see beyond a child's current struggles and into the boundless potential they carried within. She noticed Ben's quiet demeanor, his avoidance of eye contact, and the way he shuffled through the hallways like a shadow. But instead of seeing a "dummy," she saw a lantern—dim and flickering, but capable of shining brightly with the right spark.

One afternoon, Mrs. Williamson called Ben to her desk after class. Her voice was gentle but firm.

"Ben," she said, "you're not dumb. You're smart, but you have to believe it. And you have to work for it."

Ben blinked, unsure of how to respond. No one had ever told him that before. Mrs. Williamson leaned in, her gaze unwavering.

"I'm going to give you a challenge," she continued. "I want you to read two books every week and write me a report on them. It doesn't matter what the books are about—find something that interests you. But I want you to read. Knowledge is your lantern, Ben. It will light your way."

Ben hesitated. Reading two books a week? It seemed impossible for someone who struggled with basic schoolwork. But there was something in Mrs. Williamson's eyes—something that told him she believed in him. And that belief sparked something inside him.

At home, Ben's mother, Sonya Carson, reinforced Mrs. Williamson's challenge. Sonya, who had only a third-grade education herself, worked multiple jobs to keep her family afloat. Despite her limited formal education, she understood the transformative power of learning. She limited her sons' television time, insisting that they visit the library and complete their reading assignments. She didn't just push them to succeed academically—she instilled in them the belief that their circumstances did not define their future.

Together, Mrs. Williamson and Sonya Carson became the guiding lanterns in Ben's life, illuminating a path that he hadn't known existed.

At first, reading two books a week was overwhelming. Ben struggled to focus, his mind often wandering back to the cruel words of his classmates. But slowly, as he immersed himself in stories of science, adventure, and faraway places, he discovered something remarkable—he loved learning. The more he read, the brighter his internal lantern grew. Knowledge, as Mrs. Williamson had promised, became his guiding light.

Within months, Ben's grades began to improve. The boy who had once been ridiculed as a "dummy" transformed into one of the top students in his class. His classmates, who once mocked him, now marveled at his transformation. But it wasn't just his academic performance that changed—Ben's Judgment Core began to shift. He no longer saw himself through the lens of failure. He saw potential. He saw a future.

By the time Ben graduated from high school, his lantern was shining brighter than ever. He earned a full scholarship to Yale University, a feat that seemed unimaginable during his early years in Detroit. But Ben's journey didn't stop there. He pursued a career in medicine, driven by a newfound sense of purpose and the belief that he could make a difference in the world.

In 1987, Dr. Ben Carson made history by successfully performing the first separation of conjoined twins joined at the back of the head. The surgery, which lasted over 22 hours, was a groundbreaking medical achievement. But for Ben, it was more than just a professional milestone—it was the culmination of a journey that began with two women who refused to let his light go out.

Decades later, reflecting on his life, Ben Carson often credited Mrs. Williamson and his mother for his success.

"They didn't see me as a lost cause," he said in an interview. "They saw potential. They saw a lantern waiting to be lit."

But now, the question turns to you. How many lanterns do you pass by each day without noticing? How many children, burdened by self-doubt or difficult circumstances, are waiting for someone to light their way? Do you see their potential, or do you let them remain in the shadows, unseen and unheard?

Your Judgment Core—the moral compass that guides your decisions—whispers that every interaction with a child leaves a lasting imprint. Will your words kindle their light, or will they snuff it out? Will you encourage them to believe in their potential, or will you, through indifference or impatience, reinforce their doubts?

Consider this:

- Have you ever underestimated someone because of their current struggles?

- Have you taken the time to recognize the potential in those who seem to be falling behind?

- How many lanterns have you passed by without offering a spark of encouragement?

The story of Ben Carson is a powerful reminder that one small act of belief can change a life. Mrs. Williamson's challenge and Sonya Carson's unwavering support weren't grand gestures—they were simple acts of faith. Yet, they ignited a light that guided Ben through the darkest moments of his life.

The children you encounter today—whether in your home, your classroom, or your community—carry lanterns of their own. Some may be flickering, on the verge of going out. Others may burn brightly, waiting for someone to help them shine even brighter. The question is: Will you be the one to light their way?

In every child lies a lantern. In every lantern lies a future. Will you help them shine, or will you walk past, leaving them in the dark?

The choice is yours. But remember, every light you nurture today will illuminate the world tomorrow.

The Hidden Scale

Imagine holding a delicate scale in your hands. On one side sits kindness—a warm, comforting weight that reassures and nurtures. On the other side lies discipline—a firmer, heavier weight that teaches resilience and responsibility. The challenge isn't in choosing one over the other; it's in finding the perfect balance. But what happens when that balance tips too far? What happens when kindness turns into indulgence and discipline fades into neglect?

Children, like seeds, absorb what we give them. Feed them kindness without limits, and they may grow with fragile roots, unprepared to stand against the storms of life. Withhold kindness, and their growth may be stunted, leaving them hardened and distrustful. The question is: Do you know how to balance the scale?

There's a whisper that tempts many parents: "If I protect them from pain, they'll never suffer." But is that kindness, or is it a veil of indulgence that shelters children from the lessons they need to learn? Imagine a child who never hears the word "no," who never faces consequences. Will they grow up believing that the world will always bend to their will? And when reality hits, will they be ready to face it—or will they crumble under its weight?

True kindness isn't about shielding children from every hardship. It's about preparing them to navigate the complexities of life with strength and empathy. It's about teaching them that effort matters, that respect must be earned, and that failure is not the end—but a step toward growth. Kindness guides them with love, while discipline equips them with tools to stand on their own. But how often do we mistake indulgence for kindness? How often do we rob children of growth in our attempt to protect them?

Now, consider your own actions. Do you give in to every demand to avoid conflict? Do you rescue your children from the natural consequences of their choices, fearing they'll suffer too much? Or do you strike a balance, offering both comfort and accountability?

Ask yourself:

- Have I confused kindness with indulgence?

- Am I teaching my children resilience, or am I protecting them from valuable lessons?

- When they face the real world, will they be ready to thrive—or will they falter under the weight of entitlement?

The scale is in your hands. Every decision you make shapes the Judgment Core of the children you're raising—the internal compass that will guide their sense of fairness, responsibility, and empathy. Will your kindness prepare them for life's challenges, or will it leave them unprepared, believing that success comes without effort?

The balance is delicate. But remember, too much kindness without accountability tips the scale toward entitlement, while too much discipline without compassion tips it toward resentment. The key is to keep both weights in check, ensuring that the next generation inherits not only your love but also the strength to carry their own lanterns through life's storms.

So, the question remains: How are you holding the scale? Are you teaching children to grow with grace and responsibility—or are you letting indulgence quietly tip the balance?.

The Lantern and the Shadows: The Rise and Fall of John Anderson

It was a brisk autumn morning in October 1975 when John Anderson was born into one of New York's wealthiest families. His arrival was celebrated with grandeur, his parents eager to give their only son everything he could ever want. From the outside, the Anderson household seemed perfect—lavish dinners, weekend getaways, and every luxury imaginable. But behind the golden façade lay a crack invisible to most: John was never told the word "no".

As John grew older, his life resembled a lantern with an ever-burning flame. His parents held the lantern high, illuminating his path, removing obstacles before he could stumble, and shielding him from any darkness. Yet, they never taught him to carry his own light. Every time John encountered discomfort, his parents extinguished it before he had to face it.

Every mistake he made was smoothed over, every failure disguised as success.

But what happens when the lantern is taken away? What happens when the shadows close in, and you're left to navigate a dark world with no light of your own?

In the mid-1980s, John entered elementary school, and the cracks in his upbringing began to show. Teachers quickly noticed his reluctance to follow rules. When asked to complete tasks, John would argue, expecting praise without effort. His classmates teased him for his arrogance, but John never learned to handle criticism. His parents, ever the protectors, would march into the principal's office, demanding leniency for their son. "He's special," they insisted. "He doesn't deserve to be treated like everyone else."

By the time John reached high school in the early 1990s, his entitlement had grown unchecked. He coasted through classes, barely scraping by. His teachers knew he had potential, but he never pushed himself. Why would he? The lantern was always there, held by his parents, casting a comforting glow on his every move.

Fast forward to 1997: the height of the dot-com boom. John, now in his early 20s, decided to start a tech company—Anderson Tech Solutions. His parents invested heavily, giving him the capital he needed to launch. At first, the venture seemed promising. John basked in the spotlight, attending lavish tech events and boasting about his "hard-earned success." But behind closed doors, cracks were widening.

John had no idea how to lead. He couldn't handle disagreements from his employees. Any criticism felt like an attack on his identity. His Judgment Core—the internal compass that guides right from wrong—was warped by years of indulgence. When staff offered suggestions, he dismissed them. When problems arose, he avoided them, hoping they'd disappear on their own. After all, problems had always been taken care of for him.

But in business, shadows don't disappear—they grow.

By 2001, cracks became chasms. The tech bubble burst, and Anderson Tech Solutions was crumbling. Competitors adapted to the changing market; John did not. His ego told him that he was too important to fail. Investors started pulling out, and employees left in droves, tired of working for a man who couldn't see beyond his own pride.

One by one, the lanterns that had illuminated John's path began to dim. His parents' wealth could no longer save him. His entitlement had left him standing in darkness, unprepared to navigate the harsh realities of failure.

In 2006, the company filed for bankruptcy. The once-celebrated entrepreneur was now a cautionary tale—a symbol of what happens when a child is given everything except the tools to succeed on their own.

But the collapse of his business wasn't the only part of John's life unraveling. His marriage, which had begun with hope and promise, was crumbling under the weight of his ego. His wife, Sarah, had grown tired of his refusal to compromise or take responsibility. "You expect the world to revolve around you," she said during their final argument. "But the world doesn't owe you anything, John."

By 2007, John found himself alone—no company, no marriage, no friends. For the first time in his life, he stood in complete darkness. The lantern was gone. The shadows were everywhere.

It wasn't until 2008 that John began to understand the damage his entitlement had caused. He enrolled in leadership seminars and sought therapy, confronting the flaws in his Judgment Core. He realized that his parents' overindulgence, though well-meaning, had left him without the resilience to face adversity.

In therapy, John was asked a simple question: "When was the last time you took responsibility for your failures?"

The question lingered in his mind, haunting him. His entire life, he had avoided accountability. He had blamed others, expecting the world to fix his problems. Now, he realized that true growth required facing the shadows head-on.

In 2010, John launched a new venture: Anderson Solutions. This time, things were different. He hired a diverse team and listened to their ideas. He practiced humility, acknowledging when he was wrong and learning from those around him. His new approach wasn't just about rebuilding a business—it was about rebuilding himself.

As the years passed, John began to repair his personal relationships. He reached out to his ex-wife, apologizing for his past behavior. He reconnected with old friends, acknowledging his mistakes. Slowly, the shadows began to recede—not because someone else held a lantern for him, but because he had learned to light his own.

John's story is a powerful reminder of the delicate balance between kindness and discipline. His parents, in their desire to protect him from pain, had inadvertently shielded him from growth. Their constant indulgence had warped his Judgment Core, leaving him unprepared for the challenges of adulthood.

Imagine a child as a lantern, their light flickering with potential. As parents, mentors, and leaders, our role is not to shield them from every shadow, but to teach them how to carry their own light. True kindness isn't about removing every obstacle—it's about teaching resilience, accountability, and self-reliance.

Now, ask yourself:

- Are you holding the lantern too tightly for those you care about, never letting them experience the shadows?

- Are you guiding with kindness and discipline, or are you indulging at the expense of their growth?

- What kind of Judgment Core are you helping to shape in the next generation?

John Anderson learned, too late, that the world does not owe us success. The only way to thrive is to build our own light, to navigate the shadows with a strong moral compass, and to understand that true kindness is teaching others to do the same.

And so, the question lingers: Will you carry the lantern for someone else, or will you teach them to hold it on their own?

Conclusion: The Echoes in the Mirror — What Reflection Will You Leave?

There's a moment in every interaction with a child when time seems to slow. The child looks at you—wide-eyed, expectant, absorbing not just your words but the tone behind them, the emotions etched in your face. In that moment, you're more than just a caregiver or a teacher—you're a mirror. Your words, your actions, your responses reflect back into their growing minds, shaping who they will become.

But what happens when frustration takes over? What happens when ego whispers that control is easier than patience, that shouting is faster than teaching?

Shouting is easy. It's immediate. It asserts authority in a way that makes you feel heard. But have you ever considered what lingers after your voice fades? Those echoes don't die out—they stay, shaping a child's Judgment Core, that inner compass that guides their moral decisions. The child you shout at today will one day be an adult who handles conflict, emotions, and relationships the way they learned from you. Will they handle those moments with grace—or with anger?

Reports show that verbal aggression leaves lasting emotional imprints. A 2013 study in Child Development revealed that children who are frequently yelled at are more likely to experience anxiety, depression, and behavioral problems. The American Psychological Association warns that shouting can be as harmful as physical punishment. Each raised voice chips away at a child's self-worth, planting seeds of fear and insecurity. Now, pause and ask yourself:

- Are you teaching them to handle conflict with dignity, or to respond with anger?

- Are you creating a space for them to feel safe, or a space where they walk on eggshells?

- Are you guiding their inner light, or dimming it with your frustration?

But shouting isn't the only trap. Being too lenient can be equally damaging. Picture a plant overwatered out of love and care—it doesn't thrive. It wilts. Its roots, never challenged to search for water, remain weak. Kindness without boundaries creates fragile roots. Children need love, but they also need limits. They need to stumble and learn resilience. They need to face disappointment and learn perseverance. Too much sheltering creates entitlement, while too little nurturing breeds fear.

<u>The Foundation of Growth: Unconditional Love and Patience</u>

Children need something beyond discipline and boundaries. They need unconditional love and extraordinary patience to grow properly. They need to know that they are loved, not just when they succeed or behave well, but even when they fall short, make mistakes, or challenge your patience.

Unconditional love doesn't mean permissiveness. It means showing them that your love isn't conditional on their behavior. It means demonstrating, time and time again, that your care for them is unwavering, even when they frustrate you. Patience is the bridge between love and guidance. It allows you to pause, to breathe, and to respond thoughtfully rather than react impulsively.

Ask yourself:

- Do my actions show a child that they are loved, no matter what?

- Am I patient enough to guide them through mistakes, or do I let frustration take over?

- Do I respond with empathy when they need it most, or do I let ego cloud my response?

Children cannot grow properly in an environment of fear or inconsistency. They need a steady, unwavering presence—a caregiver who offers love without conditions and patience without limits. They need someone who shows them, through actions and words, that they are valued and worthy of love, even in their most difficult moments.

<u>Your Actions Shape Their Judgment Core — What Will They Mirror?</u>

Children are not blank slates; they are mirrors. They reflect what they see. If they see anger, they learn anger. If they see compassion, they learn compassion. If they see accountability, they learn responsibility. Your actions, whether intentional or impulsive, are carving their Judgment Core—a moral compass they will carry for life.

But have you ever paused to listen to your own whispers?

Ego whispers: "Raise your voice. Prove you're right. They need to respect you."

But your Judgment Core whispers a different truth:

- "Pause. Reflect. Teach, don't control. Guide, don't overpower."

The next time you're about to raise your voice, ask yourself:

- Is my reaction coming from ego, or empathy?

- Am I showing them the best version of myself, or letting my impatience take over?

- Will my words plant seeds of confidence and resilience, or seeds of fear and insecurity?

Pause. Take five seconds before you react. Those five seconds could change a child's future.

<u>The Balance of Guidance: Roots Must Grow Strong</u>

Imagine standing in front of a garden. Your role is not to control its growth, but to guide it. You must water it with kindness, but not drown it.

You must provide support, but not overprotect it. Children are like that garden—they need boundaries to develop strength and resilience, but they also need warmth and care to thrive.

Ask yourself:

- Am I giving them the tools to navigate life's challenges, or shielding them from growth?

- Am I overprotecting them to avoid conflict, or am I allowing them to build resilience through experience?

- Will they face life's storms with strong roots, or will they crumble when I'm no longer there to shelter them?

Finding this balance is one of the hardest tasks of parenting and caregiving. But remember: The way you guide their growth today shapes how they stand tomorrow.

The Lasting Reflection: What Legacy Will You Leave?

In the quiet moments, when no one is watching, your Judgment Core whispers: "You're shaping a life. Every action leaves a mark."

Children don't remember every word you say, but they never forget how you made them feel. They will carry those feelings into adulthood. The child who learned fear from your anger will teach fear to others. The child who learned compassion from your patience will spread kindness in their relationships.

So ask yourself:

- What reflection will they carry into the future?

- Will they mirror light and empathy, or shadows and frustration?

- When they face conflict, will they escalate it with pride or navigate it with grace?

Every child is a mirror reflecting your legacy. Will your reflection be one of compassion, resilience, and wisdom? Or will it be one of impatience, anger, and regret?

Shape the Future with Intention

The next time a child makes a mistake, pause before reacting.

- Take five seconds.

- Ask yourself: Am I teaching them to handle conflict with empathy, or to escalate it with frustration?

- Choose to guide with your Judgment Core—not with ego.

Every action you take is shaping their internal compass—their Judgment Core—which will guide them for life. Your words today will echo in their future. Will those echoes bring light, or will they cast shadows?

Children need unconditional love, patience, and guidance to grow properly. They need boundaries to learn resilience and accountability. They need your kindness to understand compassion. What you show them now is what they will carry forward.

<u>The Final Question: What Reflection Will You Leave in the Mirrors of Tomorrow?</u>

Every child is a mirror, reflecting your actions into the future. They carry the legacy of your words, your patience, your love, and your mistakes. The choice is yours:

Will you be the light they follow? Or will you be the shadow they must overcome?

What reflection will you leave in the mirrors of tomorrow?

7.7 The Dignity of the Elderly: Honoring Our Parents and Elders

You're standing before an ancient tree—its roots deep, its branches wide, its leaves whispering stories of seasons gone by. This tree once stood tall and unwavering, offering shade, shelter, and fruit. You once relied on it to survive—its branches shielding you from harsh winds, its fruit easing your hunger, and its sturdy trunk providing you with a sense of safety. Without it, you would have suffered in the cold, starved in barren seasons, and wandered vulnerable without protection. But now, weathered by time, its bark is cracked, its limbs slower to sway in the wind. Do you dismiss it as weak and withered? Or do you honor it for the life it has given, the roots it has laid, and the security it once provided?

Now, shift your focus to the people in your life. Do you see the elders around you as fragile, past their prime? Or do you recognize them as the trees that once stood strong—carrying the weight of families, communities, and history on their shoulders? Just as you once depended on that ancient tree for survival, you have depended on these individuals for guidance, care, and love. Their roots are your roots. Their sacrifices are the foundation of everything you stand on today. Yet, how often do we overlook this truth?

As we journey through life, the significance of honoring and respecting the elderly becomes more profound, especially when it comes to our parents. These individuals, once vibrant and strong, have weathered the challenges of life, offering wisdom that comes from their unique experiences. Their contributions to society, family, and the world around us are immeasurable, forming the foundation upon which younger generations stand.

For our parents, in particular, their influence on our lives cannot be overstated. From nurturing us as infants to guiding us through childhood, they invested their energy, time, and love, often sacrificing their own needs for our well-being. It is easy to overlook these sacrifices, especially as we become independent and focus on our own lives. However, their tireless efforts, even if flawed at times, were born out of a deep desire to provide the best for us, laying the groundwork for the people we are today.

Honoring the elderly, especially our parents, is more than a matter of duty—it is a reflection of our humanity. In a world that often prioritizes youth and productivity, it is vital to recognize the inherent dignity of those who have given so much. Showing kindness, patience, and respect not only acknowledges their sacrifices but also preserves their sense of worth. As their physical strength wanes and their roles in society shift, they should be cherished, not forgotten, for the wisdom they hold and the legacy they leave behind.

Furthermore, the way we treat our elders sets a powerful example for the younger generations. By treating the elderly with care and reverence, we instill in our children the values of gratitude, respect, and empathy. In doing so, we create a ripple effect that carries these values forward, ensuring that when our time comes, we too will be treated with the dignity we offered to those who came before us.

Ultimately, honoring the elderly is a reminder of the cyclical nature of life. Just as they cared for us when we were vulnerable, it becomes our responsibility to support and uplift them in their later years. In this reciprocity, we uphold the bonds of family and community, fostering a society where every individual, regardless of age, is valued and respected.

Now, ask yourself: How do you treat the tree that once sheltered and nourished you? Are you showing gratitude, or have you forgotten its importance? The way you care for the people who once provided for you shapes not only their dignity but your own moral compass. Your Judgment Core whispers that every act of respect toward the elderly strengthens the roots of empathy, gratitude, and compassion in future generations.

Will you be the one who keeps the tree standing strong, honoring it for the life it gave you? Or will you let it wither, forgetting the vital role it played in your survival? The choice is yours. What legacy will you leave for those who follow?

Anil Kumar: The Reflection of Forgotten Sacrifices

It was the autumn of 1991 in Bangalore, India. The air was crisp, the streets bustling with life, and inside a grand villa stood Anil Kumar, a man at the pinnacle of success. His name was synonymous with wealth, prestige, and influence in the corporate world. But the foundation of this success? It was a story buried under layers of neglect—a story of sacrifices that had been quietly forgotten.

Anil was born in 1953 to a modest family living in a small village outside of Bangalore. His father, Rajan Kumar, worked tirelessly as a factory laborer, while his mother, Lakshmi, managed their small household and ran a roadside vegetable stall. Their dreams revolved around Anil's future. Rajan believed education was the ladder that would lift his son out of poverty, and Lakshmi, despite her exhaustion, would spend her evenings tutoring Anil by the dim light of an oil lamp.

Every penny they earned was invested in Anil's education. Rajan would often skip meals to save money for Anil's school fees, and Lakshmi wore the same faded sari for years, unwilling to spend on herself. Their sacrifices were invisible, but they were there in every step Anil took toward success.

By the early 1970s, Anil had earned a scholarship to a prestigious university. His parents' joy knew no bounds. When he graduated with honors and secured a high-paying job in the city, Rajan and Lakshmi believed their hardships had paid off. They saw Anil's success as their own and dreamed of spending their later years basking in the warmth of family.

But life took a different turn.

In 1985, Anil married Priya, a woman from an affluent family in Bangalore. Priya's lifestyle and social circle were worlds apart from Anil's humble roots. Slowly, Anil began to distance himself from his parents, ashamed of their simplicity and their old ways. He moved them into a small annex behind his sprawling mansion, out of sight from his high-society friends.

Rajan and Lakshmi, who had once been the center of Anil's world, now found themselves isolated. The warmth of family dinners and shared laughter had been replaced by silence. Their grandchildren barely knew them, and Priya's disdain for their presence was palpable.

Despite the growing distance, Rajan continued to hold on to hope. He believed Anil was just busy, that one day his son would come back to them. Lakshmi, however, saw the truth—they had been cast aside, their sacrifices forgotten.

In 1994, Rajan's health began to decline. He suffered from chronic back pain from years of hard labor, and Lakshmi developed arthritis. When they sought Anil's help, he hired caretakers—not out of love, but to ease his own guilt.

By the winter of 1994, both Rajan and Lakshmi passed away within months of each other. Their funerals were modest affairs. Anil attended, but his mind was elsewhere—focused on his next business deal. He hadn't allowed himself to process the loss, let alone reflect on the life his parents had lived for him.

Years went by. Anil continued to climb the corporate ladder, his name appearing in business magazines and newspapers. But as time passed, life began to change for him too.

By 2010, Anil's health started to deteriorate. He developed diabetes and struggled with mobility. His wealth and success no longer brought him joy—he needed companionship, care, and love. Expecting his children to step in, he reached out to them. But they, like he once had, were too busy. They rarely visited, only calling out of obligation.

Sitting alone in his lavish home, Anil began to reflect on his life. The room where his parents had once lived now stood empty, filled only with memories and regret. He realized he had created a legacy of indifference. His children had learned from him—they had mirrored his behavior.

One evening, Anil sat by the window, staring at the sunset. His mind wandered back to his childhood—to his father's rough hands helping him with homework, to his mother's gentle voice encouraging him to dream big. The sacrifices they had made, the love they had given, all flashed before his eyes.

His Judgment Core—that inner moral compass we all carry—stirred. It whispered questions he could no longer ignore:

How did I become this person?

Why did I let pride overshadow gratitude?

What kind of legacy am I leaving for my children?

The answers were painful. Anil had prioritized wealth over relationships, appearances over love. He had forgotten the hands that had lifted him when he couldn't stand on his own.

Anil's story is not just a personal tragedy—it's a cautionary tale about the consequences of neglecting our elders. The way we treat those who sacrificed for us shapes the values of future generations. Children learn from what they see. If they see indifference, they will replicate it. If they witness respect and care, they will carry those values forward.

Anil's life, once defined by success, became a reflection of his choices. His loneliness was a result of the seeds he had sown—seeds of neglect and indifference.

Now, imagine yourself in Anil's place. Picture the faces of those who raised you, who stood by you during your hardest moments. How do you treat them today? Are you showing them the respect and gratitude they deserve, or are you allowing pride and ego to create distance?

Ask yourself:

When was the last time I truly listened to my parents or elders?

Have I shown them the same patience and care they once showed me?

What example am I setting for my children?

The Judgment Core whispers to all of us. It reminds us that life is a cycle—the care we give will one day be the care we receive. The respect we show today will shape how we are treated tomorrow.

So, what kind of reflection will you leave in the mirrors of tomorrow? Will your legacy be one of love and gratitude, or one of regret and loneliness? The choice is yours—but remember, the seeds you plant today will shape the world you live in tomorrow.

The Forgotten Carpet: A Tale of Judgment and Redemption

It was a cold autumn evening in 1823, and the streets of Fez, Morocco, glowed faintly under the flickering lanterns. The city, with its maze-like alleys and ancient walls, carried the whispers of centuries-old traditions, where stories of honor, sacrifice, and family bonds were passed down from one generation to the next. Yet, hidden within one of those narrow streets, a man named Ahmed Ibrahim stood at a crossroads—caught between duty and convenience.

Ahmed's father, Hassan Ibrahim, had once been a pillar of strength. In his youth, he had labored tirelessly in the fields outside the city, ensuring his family never went without. But now, in his twilight years, Hassan's hands trembled, his back hunched, and his gait slowed. His once-powerful voice, which had guided Ahmed through childhood, had softened to a frail whisper.

Despite his father's sacrifices, the weight of caring for him began to strain Ahmed's household. His wife, Amina, grew increasingly resentful.

"He spills his food. He forgets things. It's too much," she complained one evening. "We have our own family to think about."

Ahmed remained silent, but the words gnawed at his heart. He had tried to be patient, reminding himself of all his father had done for him. But as the weeks passed, Amina's words became harder to ignore. The tension in the house grew, and Ahmed's resolve weakened.

One evening, under the crimson glow of the setting sun, Ahmed made a decision that would change his life forever. He found an old handwoven carpet, a family heirloom his father had used for prayer for decades. The carpet, worn but still sturdy, had witnessed countless moments of devotion and faith. Ahmed gently rolled it up and approached his father.

"Come, Father," Ahmed said softly, his voice betraying the conflict within him.

Hassan, trusting his son without question, slowly rose and sat on the carpet. Without a word, Ahmed began pulling the carpet through the winding streets of Fez. The city's chatter faded into silence as they ventured toward the mosque on the outskirts of town, where Ahmed planned to leave his father, hoping someone would take him in.

Unbeknownst to Ahmed, his eight-year-old son, Youssef, had been watching from the shadows of their courtyard. Curious and confused, Youssef followed them, keeping a careful distance. The boy's small footsteps echoed softly against the cobblestone streets as he trailed his father through the labyrinth of Fez.

When they reached the mosque, Ahmed unrolled the carpet and gently helped his father sit down on the cold stone steps. For a brief moment, the two men sat in silence—one resigned to his fate, the other consumed by guilt. Ahmed stood, bowed his head, and whispered, "Forgive me, Father," before turning to leave.

As he walked back home, Ahmed's heart was heavy with conflicting emotions. Relief mixed with guilt, but he convinced himself it was the right thing to do.

When Ahmed entered his home, he found Youssef sitting on the floor, scissors in hand, cutting the remaining portion of the carpet into smaller pieces.

"Youssef!" Ahmed's voice was sharp. "What are you doing? Why are you cutting your grandfather's carpet?"

Youssef looked up, his innocent eyes wide with determination. "I'm keeping this part of the carpet for you, Father," he said calmly. "When you grow old, I'll use it to take you to the mosque, just like you did with Grandfather."

Time seemed to freeze. Ahmed stared at his son, the weight of those simple words pressing down on him like a mountain. His Judgment Core—the inner compass that guides moral decisions—roared to life. In that moment, the layers of denial and justification he had built crumbled, exposing the raw truth.

The way we treat our elders shapes how we will be treated in return.

Ahmed's knees buckled as he sank to the floor. His mind raced through memories—his father teaching him to read under the flickering light of an oil lamp, guiding him through the bustling markets of Fez, and sacrificing his own comforts to ensure Ahmed's success.

Without hesitation, Ahmed sprang to his feet and rushed back through the dark streets. His heart pounded with urgency as he retraced his steps to the mosque. There, sitting quietly on the carpet, was his father. Hassan's tired eyes met his son's, filled with a mix of understanding and sadness.

"Father," Ahmed whispered, his voice breaking, "forgive me. I was blinded by my own selfishness."

Hassan said nothing but placed a trembling hand on his son's shoulder, a gesture of unspoken forgiveness and unconditional love.

When Ahmed returned home with his father, the atmosphere in the house shifted. Amina, seeing the transformation in her husband, softened her stance. She began to show more kindness toward Hassan, and slowly, the family's fractured bonds began to heal.

But the greatest change was in Youssef. The boy, who had been a silent observer, grew up carrying the lesson he had unknowingly taught his father. The way we honor our parents is the blueprint for how future generations will treat us.

Years later, when Ahmed himself grew old and frail, Youssef cared for him with unwavering dedication. He never forgot the lesson of the carpet—the unbreakable bond of family and the importance of treating elders with respect and dignity.

As you read Ahmed's story, ask yourself:

- How do you treat the elders in your life?

- Are you showing them the respect they deserve, or are you allowing the burdens of life to cloud your sense of duty?

- What legacy are you passing down to the next generation?

The Judgment Core whispers that every action leaves an imprint—not just on those we care for but on those who are watching. The way you honor your parents today shapes the future of your family. The choices you make now will ripple through time, becoming the guiding light—or the shadow—that future generations will follow.

The carpet you lay down today will be the one your children carry tomorrow. Will it be a carpet of kindness, respect, and love—or one of regret? The choice is yours.

The Silent Sacrifice: A Story of Love and Redemption

In the summer of 1967, Amman became a city of refuge for countless families fleeing the Israeli occupation of the West Bank. Among the many displaced was Leila Al Tareq, cradling her infant son, Sami Amaar Al Tareq, in her arms as they made their escape. The journey was perilous, filled with uncertainty, as they traveled through Israeli Airstrikes.

Their ordeal took a horrifying turn when an Israeli airstrike erupted nearby. Leila instinctively shielded Sami with her body, enduring the brunt of the blast. When she awoke in a hospital in Amman, her body bore deep scars from the shrapnel, and her left eye was heavily bandaged. She had saved her son, ensuring he was protected as much as possible, though the attack had left its mark on both their lives.

From that moment on, Leila was determined to rebuild their lives. Despite her injuries and the trauma of their escape, she focused all her energy on Sami's future.

As Sami grew, he became known for his striking eyes—one a piercing blue, the other a deep brown. His mother often smiled when people commented on them, explaining warmly, "Your blue eye comes from me, and your brown one from your father. It's a gift from both of us."

Cherishing the thought that his unique eyes symbolized the love of his parents. But as he grew older, his blue eye, so distinct, became a source of teasing among his classmates. Children at school would call him "odd" or "mismatched," and their taunts weighed heavily on him.

"Why couldn't I just look normal?" Sami would complain.

Leila, working long hours in a plastic factory to provide for him, always responded with patience and encouragement. "Your eyes are special, my son," she would say. "They're a reminder of where you come from and how much you're loved."

Though Leila poured her energy into providing Sami with opportunities, including a good education, he began to grow distant as he became more aware of their modest life. He felt embarrassed by her worn clothes and the faint chemical smell that clung to her after long shifts. The sacrifices she made were invisible to him, overshadowed by his frustration with their circumstances.

Sami's hard work paid off when he earned a scholarship to study in the United States. It was a dream come true, made possible by his mother's unwavering determination and tireless efforts. Their farewell was bittersweet—Leila, proud and hopeful, and Sami, eager to leave behind the struggles of his past.

In America, Sami thrived. He graduated with honors and secured a prestigious job, building a life far removed from his humble beginnings. Though he sent money to his mother regularly, their conversations dwindled to occasional phone calls. The physical distance mirrored the emotional distance that had grown between them.

By 1995, Sami was living a life of comfort and success, far from the memories of Amman. He seldom thought about his mother's sacrifices, focusing instead on his achievements and future.

One day, Sami received devastating news—his mother, Leila, had passed away. The news shattered him, and he immediately flew back to Amman. Their modest home, filled with echoes of his childhood, now felt unfamiliar and heavy with loss.

After her burial, Sami began sorting through her belongings. Among them, he found an old wooden box tucked away in a corner. Inside were photographs and documents that unraveled a truth he had never imagined.

The first photograph was of Leila cradling him as a baby. Her face bore faint scars, and her left eye was heavily bandaged, though her smile was radiant. Sami felt a pang of guilt, realizing how much she had endured to protect him.

Next, he found medical reports dated 1967. They detailed a severe injury to Leila's left eye from shrapnel during their escape. The reports revealed something that took Sami's breath away: a surgical procedure in which Leila had donated her left eye to him. She had endured a life with only one eye, all so her son could grow up with clear vision in both.

The blue eye he had always thought was a genetic gift from his mother was, in fact, her literal gift—one she had never spoken of.

Sami sat frozen, the documents trembling in his hands. His mother's sacrifice, which he had been oblivious to all his life, now shone with heartbreaking clarity. The eyes he had resented were a testament to her boundless love and devotion.

In that moment, Sami's Judgment Core, his inner moral compass, stirred deeply. He realized how far he had strayed from the values of gratitude and respect that his mother had embodied. Her selflessness had given him the opportunities he now enjoyed, and he had taken it all for granted.

Returning to the United States, Sami was a changed man. He dedicated himself to honoring his mother's memory by helping others. He volunteered with organizations supporting refugees and shared his story to inspire gratitude and selflessness in others.

Every time Sami looked in the mirror, his mismatched eyes reminded him of Leila's ultimate sacrifice and her unwavering love. The blue eye, once a source of shame, became his greatest treasure—a symbol of his mother's boundless devotion and a guide for living with compassion and humility.

Through her sacrifice, Leila had not only shaped Sami's future but had also given him a profound lesson in love and humanity—one he would carry for the rest of his life.

Conclusion: Honoring the Hands that Raised You

You're standing before a mirror—not one that merely reflects your current self, but one that reveals the entirety of your life. In its surface, you see your past, your present, and a glimpse of your future. The mirror whispers truths you cannot ignore: every act of kindness, every word of gratitude, and every moment of care toward your parents and elders shapes the reflection of your own later years.

Our parents and elders, who once stood strong, made countless sacrifices to build the foundation upon which we stand. Yet, they were not perfect. They made mistakes—some we may still struggle to understand, and others they may not even realize they made. Despite their imperfections, their sacrifices, love, and guidance have shaped us into who we are today. They gave us their best, often at the cost of their own dreams, comforts, and desires.

And now, as time takes its toll, the roles have reversed. They stand where we will one day stand—vulnerable, in need of care, craving respect and connection. As they age, our treatment of them becomes a reflection of our moral compass and the values we hold dear.

Your Judgment Core, your inner guide to right and wrong, poses critical questions:

- When you look in the mirror of your future, do you see someone who honored the hands that raised them, despite their flaws?

- Can you recognize the sacrifices your parents made, even if they were imperfect?

- Do you show gratitude for what they gave, knowing that without them, you would not be who you're today?

The truth is, none of us reach adulthood unaided. Every step of our journey was shaped by the love, patience, and sacrifices of those who came before us. Their efforts—whether flawless or flawed—paved the way for our opportunities, shaping not just our lives but also our ability to navigate the world with strength and resilience.

The Reflection of Compassion

Honoring our parents and elders is not about overlooking their mistakes but about acknowledging the humanity within them. They, like us, were navigating life without a perfect guidebook, learning as they went. Their missteps were part of their journey, but so too were their triumphs—the moments they chose to give us more than they ever had.

Now, the mirror turns to you. Ask yourself:

- Do you offer forgiveness for the mistakes your parents made, knowing they likely did their best?

- Are you treating them with the same patience and care they once extended to you?

- What kind of legacy are you creating for the generations that watch how you honor them?

A Call to Action

Life is cyclical. The way you treat your parents and elders today sets the tone for how you will be treated tomorrow. Children observe, absorb, and mimic the respect—or lack thereof—that you demonstrate. Your actions are not just for the elders in your life but for the generations that will follow.

The Judgment Core calls on you to act:

- Forgive the imperfections of your parents and focus on the love they gave.

- Express gratitude for the sacrifices they made, whether big or small, acknowledged or unseen.

- Offer them dignity and care, not as a duty, but as a reflection of the love that shaped your own life.

Your Future in the Mirror

As you gaze into the mirror of your life, remember that time spares no one. One day, you too will grow old, reliant on others for care and compassion. How will you want to be treated? What lessons are you teaching your children and community today about how to honor those who came before them?

When your reflection shows an elder, will it reflect pride in the care and respect you once gave, or will it carry the shadows of missed opportunities and regret? The choice is yours. What will your Judgment Core guide you to do today to ensure that the mirror reflects a life lived with empathy, gratitude, and love tomorrow?

7.8 Embrace Generosity Without Expectation

You're walking through a bustling market, where people of all walks of life converge. Some are surrounded by laughter, their arms full of goods to share with loved ones. Others wander alone, their eyes scanning the crowd, carrying only the weight of solitude. A merchant offers an apple to a hungry child who clutches at his mother's frayed cloak, while another vendor watches silently, consumed by his own struggles. In this moment, you see it—the stark reality that life is not always fair. Some receive plenty, while others barely scrape by. And yet, within this unfairness lies the opportunity for a simple, profound truth: generosity can bridge the gap.

Life's inequities are unavoidable. Some are born into privilege, with access to wealth, education, and opportunity, while others face barriers that seem insurmountable. Some enjoy the warmth of family gatherings, while others endure empty rooms and silent evenings. Some are blessed with robust health, while others battle unseen ailments or face limitations that reshape their dreams. The uneven distribution of fortune is a constant reminder that fairness is not guaranteed. But in this imbalance, there is a call to action: to share what we can, not just materially but emotionally, to extend kindness, love, and connection to those who may lack what we take for granted.

Generosity, in its truest form, is not confined to money or possessions. It is found in the warmth of a shared moment, in offering time to someone who feels forgotten, in opening your heart to those who long for connection. It is a smile for a stranger, a listening ear for a friend, or an embrace for someone navigating a storm. To be generous is to recognize the humanity in others and to give freely—not out of obligation, but because the act itself enriches both the giver and the receiver.

But generosity also tests your Judgment Core—that inner compass guiding your moral decisions. It asks:

- When faced with life's unfairness, do I respond with empathy or indifference?

- Do I share what I have—be it time, love, or resources—without expecting anything in return?

- Can I celebrate my own blessings while still reaching out to lift others who have less?

Being generous with others is a way of balancing life's scales, even if just slightly. It is a way of saying to those who struggle: You're not alone. Your existence matters. I see you. Whether you have wealth to share or simply the gift of your presence, the act of giving becomes a powerful antidote to life's inherent inequities.

Consider this: some have families to lean on, others do not. Some have children who bring joy to their lives, while others yearn for that gift. Some move through life with ease, while others fight battles invisible to the world. By choosing generosity, you create moments of equity within life's imbalance. You remind yourself—and those around you—that the value of a person is not measured by what they have but by the love and kindness they extend.

And so, the mirror turns to you:

- When you look at your own blessings, do you see opportunities to uplift others?

- Do you acknowledge the unfairness of life, not with bitterness, but with a commitment to be a source of light?

- How would you hope to be treated if your fortunes changed?

Life's unfairness is undeniable, but generosity allows us to transcend it. Through giving—of love, time, and care—we weave a tapestry of connection that binds us together. The question is: will you choose to be part of that thread?

The Caravan of Generosity: Uthman ibn Affan's Defining Choice

Medina, 638 CE. The scorching sun hung unrelenting over Medina, its rays baking the earth and intensifying the city's plight. The drought had gripped the land for months, depleting food and water supplies, leaving families to ration their remaining resources with increasing desperation. The once-bustling markets had grown quieter, and the faces of the townspeople bore the strain of uncertainty.

But on this fateful afternoon, a caravan appeared on the horizon, its thousand camels laden with sacks of grain, barrels of water, and other essential supplies. The caravan belonged to Uthman ibn Affan, a man of immense wealth and unwavering faith, known throughout Medina for his acts of charity and humility.

As the caravan entered the city, the atmosphere shifted from despair to hope. Word spread rapidly, and soon, a gathering of eager merchants approached Uthman. They saw an opportunity in the desperation that hung thick in the air—an opportunity to buy the goods, inflate their prices, and sell them at exorbitant rates to the starving population.

One by one, the merchants approached Uthman, each vying to strike a deal.

"We'll pay you 10 dirhams per sack of grain," one merchant began, confident in his bid.

"I'll offer 12 dirhams," another quickly countered, determined to outdo his competitor.

"15 dirhams per sack!" a third merchant declared, his voice tinged with urgency.

The bidding war escalated rapidly as the merchants grew increasingly competitive, each raising their offer in an attempt to secure the goods. The air buzzed with their negotiations, and the crowd watched intently, anticipating Uthman's response.

Uthman, however, remained silent. His calm demeanor was unshaken by the escalating offers. He stood quietly, listening as the merchants raised their bids to amounts far above the usual market price.

Sensing his hesitation, one merchant stepped forward, his tone almost pleading. "20 dirhams per sack! Surely, Uthman, this is the best offer you'll receive. Think of the fortune you could make!"

Another merchant, determined to outbid the rest, added, "I'll pay 25 dirhams per sack! No one else will offer you more."

The offers had reached extraordinary heights, and the merchants, certain they had swayed Uthman, waited for his answer. After all, who could refuse such profits?

Finally, Uthman spoke, his voice steady and deliberate. "I appreciate your offers," he began, his gaze sweeping over the assembled merchants. "But I have already received a better offer."

The merchants were stunned. Whispers rippled through the crowd. Who could have outbid them? They had raised their offers to levels no one else could match.

"Who has outbid us?" one merchant demanded, disbelief lacing his words.

Uthman's eyes softened, and a faint smile crossed his face. "Allah has offered me ten times more for every dirham," he said calmly. "For every act of charity, He has promised a reward far greater than anything I could earn here. I will not sell these goods to you. Instead, I will give them freely to the people of Medina."

A stunned silence followed. The merchants, caught between admiration and disappointment, could only watch as Uthman turned to his attendants and ordered them to begin distributing the goods.

"But Uthman," one merchant protested, his voice tinged with frustration, "you're walking away from a fortune!"

Uthman's expression grew resolute. "True wealth is not found in what we hoard," he replied, "but in what we give. These goods are not mine to profit from; they are a trust given to me to ease the suffering of others."

As the townspeople gathered, Uthman's men began distributing the supplies—sacks of grain, barrels of water, and other essentials—to families, widows, and travelers. Many of them wept as they received the goods, their hearts overwhelmed by relief and gratitude.

Uthman's actions sent ripples through Medina and beyond. His refusal to profit from the suffering of others was a testament to his faith, his unwavering belief in justice, and the strength of his Judgment Core—the inner compass that guided him to prioritize compassion over greed.

Uthman's story is not just a tale of generosity but a profound challenge to us all. Imagine yourself in his position. Would you have resisted the merchants' offers, choosing instead to give freely to those in need? Or would the allure of profit have clouded your judgment?

- What does your moral compass tell you about prioritizing the needs of others over personal gain?

- How do you navigate the imbalance of privilege in the world? Do you act to close the gaps, or do you allow them to persist?

- What legacy will you leave behind—one defined by wealth or by the lives you uplifted?

Uthman ibn Affan's decision reminds us that true wealth is measured not by the treasures we accumulate but by the lives we touch. Generosity without expectation is a beacon of hope, illuminating the path toward a more just and compassionate world.

What will you do when the choice is yours? Will you embrace generosity, or will you let the moment pass, lost in the shadow of self-interest? The decision lies within you—and it shapes not only your legacy but the world you leave behind.

The Stranger Who Held a Key

Detroit, Michigan – 1971. In a city marked by struggle, where boarded-up windows and cracked sidewalks told stories of hardship, a young boy named Sami Walker wandered through his school library, his head hanging low. The sound of distant laughter and chatter echoed through the halls, but it wasn't for him. Sami lived in a world of quiet defeat. At just 11 years old, he had been labeled "the dumbest kid in class," a title that weighed on him like a chain.

Detroit wasn't kind to kids like Sami. His father had walked out when he was only six, leaving his mother, Martha Walker, to raise him and his older brother on her own. Martha worked tirelessly as a domestic cleaner, juggling multiple jobs just to keep a roof over their heads. Despite her exhaustion, she was determined to give her boys the one thing no one could take away: an education.

But for Sami, school was a battlefield, and he was losing. Words on a page jumbled together, numbers danced mockingly in his notebooks, and every test felt like a mountain too steep to climb. The taunts of his classmates echoed louder than the encouragement of his teachers. "You'll never make it," they sneered, and in his heart, Sami feared they were right.

One gray afternoon, seeking a place to hide from the world, Sami found himself in the far corner of the school library. The air smelled of old paper and dust, and the shelves loomed like silent sentinels. He sat at a small wooden table, his head resting on his folded arms, trying to block out the overwhelming sense of failure that had become his constant companion.

From behind the shelves, an older woman with kind eyes and graying hair noticed him. She was the librarian, Mrs. Evelyn Harper, a quiet observer of the countless children who passed through her domain. There was something about Sami that tugged at her—a sadness in his eyes, a heaviness in his posture.

Without a word, Mrs. Harper approached him, carrying a slim, brightly colored book. It wasn't a textbook or something dense with facts, but a simple story about a boy who faced challenges and discovered courage along the way. She placed the book gently on the table in front of him.

"This might take you somewhere special," she said softly. Her voice was calm, almost musical, and it startled Sami out of his thoughts.

He looked up, puzzled. "I'm not good at reading," he mumbled.

Mrs. Harper smiled, unbothered by his hesitation. "That's okay," she replied. "You don't have to be good. Just try. Every story starts with a first step."

There was something in her tone—an unshakable belief in him—that Sami hadn't felt before. Reluctantly, he opened the book, his fingers trembling slightly as he turned the first page. The words seemed foreign at first, but with each sentence, they began to make sense.

For the first time, Sami didn't feel like the world was mocking him. Instead, the story pulled him in, offering a quiet escape and a glimpse of something he hadn't known before: possibility.

That small act—a stranger offering a book—became the spark Sami needed.

Encouraged by that single experience, Sami began to visit the library more often. Each time, Mrs. Harper was there, quietly guiding him toward books that matched his growing confidence. At home, Martha noticed the change. She saw Sami reading late into the night, his brow furrowed in concentration, and she seized the moment to set a rule: two books a week, with written reports for her to review. She could barely read the reports herself, but that didn't matter. What mattered was the discipline, the drive, and the hope she saw blossoming in her son.

Within months, Sami's reading skills improved dramatically. Words no longer felt like enemies; they became tools, opening doors to worlds he had never imagined. He discovered a love for science, devouring books about the human body, space, and the mysteries of the natural world. His grades soared, and the boy who had once been dismissed as "the dumbest" climbed to the top of his class.

Years later, Sami reflected on the pivotal moment that had changed everything. He realized that Mrs. Harper's small act of generosity wasn't about giving him a book; it was about seeing him—truly seeing him. Her kindness ignited a spark in his Judgment Core, the inner compass that guides one's sense of right and wrong. It reminded him that even in a world that feels indifferent, small acts of care can transform lives.

Sami understood that life wasn't fair. Some were born into privilege, while others, like him, had to fight for every inch of progress. But generosity—whether in the form of time, attention, or belief—could bridge those gaps.

In 1987, at just 27 years old, Dr. Sami Walker performed his first major neurosurgical procedure, earning international recognition for his skill and precision. As his career flourished, Sami never forgot the librarian who had believed in him when no one else did.

Sami's story became a testament to the power of generosity without expectation. It wasn't Mrs. Harper's job to change his life, yet her small act of kindness set in motion a ripple effect that would touch countless others.

Now, imagine yourself in Mrs. Harper's place—or Sami's. How often do you extend a hand to someone in need, even when it isn't your responsibility? And how often do you overlook the opportunities to inspire someone, believing that your actions won't matter?

- What does your Judgment Core tell you about the power of small acts?

- How do you measure generosity—in the size of the gift or the depth of its impact?

- And when life offers you a chance to be a "stranger" in someone else's story, will you take it?

The world is filled with people like Sami, waiting for someone to hand them their first "book." Will you be the one to offer it?.

The Science of Generosity

Modern research supports what many spiritual and philosophical traditions have long claimed: generosity brings joy, fulfillment, and a sense of purpose. According to studies conducted by the Greater Good Science Center at the University of California, Berkeley, acts of generosity are closely tied to increased happiness, improved health, and greater life satisfaction. Research published in the Journal of Happiness Studies (2010) and Social Psychological and Personality Science (2013) further supports the idea that generosity, whether through time, money, or emotional support, activates key areas of the brain associated with pleasure, social connection, and trust, creating what is often called the "warm glow" effect.

<u>How Generosity Affects the Brain and Body</u>

The act of giving triggers the release of chemicals such as dopamine and oxytocin, both of which are linked to feelings of pleasure and bonding. Dopamine, often referred to as the "feel-good" chemical, floods the brain when a person performs an act of kindness, leading to a sense of joy and satisfaction. Oxytocin, sometimes called the "love hormone," promotes feelings of empathy, connection, and trust. These effects were explored in a study published in Nature Communications (2017), showing how acts of generosity create long-lasting positive effects on mental health by reinforcing these social bonds.

Generosity has also been shown to reduce levels of cortisol, the body's primary stress hormone. High levels of cortisol over prolonged periods can contribute to anxiety, depression, and a weakened immune system. In a 2006 study by the University of British Columbia, researchers found that acts of kindness significantly reduced participants' stress levels, thereby enhancing immune function, lowering blood pressure, and potentially extending life expectancy. Additional research published in the American Journal of Public Health (2013) found that individuals who regularly engage in acts of kindness have a 44% lower risk of early mortality, further underscoring the health benefits of generosity.

Research on Spending and Happiness

A fascinating study on generosity and happiness, cited by the Greater Good Science Center and published by Harvard Business School (2008), involved participants receiving a sum of money and being instructed either to spend it on themselves or to donate it to someone else. The study found that those who spent the money on others reported significantly higher levels of happiness compared to those who spent it on themselves. These results, published in the Journal of Personality and Social Psychology, highlight the joy of giving, suggesting that generosity is a natural and integral part of human behavior that enhances overall well-being.

The study further illustrated that generosity fosters a sense of purpose and fulfillment. When we give to others—whether financially, emotionally, or through acts of service—we feel connected to a larger community. This sense of belonging and contribution is essential for mental health and personal happiness. The findings, backed by Social Psychological and Personality Science (2015), challenge the idea that material wealth alone can bring fulfillment, showing that the act of giving is fundamental to a balanced, meaningful life.

The Ripple Effect of Generosity

One of the most profound aspects of generosity is its ripple effect. Acts of kindness, no matter how small, inspire others to be generous in turn, creating a cycle of positive interactions that strengthen social bonds. A 2017 study published in Nature Communications demonstrated this "contagious generosity" effect. Participants who observed acts of kindness were significantly more likely to engage in prosocial behavior themselves, amplifying the impact of generosity within a community.

This ripple effect was further examined in a 2019 report by the Greater Good Science Center, which showed that when individuals witness generosity, they are more likely to act kindly toward others, creating a wave of positive change that enhances lives within the community.

Conclusion: When Roles Reverse, Will Your Judgment Core Hold?

You're walking a narrow bridge suspended over a vast chasm. On one side, you stand strong, supported by the blessings of good fortune, love, or opportunity. But with just one unexpected shift—a lost job, a health crisis, or an emotional struggle—you could find yourself on the other side of that bridge, needing someone to hold out their hand, to show you generosity in your moment of need.

Life's inequities are stark and unavoidable. Some are born into privilege, while others begin their journey with fewer opportunities. Some find warmth in the embrace of a family, while others face the chill of solitude. Some thrive in health, while others endure silent battles with illness. Today, you may stand on the side of the giver, offering support, kindness, or resources. But life's unpredictability serves as a humbling reminder: what if, one day, you're on the other side, waiting for someone to extend their hand to you?

Generosity, when embraced without expectation, is more than an act of kindness—it is a lifeline that bridges these divides. It calls upon your Judgment Core—your internal moral compass—to recognize the shared humanity in others and to act with compassion and empathy. Each act of giving is a choice that shapes your moral identity, asking:

- If our positions were reversed, how would I hope to be treated?

- Do I give freely, knowing one day I might need the generosity of others?

- Am I building connections of support, or am I letting opportunities to care slip by?

True generosity transcends material wealth. It exists in the willingness to offer emotional support, a listening ear, or a comforting presence. It's found in the courage to say, "You're not alone," and the humility to know that one day, you might need to hear those same words. How do you want the world to respond when it's you on the other side of the equation?

When we give—whether time, love, or resources—we create moments of balance in an inherently unbalanced world. Generosity reminds us that we are all interconnected, and the life you uplift today could very well be the hand that reaches back to steady you tomorrow. Are you contributing to this cycle of connection, or are you standing apart, blind to the threads of mutual support that bind us all?

Consider this deeply. Life's tables can turn, often when we least expect it. The same hand you extend today could inspire others to act, creating a ripple of generosity that shapes a more compassionate world. What kind of legacy are you leaving?

Through giving, you strengthen your Judgment Core. You align yourself with principles of fairness, empathy, and love, ensuring that your moral compass guides you toward building a just and supportive community. In doing so, you remind others—and yourself—that even in a world of inequity, we have the power to make a difference, one act of generosity at a time.

Today, you have the chance to be a giver, to weave threads of light into the fabric of someone's life. Tomorrow, you might find yourself needing those same threads to hold you. What kind of bridge are you building? Will it be strong enough to carry someone else across—or one day, yourself? The choice is yours.

7.9 Upholding Integrity

You're standing at a crossroads in a silent, moonlit city. To your left lies a forgotten wallet on a deserted bench, brimming with cash. To your right, an unlocked door leads into a store closed for the night, shelves stocked with valuable goods. The street is empty; no one is watching. The question is not just whether you take what isn't yours, but what that choice will mean—not only for the people who lose but for the person you become. Would you still make the same decision if someone were watching? And, more importantly, how will this moment echo in the story of your life?

Integrity is the silent witness of our choices, shaping who we are when no one else is looking. It forms the bedrock of trust, the foundation upon which communities thrive, and the compass that guides moral judgment. Cheating and stealing, whether minor or monumental, may seem like shortcuts to gain or survival, but their consequences ripple far beyond the immediate act, disrupting not only lives but the delicate balance of trust that sustains societies.

When we cheat or steal, we create invisible fractures—within ourselves, in the lives of others, and in the broader community. Consider a seemingly small act: taking office supplies from work or fudging numbers on a report. To the individual, these may appear harmless, but to the business, they represent losses that accumulate, forcing cost-cutting measures that might lead to layoffs or reduced benefits. Behind those numbers are real people—families who depend on stability, children whose futures may be altered, and communities that feel the shock of every ripple.

On a personal level, dishonesty corrodes the Judgment Core (JDC)—the internal framework of values that shapes our decisions. Each dishonest act chips away at the clarity of this moral compass, making it easier to justify further actions that serve the self at the expense of others. The cracks in the JDC grow, distorting perceptions of right and wrong, and transforming one's character in ways that undermine trust, empathy, and dignity.

But integrity is about more than simply avoiding harm. It is about embracing a framework that respects the interconnectedness of our actions. Upholding integrity means making decisions that align not only with personal values but also with the greater good—recognizing that every choice we make reverberates through the lives of others.

Ask yourself:

- What does your Judgment Core reveal about your choices when no one is watching?

- Can you resist the allure of shortcuts, knowing the unseen damage they may cause to others and to yourself?

- Are your actions building trust and strengthening the community, or are they creating fractures that others must bear?

Upholding integrity is a commitment to living with purpose and authenticity, ensuring that our actions contribute to a more resilient and just society. When we choose honesty over deceit, fairness over exploitation, and empathy over indifference, we reinforce the bonds that hold humanity together. The question is: when faced with the crossroads of temptation, which path will you take—and what kind of person will you leave behind?

The Shadows of Craft Haven

In the heart of Portland, Oregon, where cobblestone streets met the aroma of fresh coffee and rain-soaked pine, Craft Haven stood as a beacon of creativity and community. Nestled on Alder Street, this small family-owned craft store had been a sanctuary for artists, teachers, and families since its founding in 2009 by Emma and Ray Spencer. Its shelves brimmed with vibrant paints, intricate beads, and hand-spun yarns sourced from local artisans across the Pacific Northwest. More than just a store, Craft Haven was a hub of inspiration, offering art workshops, school donations, and a sense of belonging to all who entered.

But by 2021, shadows began to creep into Craft Haven's story. The COVID-19 pandemic had strained small businesses nationwide, but for Emma and Ray, another invisible challenge began taking its toll—shoplifting. At first, the losses seemed minor: a missing brush set here, a few paint tubes there. However, as the months passed, the trickle of thefts became a steady drain on their already tight margins.

One crisp October morning, as Emma opened the store, she noticed an empty shelf where an expensive set of calligraphy pens had been the day before. She sighed and turned to Ray, who was restocking the cashier counter. "Another one gone," she muttered, her voice tinged with frustration.

Ray frowned. "That's the third time this week. These small losses are adding up, Emma. We're barely breaking even."

The thefts weren't just affecting their bottom line. Every stolen item represented a ripple effect that touched not only their family but also the wider community. Emma and Ray were faced with a heart-wrenching decision: raise prices or cut back on their cherished community contributions.

"We knew what it would mean," Ray later reflected. "Our regular customers are artists and teachers, many of them living paycheck to paycheck. We didn't want to make it harder for them, but what choice did we have?"

Reluctantly, Craft Haven raised prices by 15%. The cost of canvases and paints rose, and the once-thriving donation program that supplied free art materials to local schools and senior centers came to a halt. Teachers, who had relied on the store for their students' art projects, sent emails and handwritten letters, pleading for assistance. "It broke my heart every time I had to say no," Emma admitted.

The repercussions extended beyond the classroom. Craft Haven had long been a lifeline for local artisans who supplied handmade goods. With reduced revenue, the store could no longer afford to place large orders, forcing several small artisans to find other, less reliable avenues for income.

Among them was Lisa Morales, a jewelry maker whose delicate wire-wrapped earrings had been a bestseller at Craft Haven. "When they reduced their orders, I lost half my monthly income," Lisa shared. "It wasn't their fault—they were just trying to survive—but it hit me hard."

As the impact of the thefts spread like cracks in a glass window, the vibrant community Craft Haven had nurtured began to fracture. Longtime customers noticed the higher prices and fewer workshops. Some voiced disappointment, while others quietly drifted to big-box stores, oblivious to the silent struggle unfolding behind the scenes.

The story of Craft Haven is not just about a small business battling theft; it is a testament to how individual choices can ripple outward, affecting lives in unexpected ways. Each stolen brush or tube of paint may have seemed insignificant to the thief, but the consequences were profound: a child losing the chance to explore their creativity, a teacher struggling to inspire their students, an artisan grappling with lost income.

For Emma and Ray, the struggle wasn't just financial; it was a battle of values. Their Judgment Core, the inner moral compass guiding their decisions, was tested daily. Should they install invasive security measures and sacrifice the welcoming atmosphere their store was known for? Should they close their doors to prevent further losses, abandoning the community that had supported them for over a decade?

One rainy evening, as Emma closed the shop, she stared at the shelves and whispered to herself, "How did it come to this? We built this place to bring people together, not to watch it fall apart."

The story of Craft Haven challenges us all to reflect on the unseen consequences of dishonesty:

- When faced with temptation, do we consider how our actions might harm others?

- If the roles were reversed, and we were the ones struggling to make ends meet, how would we hope to be treated?

- Can we strengthen our own Judgment Core to prioritize integrity, knowing that even small choices can have far-reaching effects?

Craft Haven's tale is a somber reminder that life's challenges often test not just our resilience but our moral compass. In a world where small acts of dishonesty can lead to disproportionate harm, the true measure of character lies in choosing integrity—even when it's difficult.

As you consider this story, ask yourself: What would you do if you were Emma or Ray? Or Lisa? Or the teacher who depended on those art supplies? The answers may not be easy, but they reveal the essence of who we are—and who we strive to become.

The Rise of Theranos

In the heart of Silicon Valley, where innovation thrives and dreams are forged, 2003 marked the beginning of a story destined to captivate the world. Palo Alto, California, became the stage where a 19-year-old Stanford dropout, Elizabeth Holmes, introduced an idea she claimed would redefine healthcare forever. With her signature black turtleneck, piercing blue eyes, and an unwavering conviction, she unveiled Theranos, a company promising to perform hundreds of diagnostic tests from a single drop of blood. It was a vision of accessibility and affordability—a vision that, on the surface, seemed too good to be true.

By 2010, Holmes's charisma and ambition had drawn some of the most powerful figures into her orbit. Former Secretary of State Henry Kissinger, ex-Defense Secretary James Mattis, and media mogul Rupert Murdoch became advocates and board members, lending her legitimacy. Her pitch resonated across industries, and soon, Walgreens and Safeway signed multimillion-dollar contracts to bring Theranos blood-testing centers to their stores. Investors poured in over $700 million, catapulting the company's valuation to $9 billion and Holmes herself to billionaire status.

Despite the glamour, whispers of discontent surfaced within Theranos. By 2013, behind closed doors, engineers and lab technicians were grappling with a sobering reality: the Edison, the device central to Holmes's promise, didn't work as claimed. Results were often inconsistent, unreliable, and dangerously misleading. Inside the labs, panic simmered as pressure mounted to meet Holmes's public guarantees.

Holmes, however, was relentless. Employees who raised concerns faced immediate dismissal, silenced by nondisclosure agreements and threats of lawsuits. To the outside world, she maintained an unflappable image of confidence, her every word carefully curated to fuel the myth of Theranos's infallibility.

In 2014, Theranos was at its peak. Holmes graced the covers of Fortune and Forbes, hailed as the female Steve Jobs. Her technology was touted as a revolution in healthcare, one that could save lives and democratize medicine. Investors and the media were entranced, and few questioned the legitimacy of her claims.

The illusion began to crumble in 2015, when investigative journalist John Carreyrou of The Wall Street Journal received a tip from a former Theranos employee. The tip alleged that the Edison machines were a façade, incapable of performing the tests Holmes had promised. Instead, the majority of diagnostics were secretly conducted using standard equipment from other companies.

Carreyrou's investigation deepened, and his findings were damning. Theranos's technology was not just flawed—it was putting lives at risk. Patients received inaccurate results, leading to unnecessary treatments and devastating emotional tolls. In one case, a woman was falsely told she had HIV; in another, a man received incorrect cancer markers that upended his life.

In October 2015, The Wall Street Journal published its first exposé, setting off a chain reaction. Investors, once enamored by Holmes, now demanded answers. The FDA and SEC launched investigations, uncovering a web of deception that spanned years. By 2018, Holmes and her business partner, Ramesh "Sunny" Balwani, faced federal charges of wire fraud and conspiracy to defraud investors, patients, and doctors.

The fallout was catastrophic. Theranos dissolved, its assets auctioned off. Holmes, once celebrated as a pioneer, became a symbol of Silicon Valley's dark side—a cautionary tale of unchecked ambition and the consequences of prioritizing profit over integrity.

Elizabeth Holmes's story transcends the boardrooms and laboratories of Silicon Valley. At its heart lies a profound challenge to the Judgment Core—the moral compass that governs our choices and defines our character.

- What is the cost of ambition without integrity? Holmes's pursuit of success blinded her to the ethical boundaries she crossed, harming countless lives in the process.

- Can trust, once broken, ever be restored? The investors, patients, and professionals who believed in Holmes faced financial and emotional devastation.

- How do we balance innovation with accountability? Theranos promised a revolution but delivered a cautionary tale, reminding us that progress must never come at the expense of honesty and humanity.

Holmes's rise and fall is a stark reminder that even the most visionary ideas require a foundation of truth. Without it, ambition turns toxic, and the ripple effects of deceit can destroy not only careers but lives.

As you consider the story of Theranos, ask yourself:

- When faced with the allure of success, would you compromise your values for personal gain?

- How do you ensure that your Judgment Core remains intact, even in the face of immense pressure?

- If you were one of Theranos's investors or patients, how would this betrayal shape your trust in others?

The story of Theranos is not just about one woman's deception. It is a reflection of the choices we all face in moments of ambition, power, and opportunity—a mirror held up to our own Judgment Core.

A Dark Tale of Deception and Betrayal

In the misty hills of Parkersburg, West Virginia, where the Ohio River wound its way through tight-knit rural communities, life unfolded at a steady, predictable rhythm. Families thrived on hard work, trust, and the shared assurance that their land and water—gifts passed down through generations—would sustain them. But in the shadows of this picturesque setting, an invisible menace was spreading, one that would upend lives and forever alter the moral fabric of the region.

It began in the early 1980s, unnoticed at first. Families started whispering about strange ailments, unexplainable illnesses, and rising cancer diagnoses. Local farmers observed eerie patterns: crops withering inexplicably, livestock succumbing to diseases that defied explanation, and water that no longer tasted as pure as it once had. The epicenter of these mysterious occurrences seemed to point to one looming presence: the sprawling DuPont chemical plant on the outskirts of town.

For decades, DuPont had operated as a lifeline to Parkersburg, providing jobs and economic stability. But behind the plant's gates, a dangerous secret simmered. The company had been using a chemical called perfluorooctanoic acid (PFOA)—a key ingredient in the production of Teflon. Internally, DuPont scientists and executives had known for years that PFOA was highly toxic, linked to cancer, liver damage, birth defects, and other severe health issues. Instead of addressing the risks, they chose to bury the evidence, quietly disposing of PFOA waste into the waterways and landfills surrounding the plant.

By the late 1980s, the subtle signs of devastation could no longer be ignored. Wilbur Tennant, a local farmer, was one of the first to connect the dots. His cattle, once healthy and thriving, began dying at an alarming rate. Tumors disfigured their bodies, their teeth turned black, and their organs swelled grotesquely. Nearly 200 of his cows perished in just a few years. Wilbur was certain the plant was to blame. His farm bordered land sold to DuPont, and the stream running through his property was filled with foamy, discolored water emanating from the plant's waste.

Tennant's complaints fell on deaf ears. Local officials, many influenced by DuPont's economic power, dismissed his concerns as baseless. Desperate, Wilbur turned to Rob Bilott, a Cincinnati-based environmental lawyer with no ties to Parkersburg. Bilott, who had spent his career defending large corporations, initially hesitated. But as Tennant shared his evidence—disturbing photos, videos of the sickened cattle, and water samples that reeked of chemicals—Bilott felt an undeniable pull. Something was deeply wrong.

Bilott embarked on a journey that would consume nearly two decades of his life. Through painstaking research and legal maneuvering, he uncovered a trove of internal DuPont documents. These files painted a chilling picture: the company had been aware of PFOA's dangers since the 1960s. Their own studies revealed the chemical's harmful effects on animals and its potential to cause cancer in humans. Despite this knowledge, DuPont continued using PFOA, hiding its toxic legacy from regulators, employees, and the community.

The documents exposed how DuPont had systematically dumped PFOA waste into the environment, knowing it would seep into the drinking water of tens of thousands of residents. The company prioritized profit over ethics, gambling with the health of an entire region. Each decision, each cover-up, represented a choice to sacrifice integrity for economic gain—a stark violation of the Judgment Core, that internal compass guiding right from wrong.

By the time the scandal came to light in the early 2000s, the damage was irreversible. Residents who had unknowingly consumed tainted water for decades suffered from kidney and testicular cancer, thyroid disease, and a host of other ailments. Pregnant women feared for their unborn children, and families mourned loved ones lost to preventable illnesses. Trust in DuPont—once the town's benefactor—shattered like glass underfoot.

In 2017, after years of legal battles led by Bilott, DuPont settled with affected residents for $671 million. The victory was bittersweet. For many, the compensation felt hollow, a mere acknowledgment of lives already irreparably changed. Farmers had lost their livelihoods, children faced lifelong health challenges, and a once-thriving community had been fractured by betrayal.

The DuPont scandal serves as a chilling reminder of how far-reaching the consequences of deception can be. It challenges us to confront uncomfortable questions about our own Judgment Core:

- When faced with the opportunity for personal or professional gain, would you compromise the well-being of others?

- How do you ensure your actions today uphold the integrity needed to build trust and resilience in your community?

- What is the true cost of prioritizing profit over people?

The actions of DuPont executives not only poisoned the water but also eroded the moral foundation of the community they claimed to support. Their decisions remind us that every act of cheating, every corner cut, creates ripples that can devastate lives far beyond the immediate moment.

As you reflect on this story, consider: If you were one of the decision-makers at DuPont, would your Judgment Core have guided you differently? And if you lived in Parkersburg, what would justice mean to you? These are questions that challenge the very essence of integrity and accountability, urging us to look inward and ensure that our own actions contribute to a better, more just world.

Conclusion: What Path Are You Paving?

You're walking a narrow path where each step leaves an imprint—not just on the ground beneath you but on the lives of those who follow. Every choice you make shapes the trail ahead, either paving a road of trust or carving fractures that others must navigate. Integrity is the compass that ensures each step leads toward fairness, empathy, and collective well-being. But what happens when the compass falters? What happens when small acts of dishonesty distort the path for everyone?

Integrity is more than a personal virtue; it is a bridge that connects individuals, communities, and industries. It ensures that trust remains unbroken, that justice prevails, and that progress benefits all. When integrity is compromised, as seen in the stories of DuPont's negligence or Theranos's deceit, the ripples of harm extend far beyond the immediate act. Entire ecosystems of trust collapse, leaving individuals and communities to bear the burden of broken promises and shattered expectations.

But the erosion of integrity does not happen in dramatic leaps—it begins subtly, with small compromises. A white lie here, a misstep there, each seemingly harmless in isolation, gradually corrodes the Judgment Core—the inner moral compass that guides our sense of right and wrong. Over time, what once felt unacceptable becomes routine. The question is: How do you ensure that your Judgment Core remains intact, even when no one is watching?

As you consider this, reflect on the stories of harm caused by compromised integrity:

- What is the cost of small dishonest acts that seem justified in the moment?

- How do you weigh personal gain against the unseen harm to others?

- When faced with temptation, do you pause to consider the ripple effects of your choices?

Integrity is not just about avoiding harm; it is about creating a foundation of trust and accountability. Each honest decision reinforces the Judgment Core, aligning actions with values and ensuring that trust, empathy, and fairness remain at the forefront of our choices.

Now, turn the mirror inward:

- If your actions today were to shape the ethical landscape of tomorrow, what legacy would you leave behind?

- If the roles were reversed and you found yourself at the mercy of someone else's choices, how would you hope to be treated?

Choosing integrity is not always easy, especially in a world filled with shortcuts and temptations. But it is in these moments of difficulty that the strength of your Judgment Core is truly tested. Upholding honesty, fairness, and empathy is not just about avoiding personal guilt—it's about actively contributing to a society where trust is cherished, and everyone feels the impact of collective responsibility.

So, the next time you stand at a crossroads, ask yourself: Will your choice strengthen the bridge of integrity, or will it add another crack? The answer shapes not only your character but the world you leave for those who come after you.

7.10 Control Your Beast: Patience and Suppressing Anger

A quiet forest at dusk. The air is still, the ground damp, and a shadow moves just beyond your sight—a powerful beast prowling silently, waiting for the right moment to act. It's neither friend nor foe; its nature depends entirely on how you approach it. Do you command it with calm resolve, keeping it at bay? Or do you let it loose, unleashing chaos on everything around you?

This beast is your anger—an ancient, primal force dwelling within. It's a double-edged sword: protective in some moments, destructive in others. The challenge is not to deny its existence but to master it. The question is: when the beast stirs, will you hold the reins or let it dictate your actions?

Anger is a part of us, a natural instinct that has evolved to protect and empower. At its best, it drives action against injustice, asserts boundaries, and fuels determination. But when anger takes control, it transforms into a destructive force, breaking trust, severing relationships, and leaving scars—on others and yourself.

Uncontrolled anger blinds reason and distorts your Judgment Core, the internal compass that guides your moral decisions. Like a fire left unchecked, it consumes everything in its path, leaving behind irreparable damage. Taming this beast is not about suppressing it but about harnessing its power. The goal is to transform raw emotion into measured action.

Imagine your anger as a wild animal on a leash. If you tug too tightly, you risk suppressing something that could protect you. But if you let it roam unchecked, it can wreak havoc. The art lies in balance—knowing when to pull back and when to let it stride forward with purpose.

Words spoken in anger are like arrows shot blindly—they may hit their target, but the wounds they leave may never fully heal. In the heat of the moment, a single cruel remark can unravel years of trust, love, or respect. The temporary satisfaction of lashing out often gives way to deep regret and an aftermath that lingers far longer than the flash of rage.

Ask yourself:

- How many relationships have suffered because of words said in anger?

- How often have you wished to take back something you said, only to realize it's too late?

Anger, when left unchecked, not only harms those around you but erodes your own sense of integrity. It becomes a test of your Judgment Core, challenging whether you can pause long enough to avoid inflicting unnecessary pain.

The next time anger surges, imagine the long-term consequences before you speak. Can you hold back, breathe deeply, and reflect on whether the momentary release is worth the lasting damage? Often, the answer lies in patience.

Patience is a virtue, but it is not infinite. Smart patience means discerning when to extend understanding and when to set firm boundaries. It's the balance between staying calm in the face of provocation and knowing when to walk away from harmful situations. Patience isn't about enduring mistreatment—it's about choosing your battles wisely and asserting yourself with clarity.

There are times when anger is justified—when boundaries are violated or values are threatened. In these moments, suppressing anger entirely may be counterproductive. Instead, channel it into constructive communication. Calmly asserting your feelings and setting boundaries can be more powerful than an outburst of rage.

Smart patience is the ability to weigh the cost of your reactions. It's not about silencing your anger but about ensuring it serves a purpose rather than becoming a weapon.

At its core, controlling your anger is about strengthening your Judgment Core—the internal framework that helps you navigate moments of frustration and conflict. Each time you pause, reflect, and choose patience over impulsivity, you reinforce the integrity of your moral compass.

Anger will always be a part of you, but its impact is determined by how you wield it. Will you let the beast control you, or will you guide it with intention and care? The choice is yours, and every choice shapes the person you become.

So, the next time the beast stirs, take a moment. Breathe. Reflect. And ask yourself: Who will hold the reins—you or the beast?

The Clash Under the Lights

September 8, 2018 – New York City. The Arthur Ashe Stadium buzzed with electric energy as the sun dipped behind the Manhattan skyline. It was the final of the U.S. Open, and a record-breaking crowd of nearly 24,000 fans had gathered to witness history. On one side of the court stood Serena Williams, a titan of the sport with 23 Grand Slam titles, revered as one of the greatest athletes of all time. On the other side, Naomi Osaka, a soft-spoken rising star from Japan, prepared to challenge her idol and etch her name into tennis history.

The stakes were monumental. For Williams, this was a chance to tie Margaret Court's elusive record of 24 Grand Slam titles, a milestone that had eluded her since her return to tennis after giving birth. For Osaka, this was an opportunity to become the first Japanese player to win a Grand Slam, a victory that would inspire millions back home.

The match began with the precision of a chess game and the tension of a tightly wound spring. Williams's powerful serves reverberated like gunshots, while Osaka countered with her sharp angles and unwavering calm. But as the game progressed, the narrative shifted in an unexpected and unforgettable way.

In the second set, with Osaka leading, the first spark of controversy ignited. Umpire Carlos Ramos, a seasoned official known for his strict adherence to the rules, issued Williams a warning for receiving coaching from the stands. Her coach, Patrick Mouratoglou, had been spotted gesturing from the player's box, a violation of the rules.

Williams was incensed. "I don't cheat!" she declared, her voice resolute and her eyes blazing. To her, the accusation wasn't just a penalty—it was an attack on her character, her integrity, her very identity as an athlete. The crowd murmured in unease as the tension between Williams and Ramos escalated.

Moments later, frustration overwhelmed her. After losing a critical point, Williams slammed her racket into the court with a force that echoed through the stadium. The frame shattered, its strings curling like a wounded animal. Ramos issued a second penalty—this time for racket abuse—costing Williams a point.

The crowd gasped, and Williams's anger boiled over. "You're a thief!" she shouted at Ramos, her voice cutting through the din. "You stole a point from me!" It was a raw, unfiltered eruption of emotion, one that laid bare the immense pressure she carried on her shoulders.

Ramos, unmoved, issued a third penalty—a game penalty—effectively handing a game to Osaka. The air in the stadium grew thick with tension, the cheers and boos blending into a cacophony of confusion and disbelief.

Osaka, caught in the crossfire, retreated into herself, her quiet determination battling the overwhelming spectacle unfolding around her.

When the match finally ended, it was Osaka who emerged victorious, securing her first Grand Slam title with a display of precision and poise. Yet, her triumph was overshadowed by the storm of controversy that had engulfed the court.

As the trophy ceremony began, Osaka stood with tears streaming down her face, apologizing to the crowd despite her historic achievement. Williams, in a gesture of grace, wrapped her arm around the young champion and urged the crowd to celebrate Osaka's win. But the damage had been done. The moment that should have belonged to Osaka was forever stained by the clash of emotions that had unfolded on that stage.

The events of that evening became a flashpoint in sports history, sparking debates about sexism, fairness, and the role of emotion in competition. For Williams, the match became a defining moment—not for her athletic prowess, but for the powerful reminder it offered about the beast of anger and the delicate balance of control.

Anger, like a wild animal, has its purpose. It can protect and motivate, serving as a rallying cry against perceived injustice. But unchecked, it becomes destructive, overshadowing the very values it seeks to defend. Williams's outburst, though deeply human, highlighted how even the strongest among us can falter when the beast takes control.

The incident also challenged the Judgment Core of everyone who witnessed it.

- Could the umpire have shown more empathy in such a high-stakes moment?

- Should Williams have managed her emotions differently to protect her legacy and Osaka's spotlight?

- And as spectators, how do we judge moments of vulnerability in our heroes?

The U.S. Open final of 2018 wasn't just a tennis match—it was a mirror held up to human nature. It reminded us of the thin line between passion and loss of control, between standing firm and stepping too far. Williams's struggle was a cautionary tale, urging us to reflect on our own capacity for patience, empathy, and self-control.

As you think about that night, ask yourself:

- How do you react when your integrity feels under attack?

- Can you tame your inner beast when the stakes are highest?

- And when the moment demands it, will your Judgment Core guide you toward control—or let the beast dictate your path?

The answers lie not just in the heat of competition but in the quiet moments of reflection that follow. What will your answer be when it's your turn to stand at the crossroads?

The Day the Beast Took Over

May 19, 1996 – Kent, England. The late spring sun bathed the Kent motorway in a pale golden light as cars sped toward their destinations, the hum of engines blending into the rhythm of a typical Sunday afternoon. Among the travelers that day was Kenneth Noye, a wealthy British businessman whose reputation hinted at a darker past—a man known for his sharp temper and willingness to cross lines others dared not. In another car just ahead was Stephen Cameron, a spirited young man in his twenties, accompanied by his fiancée. Neither knew that their lives were about to intersect in a way that would leave a permanent scar on both their families and the nation's collective memory.

It began with a minor incident—an accidental cut-off on the road. A flash of brake lights, a honk of a horn, and a flurry of frustration ignited tensions between the two drivers. What could have ended with a wave of apology or averted glance quickly escalated. Noye and Cameron pulled over on the roadside, their simmering anger urging them to settle the matter face-to-face.

Witnesses would later describe the scene: two men standing inches apart, voices raised, fists clenched. The argument, fueled by pride and unchecked tempers, spiraled into something far more dangerous. Cameron, youthful and fiery, refused to back down. Noye, seasoned and hardened, allowed his frustration to boil over into fury.

And then it happened—the moment where reason gave way to rage. Noye reached into his car, pulling out a knife. In one swift, unthinking act, he plunged it into Cameron. The younger man collapsed to the ground as his fiancée screamed in horror. The golden afternoon now seemed steeped in shadow, the motorway silenced by the weight of a senseless tragedy.

Noye, realizing the gravity of what he'd done, fled the scene. His car roared away, leaving Cameron's fiancée cradling her dying partner, her cries echoing across the quiet motorway. A routine drive had become an unspeakable nightmare, one that would haunt everyone involved for the rest of their lives.

As news of the stabbing spread, Kenneth Noye became the target of a nationwide manhunt. His past—a criminal history involving gold smuggling and suspicions of ties to organized crime—painted him as a man familiar with evasion. True to form, Noye disappeared, slipping through the cracks of justice and vanishing into the shadows of Europe. For two years, he lived as a fugitive, moving between safe houses, his face plastered on wanted posters across the UK.

The Cameron family, meanwhile, grappled with the devastating loss of Stephen. The young man, full of life and promise, was gone in an instant, leaving behind a void that no trial or conviction could ever fill.

Noye's escape ended in 1998, when Spanish authorities tracked him down and arrested him in a quiet coastal town. Extradited to the UK, he stood trial in 2000, facing the full weight of the law. The court heard chilling testimony about the events of that day, and the jury returned a verdict of guilty. Noye was sentenced to life imprisonment, the final chapter in a story of rage and recklessness.

The murder of Stephen Cameron serves as a grim testament to the destructive power of unchecked anger. In a fleeting moment of fury, Noye allowed his "inner beast" to dictate his actions, obliterating not only Cameron's life but his own future and the peace of two families. For the Camerons, the loss of their son was an irreparable wound. For Noye's family, the knowledge of his crime became a lifelong burden.

This tragedy challenges us to confront the fragility of self-control. Anger is a natural emotion—an ancient survival mechanism designed to protect us—but when unleashed without restraint, it can spiral into violence, leaving devastation in its wake. Moments like these test the Judgment Core, the internal compass that guides our moral decisions and helps us navigate the gray areas of human behavior.

- What stops a fleeting moment of anger from turning into irreversible action?

- How do we ensure that our moral compass remains intact in the face of provocation?

- And when the beast within threatens to rise, can we summon the strength to tame it?

The story of Kenneth Noye and Stephen Cameron is more than a cautionary tale about road rage—it is a mirror reflecting the choices we all face when anger beckons. It reminds us that while anger is universal, our response to it defines who we are.

In moments of frustration, ask yourself:

- Will you let a fleeting emotion dictate your actions, or will you pause to reflect on the consequences?

- When faced with provocation, can you draw on your Judgment Core to guide you toward restraint?

- How would you want to be remembered—in control of your emotions or consumed by them?

Life is filled with moments where anger flares and choices must be made. The tragedy on the Kent motorway stands as a stark reminder that those choices, however brief, can echo for a lifetime. What will your choice be when the beast within stirs?

The Melody of Justice: A Tale of a Broken Guitar

March 2008 – Chicago O'Hare International Airport. The hustle and chaos of Chicago O'Hare hummed in the background as Dave Carroll, a Canadian musician, peered out the window of a United Airlines plane during a layover. He had spent years on the road with his band, Sons of Maxwell, but this flight to Omaha, Nebraska, carried an air of routine. That is, until he noticed something unsettling on the tarmac.

There they were—United Airlines baggage handlers, tossing suitcases and bags with little care. His stomach sank as he saw his prized possession, a $3,500 Taylor guitar, sail through the air and land with a sickening thud. He couldn't unsee it. The crack of his guitar's neck played in his mind before he even opened the case.

When Carroll arrived in Omaha and unlatched the guitar case, his worst fears materialized. The neck of his beloved Taylor was splintered. His constant companion, the instrument that carried the soul of his music, was broken. Disheartened but determined, Carroll did what anyone might do—he reported the incident to United Airlines, trusting they would take responsibility for the damage.

What followed was a frustrating spiral into corporate apathy. Carroll's complaint was met with redirection, denial, and indifference. Weeks turned into months as he navigated the labyrinth of United Airlines' customer service. His calls were shuffled between departments. Emails went unanswered. Every interaction ended in the same refrain: "We are not liable."

Nine months of relentless effort led nowhere. Carroll's patience wore thin as his pleas for justice seemed to evaporate into the void. At every turn, he faced a wall of bureaucracy, the airline's apathy eroding his faith in fairness

Carroll stood at a crossroads. He could let his frustration consume him, lashing out in anger, or he could take a different path—a path guided by creativity and resilience. His Judgment Core, that inner moral compass that guides decisions, whispered a third option.

"If they won't hear my words," Carroll mused, "perhaps they'll listen to my music." And so, he turned to what he knew best: storytelling through song. In July 2009, he released "United Breaks Guitars," a satirical anthem recounting his experience with the airline.

The song's catchy lyrics and biting humor resonated with travelers worldwide:

"I should have flown with someone else, or gone by car,

" Cause United breaks guitars."

He uploaded the video to YouTube, expecting a modest reaction. Instead, the response was electric. Within hours, the video began to spread like wildfire, racking up millions of views. Travelers across the globe related to his plight, sharing their own tales of mistreatment. Carroll had struck a chord—not just with his music, but with a universal frustration.

The impact was immediate and devastating for United Airlines. Public backlash mounted as Carroll's song became a rallying cry for dissatisfied customers. Social media lit up with conversations about poor customer service, and United's reputation took a nosedive. Reportedly, the airline's stock value dropped by 10%, costing shareholders roughly $180 million.

United Airlines finally reached out to Carroll, offering compensation and an apology. But the damage was done. The viral storm had changed the narrative. Carroll's creative approach to injustice had shone a harsh light on corporate indifference, forcing the airline to reckon with its neglect.

For Carroll, the experience was transformative. His measured response, born out of frustration, launched him into a new role as an advocate for customer service reform. He became a speaker, using his story to highlight the importance of integrity in business and the power of respectful engagement.

Dave Carroll's tale is more than a viral success story—it is a reminder of the profound impact of the choices we make in moments of anger. When faced with injustice, Carroll's Judgment Core guided him to channel his frustration into something meaningful. Instead of succumbing to the destructive power of rage, he harnessed his creativity, proving that patience and ingenuity can transform even the most frustrating circumstances into powerful lessons.

- What would you do if faced with similar indifference? Would your anger consume you, or could you find a way to create change?

- When systems fail and frustrations mount, can your Judgment Core guide you to a response that uplifts rather than destroys?

- What legacy will your actions leave behind—a trail of conflict, or a melody that inspires others to act with integrity?

Carroll's story challenges us to reflect on how we handle adversity. His path—marked by creativity, resilience, and integrity—reminds us that even when others fail us, we have the power to rise above, leaving behind not just lessons, but a lasting legacy.

So, the next time you face an unjust moment, ask yourself: What song will you write?

Conclusion - Taming the Beast: Who Holds Your Leash?

A shadowed forest at dusk, the air thick with tension as an unseen predator prowls nearby. You hear its heavy breath, feel its raw power, and know it could either protect or destroy. This is your beast—anger—ancient, primal, and powerful. It waits within, coiled and ready, watching for the moment when your guard falters. But here's the truth: the beast isn't your enemy. It is a force you can command, or it can command you. The choice is yours.

Anger, like a wild beast, has its place. It can shield you, give you strength, and ignite action when faced with injustice. Yet, when unleashed without control, it ravages everything in its path—relationships, reputations, and your sense of self. Each time you let the beast slip its leash, you risk becoming its prey, consumed by the chaos it creates.

- How often have you released the beast in moments of frustration, only to regret the scars it left behind?

- Have you ever stopped to wonder if the wounds it inflicts—on others and yourself—are worth the fleeting satisfaction of rage?

- And when the beast rages, does it honor your values, or does it pull you further from them?

Unchecked anger isn't just a fleeting emotion; it's a test of your Judgment Core, the moral compass that guides your actions. Like a trainer with a wild animal, you must learn to tame the beast within—not by suppressing it, but by understanding its purpose. Each time you pause before reacting, each moment you choose reflection over impulsivity, you strengthen the chains of control and reinforce your inner strength.

But taming the beast doesn't mean silencing it. Even the wildest creatures have their moments of purpose. Anger, when directed with precision, can be a force for justice and protection. It can help you set boundaries and stand firm against wrongdoing. The key lies in balance: knowing when to unleash the beast's power and when to hold it back.

- Can you recognize the moments when patience is the wiser choice?

- When anger stirs, will you summon the strength to leash it, or will you let it rule you?

- And when the beast is calm, do you reflect on the path it has left behind?

Every time you allow the beast to run wild, it leaves destruction in its wake. Words spoken in anger become arrows that pierce deeply, leaving wounds that may never heal. Relationships, carefully nurtured over years, can shatter in a single moment. Yet, when you guide the beast with intention, its power becomes a tool—a source of strength and a guardian of your values.

Patience, like a sturdy leash, is your greatest ally in taming the beast. But patience must be smart and deliberate. It is not about enduring harm or turning a blind eye to injustice. It is about knowing when to extend understanding and when to draw firm boundaries. Smart patience allows you to channel your anger constructively, ensuring it serves your principles rather than undermines them.

The beast within is neither good nor evil—it is a part of you, waiting to be shaped by your choices. When the moment comes and the beast stirs, the question is not whether it will act, but whether you will control it. Your Judgment Core is the trainer, the guide that ensures your anger remains a force for good rather than destruction.

- When the beast prowls, will you tame it or let it rule you?

- Can you use its power to protect what matters without losing sight of your values?

- And when the storm passes, will you look back with pride or regret?

The beast is always there, watching, waiting. It is not your enemy but your test—a reflection of your inner strength and your ability to navigate the storms of life. Each time you face it, you decide whether to let it define you or to master it.

When the beast stirs again, take a breath. Steady your hand on the leash. And ask yourself: Who will command the beast—you, or the beast itself? This choice, made in the crucible of emotion, will shape the story of who you're and the legacy you leave behind.

7.11 The Lighthouse of Family Love: Unconditional Yet Anchored

A lighthouse standing tall on a rocky shore. Its beam sweeps across the dark waters, offering guidance to ships battling turbulent seas. The light, unwavering and steady, symbolizes unconditional love—always present, always illuminating the path. But the lighthouse doesn't chase the ships or calm the storm; it simply provides direction, allowing the vessels to navigate safely. If it tried to do more, it would fail in its purpose, sinking into the sea it was meant to guide.

Unconditional love within families operates much like that lighthouse—steadfast, nurturing, and forgiving. It provides a sanctuary of trust, a haven of acceptance. Parents love their children despite mistakes; siblings forgive missteps over time; and romantic partners weather life's tempests together. This love is not transactional. It doesn't tally wins and losses but stands firm through life's uncertainties.

Yet even a lighthouse has boundaries—it cannot control the waves or pull ships from peril. Similarly, unconditional love requires limits to remain sustainable. Love without boundaries risks becoming enabling, smothering growth, and fostering dependence. Without clear limits, family relationships can become strained, turning the comfort of unconditional love into a source of exhaustion and resentment.

Families, like the ocean, are unpredictable. We do not choose our family members, but we must navigate their unique temperaments, flaws, and strengths. While familial bonds can be some of the deepest connections in life, they also test patience, challenge empathy, and push the limits of forgiveness. True unconditional love means not only accepting each other but also fostering growth through accountability and respect.

Unconditional love doesn't mean ignoring harmful behavior or shielding loved ones from the consequences of their actions. Over-supporting family members, much like oversteering a ship, can lead to dependency and fragility. By stepping back and allowing loved ones to face challenges, we equip them with the tools to navigate life's storms. This balance—between care and accountability—strengthens not only the individual but the entire family.

Your Judgment Core acts as the compass in these complex waters. It challenges you to consider the balance between love and enabling, between support and self-preservation.

- Can unconditional love exist without boundaries that protect both the giver and receiver?

- Are you empowering your loved ones to grow, or are you shielding them from necessary challenges?

- How does your moral compass guide you in setting limits that uphold respect and dignity while maintaining love?

Setting boundaries is not an act of withholding love—it is an expression of it. Boundaries allow love to thrive in a sustainable, healthy way, preserving the trust, respect, and emotional well-being that form the foundation of family relationships. Like the lighthouse, your role is not to calm the storm but to provide steady guidance.

Unconditional love, when strengthened by thoughtful limits, transforms families into safe harbors. It encourages resilience, fosters independence, and ensures that relationships remain a source of support rather than strain. As you reflect on the waters of your own family dynamics, ask yourself: Are you providing steady light, or are you being pulled into the waves? How will you navigate the balance between love and limits to keep your relationships afloat?

A Ballad of Love and Shadows: The Forsberg-Weiland Story

Los Angeles, 1997. The City of Angels pulsed with electric energy in the late '90s, where neon lights reflected off endless highways and the heartbeat of rock and roll echoed from Sunset Boulevard. It was here, amid the chaos and allure of the music industry, that Mary Forsberg and Scott Weiland first crossed paths. He was the enigmatic frontman of Stone Temple Pilots, a band that dominated airwaves and defined a generation, while she was a striking model with a magnetic presence of her own. Their meeting was as fiery as it was fateful—two souls drawn together by a shared intensity that neither could resist.

By the year 2000, their whirlwind romance had solidified into marriage. The couple settled into a family home nestled in the hills of Beverly Hills, and soon after, welcomed their two children, Noah and Lucy. To outsiders, their life seemed like a dream—music, fame, beauty, and a growing family. Yet, beneath the polished surface, shadows loomed.

Scott's struggles with addiction were no secret. Long before meeting Mary, he had battled the demons of substance abuse, and despite his best efforts, they continued to haunt him. Mary, deeply in love, was determined to help him fight. She stood by his side through countless rehab stays and sleepless nights, believing that her unwavering support and their family's love could anchor him.

Their home became both a sanctuary and a battleground—a place where hope clashed with despair. Mary often found herself playing dual roles: wife and caretaker, lover and protector. Her Judgment Core, the inner compass that guided her decisions, pushed her to give everything she could to save her husband, even when it meant sacrificing her own stability.

In the early hours of a chilly December night in 2007, an event unfolded that would alter their family's course forever. Scott, under the influence, had wandered into the kitchen, intending to cook. Distracted and disoriented, he left the stove unattended. Flames quickly spread, filling the home with thick, acrid smoke.

Mary awoke to the suffocating smell, her heart pounding as she realized the danger. Instinct took over as she rushed to Noah and Lucy's rooms, gathering them in her arms and fleeing into the driveway. As firefighters battled the blaze, she stood outside in her pajamas, holding her terrified children close, the orange glow of the fire illuminating their frightened faces.

Watching smoke pour from their home, Mary made a decision that had been building in her heart for years. Scott's addiction was no longer just his battle—it was a threat to their family's safety. For the sake of her children and herself, she had to walk away.

Shortly after the incident, Mary filed for divorce. It was a heart-wrenching choice, but one she knew was necessary. Despite ending their marriage, her love for Scott remained steadfast. She continued to visit him in rehab, offering encouragement during his relapses and cheering for his victories, however small.

In 2009, Mary shared their story with the world through her memoir, Fall to Pieces: A Memoir of Drugs, Rock 'n' Roll, and Mental Illness. It was a raw, unflinching account of their life together, filled with love, pain, and the lessons she had learned. Through her words, she revealed not only the depths of their struggles but also her enduring belief in Scott's potential for redemption.

On December 3, 2015, Scott Weiland was found lifeless on his tour bus in Minnesota. The cause: an accidental overdose of cocaine, ethanol, and MDA. He was 48 years old. The news sent shockwaves through the music world, but for Mary and their children, it marked the culmination of years of heartache.

Despite their tumultuous past, Mary chose to honor Scott's memory with grace. She became a pillar of strength for Noah and Lucy, helping them process their father's legacy—the good and the bad. Through her actions, she ensured that Scott's story would not be defined solely by his struggles but also by the love he had shared with his family.

Mary's journey is a testament to the delicate balance between unconditional love and self-preservation. Her Judgment Core, the internal moral compass that guided her through years of turmoil, allowed her to see the difference between enabling and supporting. She understood that love doesn't always mean staying—it sometimes means setting boundaries, even when it breaks your heart.

Her story prompts us to reflect on our own moral compass:

- How do we balance love and accountability when someone we care for is on a self-destructive path?

- Can we offer compassion without sacrificing our own well-being?

- When faced with the choice to let go, how do we reconcile love with the necessity of boundaries?

Mary Forsberg's life with Scott Weiland is not just a tale of rock and roll—it's a story of resilience, courage, and the enduring power of love. It reminds us that even in the face of loss, our choices define us, shaping our legacy and the lives of those we hold dear.

So, when love demands a sacrifice, where will your Judgment Core lead you? Will you find the strength to walk away, or will you stay and fight, knowing the risks? The answers lie not in easy solutions but in the quiet resolve to do what's right—even when it's the hardest thing to do.

The Al-Tabarie Brothers: A Bond Forged Through Exile and Sacrifice

Dubai, United Arab Emirates – 2008. The shimmering skyline of Dubai, with its towering skyscrapers and bustling streets, felt worlds apart from the memories of Tabariya—a tranquil city on the shores of the Sea of Galilee that Zahi and Osama Al-Tabarie's family once called home. In 1948, during the Nakba, their grandparents were forced to flee Tabariya as the Israeli invasion swept through the region. The family found refuge in Gaza, but the scars of displacement never faded, passed down through generations like an heirloom of resilience and loss.

By 2008, Zahi and Osama had made lives for themselves in Dubai, far from the struggles of Gaza but always carrying the weight of their family's history. Zahi, the younger of the two, worked as a skilled auto mechanic, known for his diligence and integrity. Osama, the elder brother, had built a career as a technician in a small engineering firm. Though their circumstances were modest, the brothers supported their families back home and found solace in the bond they shared—one forged in shared hardship and unshakable loyalty.

But that year, the global financial crisis struck with unrelenting force, its ripples reaching even the prosperous streets of Dubai. Osama's engineering firm, struggling to stay afloat, announced mass layoffs. Osama was among those let go.

For Osama, the loss of his job was devastating. With a wife and two young children depending on him, the sudden lack of income left him grappling with uncertainty and a growing sense of failure. Desperate to find another job, he combed through advertisements, sent resumes, and took on small temporary gigs, but opportunities were scarce in the shadow of the economic downturn.

Zahi, seeing his brother's distress, didn't hesitate to act. "You're my brother," he told Osama one evening as they shared tea in Zahi's modest apartment. "We've faced harder times as a family. We'll get through this together."

Despite his limited salary as a mechanic, Zahi made the decision to share his income with Osama's family. It was a sacrifice that would stretch his resources to their limits, but Zahi's sense of familial duty was deeply rooted in his identity. He couldn't forget the stories of his grandparents' struggles in Gaza after fleeing Tabariya, or the lessons they had passed down about the strength of family ties. His Judgment Core, the moral compass that guided his actions, left no room for hesitation.

For the next eighteen months, Zahi and his wife, Amal, adjusted to a frugal lifestyle. Every dirham was carefully accounted for, and luxuries were set aside. Family outings were replaced with quiet evenings at home, and any thoughts of new purchases or personal indulgences were put on hold.

Meanwhile, Osama wrestled with his own feelings of guilt and determination. He took on part-time jobs and odd tasks to contribute what he could, but it wasn't enough to sustain his family. Every time he saw Zahi handing over a portion of his hard-earned income, he felt a mix of gratitude and resolve.

"I won't let your sacrifice go to waste," Osama promised his younger brother one evening. "I'll find a way to make things right."

In June 2010, after countless interviews and rejections, Osama finally secured a stable position as a supervisor in a new engineering firm. The relief was immediate and overwhelming. For the first time in nearly two years, both families could breathe easier.

Osama never forgot Zahi's unwavering support during those difficult months. One evening, as the brothers shared a meal, Osama raised a glass of tea in his brother's honor. "You didn't just help me survive, Zahi," he said. "You reminded me of the strength of family and what it means to truly stand by someone."

Zahi smiled, his humility evident. "That's what family is for. Our grandparents survived because they stuck together. We're no different."

The story of Zahi and Osama Al-Tabarie is a testament to the enduring strength of family bonds. Their ancestors had been forced to rebuild their lives after the trauma of losing their homeland, and that resilience carried through to the brothers' actions. Zahi's choice to sacrifice for his brother was not driven by blind duty but by a deep alignment with his Judgment Core—his inner moral compass that prioritized family, loyalty, and perseverance.

Their story challenges us to reflect on our own values:

- How far would you go to support a loved one in their time of need?

- Can you find the balance between self-sacrifice and self-preservation?

- And when faced with challenges, does your Judgment Core guide you to act with compassion, even at personal cost?

The Al-Tabarie brothers' journey reminds us that family is not merely a bond of blood but a commitment to stand by one another through life's trials. Their story, rooted in the resilience of a displaced family, echoes the truth that love and loyalty can help us weather even the most difficult storms.

As you think about their journey, ask yourself:

- What legacy of love and resilience will you build for your family?

- When the time comes to sacrifice, will your Judgment Core guide you to act with strength and compassion?

The answers lie in how we choose to uphold the bonds that connect us—bonds that, like the Al-Tabarie brothers', can become a source of enduring strength in the face of adversity.

Conclusion: Balancing Love and Boundaries

A lighthouse standing resilient against the crashing waves, its beam cutting through the darkness to guide ships safely home. The light symbolizes unconditional love—steady, unwavering, and always present. But even the most steadfast lighthouse cannot chase the ships it guides, nor can it calm the storm. Its purpose is to illuminate the path, not to sail the ship. Like the lighthouse, unconditional love is a guiding force in families, offering support and strength while standing firm within its boundaries.

Unconditional love forms the foundation of family, creating a sanctuary of trust, resilience, and belonging. Parents extend this love to their children without expectation, and spouses choose it daily, nurturing their bond through mutual respect, empathy, and understanding. However, love between spouses is unique—anchored in both choice and commitment. It thrives when partners navigate life as equals, their love fortified by shared values and a continuous effort to understand each other.

In contrast, many family relationships are not chosen. These bonds, though deeply rooted, often test the limits of patience and empathy. While loyalty and support remain pillars of unconditional love in these relationships, they must be tempered by boundaries to prevent unhealthy dynamics. Even the strongest love requires balance to ensure it uplifts without enabling.

For example, the love between spouses is a daily choice, a partnership built on respect and shared effort. Yet, even here, boundaries are vital to avoid one partner's needs overshadowing the other's well-being. Similarly, in parent-child or sibling relationships, unconditional love must allow space for individual growth. Sacrifice is sometimes necessary for the greater good of the family, but even sacrifices must have their limits. True love requires trusting family members to take responsibility for their actions, face consequences, and grow from their experiences.

Stepping in to shield loved ones from every mistake can undermine their ability to develop resilience, accountability, and self-reliance. While it may be tempting to intervene, true support lies in trusting their capacity to navigate challenges and respecting their autonomy. Overextending in the name of love can foster dependency, entitlement, or even resentment, ultimately weakening the very bonds it aims to protect.

Your Judgment Core, the inner compass that shapes your decisions, plays a crucial role in maintaining this balance. It asks you to reflect:

- Are you empowering your loved ones to grow, or are you shielding them from the growth that comes through struggle?

- Can you offer support without losing sight of your own needs and boundaries?

- How do you ensure your love uplifts rather than diminishes, strengthens rather than stifles?

Setting boundaries is not an act of withholding love—it is an expression of it. By creating a space where love and respect coexist, boundaries ensure relationships remain sources of strength and trust. They allow love to thrive sustainably, protecting both the giver and receiver from the strain of imbalance.

Unconditional love is not about removing every obstacle or sparing loved ones from every hardship. It is about standing as a guiding light, steadfast but grounded, offering support without becoming the vessel that carries their burdens. Just as the lighthouse remains anchored on the shore, unconditional love requires firm roots—boundaries that preserve its strength and purpose.

So, as you reflect on the dynamics of your family relationships, ask yourself:

- Are you the lighthouse, guiding with steady light, or are you trying to weather the storm for others?

- How does your Judgment Core guide you in balancing love, sacrifice, and self-preservation?

- Are you empowering your loved ones to sail their own ships, or are you unknowingly taking the helm?

True familial love is not measured by the weight of sacrifices made but by the resilience, independence, and mutual respect it fosters. It is a bond strengthened by limits and trust—a legacy of love that shines brightly through life's darkest storms. When the waves crash and the winds howl, will your love stand tall like the lighthouse, or will it lose its purpose by chasing every ship? The answers lie in your Judgment Core, where love and limits merge to create a guiding light for those you hold dear.

7.12 Unconditional Love & Support for "Human Angel"

You're walking into a serene garden at twilight, where a single, radiant flower stands apart from the rest. Its petals are luminous, glowing softly as though lit from within. You're drawn to it, sensing its fragility and its strength. Caring for this flower requires patience and devotion, yet its radiance fills the entire garden with light. This flower is a metaphor for the "Human Angel" in your life—a sibling or child with special needs—whose presence brings profound meaning and an opportunity to grow in love and purpose.

Caring for a sibling or child with special needs is a journey that demands immense strength, patience, and sacrifice. It's natural to feel overwhelmed at times, questioning whether you're capable of handling such responsibility. But this role is not a punishment; it's a sacred trust. Some believe that children born with disabilities—whether physical, visual, or mental—are gifted souls who embody purity and innocence. In many spiritual traditions, it is said that they are already destined for heaven, untouched by the burdens of judgment on the Day of Judgment because they never had the privileges or choices the rest of us do.

These "Human Angels" are believed to be your key to heaven. Their lives, marked by challenges and struggles, offer you a unique opportunity to grow closer to the divine through your love and support. By easing their pain, sharing their burdens, and celebrating their victories, you partake in a sacred exchange. Their suffering is lessened, their lives are brightened, and in return, you're enveloped by their holy sphere—a sphere of purity and grace that blesses everyone it touches.

Their daily existence is a testament to resilience. Simple tasks that most take for granted—tying a shoe, speaking a word, or completing a chore—become monumental achievements for them. Their courage in facing these challenges reminds us of the strength of the human spirit. And while they may rely on you for support, their presence reshapes your understanding of life, teaching you compassion, humility, and the boundless power of love.

From a spiritual perspective, your dedication to a "Human Angel" is seen as an act of immense merit. By supporting them, you'ren't just helping them navigate life's difficulties—you're actively reducing their suffering and sharing in their journey. This selflessness, many believe, aligns you with divine blessings and rewards beyond measure. Through their unique light, they guide you toward a deeper connection with the divine, reminding you that your care for them is a path to spiritual fulfillment and, ultimately, heaven.

Even without a spiritual lens, the rewards of such a role are profound. Each small triumph becomes a celebration of perseverance and love. Your Judgment Core, the moral compass that shapes your actions, grows stronger with every act of kindness and every moment of patience. You learn to find joy in the simplest moments, and your empathy deepens as you walk alongside someone navigating a path filled with challenges. These experiences redefine your understanding of success and fulfillment, showing you that true happiness is rooted in love and connection.

As you reflect on your role in their life, ask yourself:

- How does caring for a "Human Angel" strengthen your Judgment Core, shaping your understanding of love and purpose?

- Can you see their challenges not as limitations but as opportunities to create a deeper bond?

- Do you recognize their presence as a source of divine blessing and guidance in your own life?

Supporting a sibling or child with special needs is not merely a responsibility—it is a profound gift. Their lives, filled with both struggles and triumphs, illuminate the path to compassion, selflessness, and spiritual growth. They are more than a loved one in need; they are a reminder of life's deeper purpose, a guiding light, and, for many, the key to heaven itself. others.

The Silent Voice: Carly Fleischmann's Journey

In the winter of 1995, as snow blanketed the streets of Toronto, Canada, Tammy and Arthur Fleischmann welcomed their daughter, Carly, into the world. Their home buzzed with excitement as they imagined a future filled with milestones, laughter, and the joy of watching Carly grow. But by Carly's second birthday, a quiet uncertainty began to take hold. Her gaze rarely met theirs, her words never came, and her reactions to the world around her seemed perplexing and, at times, overwhelming.

Doctors eventually confirmed what Tammy and Arthur had begun to suspect: Carly had severe autism and an oral-motor condition that made speech impossible. The diagnosis was both a relief and a devastating blow. Their daughter's world was locked away, and they were left with questions that no one could answer.

The Fleischmanns embarked on a path filled with challenges. Carly's autism was relentless. Sudden noises, bright lights, and even the feel of certain fabrics could trigger meltdowns. Tammy and Arthur worked tirelessly, immersing themselves in behavioral, speech, and occupational therapies. Days turned into years of appointments, routines, and adjustments, yet Carly remained a mystery—a silent presence in their lives.

By the time Carly turned eleven in 2006, the family had grown accustomed to their daily struggles but still longed for a breakthrough. Then, one day, the silence broke.

During a routine therapy session, Carly suddenly reached for a computer and typed, "Help teeth hurt." The room fell silent. Carly's therapist, Barb Nash, and her parents stared at the screen, stunned. This was no fluke. Carly had not only understood the world around her but had found a way to communicate.

That single sentence opened a floodgate. Carly began typing more, revealing the depths of her inner world. "It feels like my legs are on fire, and I want to run," she explained about her meltdowns. For the first time, her family understood the pain and chaos she endured daily. Carly's words transformed the Fleischmanns' relationship with her. She was no longer just a child lost in silence—she was a vibrant soul with thoughts, humor, and a keen awareness of the world.

Her siblings, Taryn and Matthew, adapted to this new dynamic with grace, learning patience and understanding far beyond their years. As Carly's voice grew stronger, she became an advocate not just for herself but for the broader autism community.

In 2012, the Fleischmanns published Carly's Voice: Breaking Through Autism, a memoir chronicling their journey. It became a beacon of hope for families navigating similar challenges. Carly's candid explanations about sensory overload and the behaviors it triggered dismantled stereotypes and fostered empathy.

Carly's influence extended to social media, where she used her platform to educate the world about autism. She became a voice for the voiceless, her courage inspiring countless others. Her advocacy resonated deeply, reminding people that those with special needs have rich inner lives, filled with dreams and struggles just like anyone else.

For Tammy and Arthur, Carly's breakthrough was transformative. Supporting Carly taught them the profound depth of unconditional love. They discovered that such love is not about fixing or changing someone but about creating space for them to thrive. It also meant setting boundaries—recognizing when to push Carly toward independence and when to step back and trust her capabilities.

Their journey was not without sacrifices. Managing Carly's needs tested their marriage, strained finances, and reshaped their priorities. Yet, the rewards were immeasurable. Tammy described it as a spiritual calling: "We were chosen to be Carly's parents because we had the strength to help her find her way."

Carly's story also touched on a spiritual belief held by many—that children with special needs are divine gifts. Seen as "keys to heaven," they embody innocence and purity, untouched by the complexities of moral judgment. Caring for them is seen as a sacred duty, one that aligns the caregiver's Judgment Core, their moral compass, with acts of compassion and selflessness.

As Carly continued to advocate for herself and others, the Fleischmanns embraced the lessons she brought into their lives: resilience, empathy, and the understanding that true love transcends barriers. Carly's journey reminded them—and the world—that every voice matters, even the ones that take years to emerge.

Her story leaves us with profound questions:

- How do we find strength in the face of overwhelming challenges?

- Can we see caregiving not as a burden but as an opportunity to grow?

- How does our own Judgment Core guide us in moments of struggle and doubt, reminding us of the transformative power of love?

Carly Fleischmann's journey is more than a tale of overcoming adversity—it's a testament to the enduring bond of family, the courage to persist, and the belief that every life, no matter how different, carries infinite value.

Max and Jake: The Tilk Family's Extraordinary Journey

In the quiet town of Ashland, Michigan, on a crisp autumn evening in 2003, the Tilk family gathered to welcome their newest member: a baby boy named Max. His arrival brought light and joy into their modest home, and no one was more excited than his older brother, Jake, a curious and spirited four-year-old. Jake had grand plans for his little brother—they would share toys, tell secrets, and conquer the world together.

As the years passed, however, the family began noticing subtle differences in Max's behavior. By the time he was two, it was clear that Max wasn't following the same developmental path as his peers. He avoided eye contact, didn't respond to his name, and his words came slowly, if at all. Concern turned into determination, and the Tilks sought answers. In 2006, after a series of evaluations, they were told Max had autism.

For Tammy and Mike Tilk, the diagnosis was a turning point. The future they had envisioned for Max felt uncertain, but one thing was clear: they would do whatever it took to support their son. For Jake, then seven, the news was harder to grasp. "Why doesn't Max talk like me?" he would ask, his young mind grappling with a reality he couldn't fully understand. But as time went on, Jake became more than a brother—he became Max's protector, his advocate, and his greatest cheerleader.

Navigating life with Max was a lesson in patience and adaptability. Max's autism manifested in unique ways: he found comfort in routines, struggled with sensory overload, and often grew frustrated when he couldn't communicate his needs. Simple tasks like visiting a grocery store became intricate missions requiring careful planning. Birthday parties and family gatherings, with their loud noises and chaotic energy, were often overwhelming for Max, and the Tilks learned to adapt their lives to ensure his comfort.

For Jake, growing up alongside Max was both challenging and transformative. He learned to recognize the subtle cues in Max's behavior, understanding when his brother needed quiet, comfort, or reassurance. Their bond deepened through shared experiences—building block towers, watching the same cartoon episode on repeat, and celebrating small victories that felt monumental.

"I realized pretty early that Max saw the world differently," Jake reflected years later. "But that didn't make his world any less beautiful."

In 2018, now a college student, Jake decided to share their story. He created a TikTok account, @mybrothermax, as a way to document Max's unique personality and bring awareness to autism. What began as a small project quickly gained momentum. Jake posted videos of Max's routines, their humorous banter, and heartwarming moments of connection. One particularly popular clip showed Max's reaction to a surprise birthday gift—his joyful laughter resonated with viewers around the world.

Within months, their account had millions of followers. People from all walks of life were captivated by Max's charm and Jake's unwavering dedication. Through their videos, Jake provided an honest glimpse into their lives, highlighting both the challenges and the joys of supporting someone with autism.

"Max's autism is just one part of who he is," Jake explained in one video. "He's funny, curious, and loves life in a way that inspires me every day."

In April 2022, Max and Jake's story caught the attention of CBS Mornings. The brothers appeared on the show, sharing their journey and their mission to promote acceptance and understanding for individuals with autism. For the Tilk family, this was a moment of validation—a recognition of the years of love, effort, and patience they had poured into building a life that celebrated Max's uniqueness.

Tammy and Mike watched proudly as Jake spoke on national television, describing how Max had shaped not only his life but the family as a whole. "Max has taught us to see the world differently," Tammy said during the segment. "He's shown us that love doesn't have to fit into a box—it just has to be real."

Max and Jake's story is more than a tale of sibling love; it's a testament to the resilience of the human spirit. The Tilks' journey has become a beacon for families navigating similar paths, offering hope, understanding, and community.

Max's influence extends far beyond his family. His story challenges society to rethink perceptions of autism and embrace neurodiversity as a strength rather than a limitation. Jake's unwavering support reminds us that love, when paired with patience and advocacy, can create ripples of change that reach far beyond a single family.

The Tilks' journey prompts us to examine our own Judgment Core—the moral compass that guides our choices in the face of challenges. Jake's dedication to Max wasn't born out of obligation; it stemmed from a deep-seated belief in the power of love and acceptance. Their story encourages us to ask:

- How do we respond when life presents us with unexpected challenges?

- Can we embrace differences, not as obstacles, but as opportunities to grow?

- Are we willing to see beauty in perspectives that differ from our own?

Max and Jake continue to share their lives with the world, spreading a message of hope, resilience, and understanding. Their bond serves as a reminder that unconditional love is not about fixing someone but about standing beside them as they navigate their path.

For the Tilk family, Max is not just a challenge to overcome—he is a blessing, a teacher, and a reminder that love's greatest strength lies in its ability to adapt, endure, and uplift. As Jake once said, "Max doesn't just make our family better—he makes the world better, one smile at a time."

Conclusion - Crossroads of Compassion: Embracing the Sacred Journey

You're standing at a crossroads, where the path ahead is shrouded in mystery, illuminated only by the faint glow of a distant light. Each step forward is uncertain, yet filled with purpose. Caring for a loved one with special needs is much like this journey—challenging, transformative, and ultimately profound. It is not merely a responsibility but a sacred calling that reshapes the very essence of who you're.

Supporting a family member with determination transforms ordinary moments into extraordinary milestones. A single spoken word, a calm gaze, or a gentle smile becomes a triumph worthy of celebration. Yet, along with these joys come moments of exhaustion, heartache, and self-doubt. The demands are relentless, stretching emotional, physical, and financial resources to their limits. Still, within these challenges lies the opportunity for profound growth—a chance to strengthen your Judgment Core, the moral compass that guides your actions and decisions.

Caring for someone with special needs often feels isolating. The world outside may not fully grasp the depth of your journey, but this isolation brings clarity: the realization that love transcends convenience and comfort. It pushes you to reevaluate what truly matters, aligning your values with the purest forms of compassion, patience, and resilience.

For those who view life through a spiritual lens, this journey takes on even greater significance. Many believe that individuals with determination are "keys to heaven," sent to families as divine gifts. These loved ones, unable to be judged by the same standards as others, are often seen as pure souls destined for paradise. By supporting them, families are not only helping to ease their struggles but are also earning blessings and rewards that transcend this life. If they are keys to heaven, what doors could their presence unlock in your life?

This sacred responsibility challenges us to confront profound questions about our own moral compass:

- Are we willing to see this journey not as a burden but as a privilege, shaping us into better, more empathetic people?

- How do we balance sacrifice and self-preservation, ensuring we support our loved ones without losing ourselves in the process?

- What can we learn from their resilience, their joy in simplicity, and their ability to persevere through challenges we might find unimaginable?

Your Judgment Core is tested in these moments of decision: to act with love even when you're weary, to set boundaries that preserve your well-being, and to see beauty in the struggles that others may overlook. It becomes a guide, reminding you that growth and purpose often emerge from life's most challenging trials.

For those outside these families, the question is equally poignant:

- How can you lend support to these caregivers who often bear their responsibilities in silence?

- Are you willing to offer understanding, kindness, or even a moment of respite to lighten their load?

- Can you step into their journey, even briefly, and recognize the profound courage it requires?

In the end, caring for someone with special needs is a path that reshapes your understanding of love, resilience, and humanity. It teaches that success isn't measured by external achievements but by the depth of our compassion and the strength of our connections. These individuals, the "keys to heaven," remind us that in supporting one another, we align ourselves with something eternal—an enduring truth that love, in its purest form, transforms not only those we care for but ourselves as well.

So, as you reflect on this journey, ask yourself:

- Will you embrace the sacred responsibility with an open heart and a steadfast spirit?

- How will you let this experience shape your moral compass and redefine your purpose?

- And when faced with the challenges of caregiving, will you see them as obstacles—or as opportunities to grow closer to the divine?

The answers lie not in words but in actions, in the choices you make each day to honor the gift of love and care. The journey may be arduous, but its rewards are immeasurable, echoing in this life and beyond. How will you navigate it? That is for your Judgment Core to decide.

7.13 Navigating the Gray Area: Balancing Right and Wrong

You're standing in a dense forest at dusk, where the fading light casts long shadows and distorts your path. The trail ahead splits into two, neither marked nor clear. One route appears well-trodden but veers into darkness; the other is overgrown and mysterious, offering no guarantees of safety. You must choose, but the right decision is not immediately obvious. This is the essence of navigating the gray areas of life—moments where the lines between right and wrong are blurred, and every step forward feels uncertain.

Right and wrong are rarely absolutes. They often exist on a spectrum influenced by context, intent, and consequences. Life's challenges frequently place us in situations where moral clarity seems like an unattainable ideal, and the black-and-white rules of childhood dissolve into complex shades of gray. It's in these moments that the Judgment Core (JDC)—our internal moral compass—becomes critical, guiding us through ambiguity with values shaped by experience, empathy, and introspection.

Navigating these murky waters requires flexibility and a nuanced understanding of ethics. The simplistic application of rigid moral codes often falters in the face of competing values, unforeseen outcomes, or conflicting responsibilities. Instead, one must balance competing priorities and weigh potential consequences, striving to minimize harm while remaining true to their principles.

Consider a whistleblower faced with a dilemma: expose wrongdoing within their organization, knowing it is ethically right, or remain silent to preserve loyalty, job security, and personal relationships. While unveiling corruption may seem like the "correct" choice on the surface, the repercussions—damaged trust, financial instability, or personal risk—can be profound. This scenario exemplifies the complexity of gray areas, where every option carries moral weight and personal consequences.

To navigate these challenges, one must draw on foundational principles:

- Empathy, to understand the perspectives and experiences of those affected by the decision.

- Fairness, to ensure that actions are equitable and just for all involved.

- Integrity, to stay true to one's core values, even when the path forward is unclear.

- Minimizing harm, to act in ways that reduce unnecessary suffering or negative consequences.

These principles act as anchors, helping us maintain stability when the tides of uncertainty threaten to pull us under. They align with the essence of the Judgment Core, which adapts to life's complexities without abandoning the values that define us.

As you reflect on your own journey, consider these questions:

- When faced with morally ambiguous situations, do you prioritize context or adhere strictly to established rules?

- How does your Judgment Core influence your ability to weigh competing values and responsibilities?

- Can you approach gray areas with a balance of compassion, fairness, and pragmatism, even when the stakes are high?

Navigating the gray area is not about finding perfect answers—it's about making thoughtful, principled choices in the face of uncertainty. It challenges us to grow, to question, and to act with integrity, even when the path forward is unclear. How will your Judgment Core guide you when the light fades, and the trail splits before you? The answer lies not in the destination but in the decisions you make along the way.

Edward Snowden: The Whistleblower in Exile

In the stillness of a Hawaiian night in 2013, Edward Snowden sat alone in his modest home, the glow of his laptop illuminating his face. Outside, the waves lapped gently against the shore, a serene contrast to the storm brewing in his mind. Deep in the underground corridors of the National Security Agency's (NSA) Hawaiian facility, where he worked as a contractor, Snowden had stumbled upon something unsettling—a trove of classified information revealing the staggering scope of government surveillance. It wasn't just foreign intelligence targets; it was ordinary Americans. Their phone calls, emails, and online activities were being collected, analyzed, and stored. The NSA's programs operated in the shadows, far from public scrutiny, and far from the principles Snowden believed a democracy should uphold.

For weeks, Snowden wrestled with his conscience. His Judgment Core—the internal compass shaped by his experiences, values, and principles—pulled him in opposing directions. He understood the gravity of what he had uncovered. If he remained silent, he would be complicit in what he saw as a massive violation of privacy rights. But if he spoke out, the consequences would be life-altering. Could he justify breaking the law to uphold what he believed was a higher moral obligation?

In May 2013, Snowden made his choice. Leaving behind his job, his home, and the life he had built in Hawaii, he boarded a plane to Hong Kong, carrying with him thousands of classified documents. It was a calculated and risky move. In Hong Kong, Snowden connected with journalists from The Guardian and The Washington Post. Together, they meticulously prepared to reveal the NSA's surveillance programs to the world.

On June 5, 2013, the first article broke, sending shockwaves across the globe. The leaked documents exposed a labyrinth of programs like PRISM, which allowed the NSA to access data from major tech companies, and others that indiscriminately collected phone records and online activities. Snowden's revelations ignited a fierce debate about the balance between national security and individual privacy.

The world's reaction was immediate and polarized. Privacy advocates and civil liberties groups hailed Snowden as a whistleblower, a hero who had risked everything to reveal the truth. His actions forced governments and corporations to confront uncomfortable questions about transparency, accountability, and the ethical limits of surveillance. For others, however, Snowden was a traitor. Critics argued that his disclosures jeopardized national security, endangered lives, and damaged critical intelligence operations.

As the controversy grew, Snowden's own life became a testament to the high cost of navigating the moral gray area. Charged with espionage and theft of government property, he faced decades in prison if he returned to the United States. In a desperate bid for refuge, Snowden fled to Moscow, where he was granted temporary asylum. It was a bitter irony—seeking shelter in a nation not known for its commitment to transparency and civil liberties.

Snowden's exile in Russia became as much a symbol as his revelations. Living in a country far from his ideals, he remained steadfast in his belief that the public had a right to know about the surveillance programs that shaped their lives. Over the years, Snowden transformed into a global figurehead for privacy rights and government accountability, writing books, giving interviews, and participating in digital conferences from his secluded residence.

In 2022, nearly a decade into his exile, Snowden was granted Russian citizenship. While the world debated his legacy, Snowden continued to warn of new threats. By 2024, his focus had shifted to artificial intelligence, a technology he described as "both a marvel and a menace."

He urged caution, emphasizing the need for ethical frameworks to prevent AI from becoming a tool of unchecked surveillance.

Snowden's journey is not one of simple answers. It is a story steeped in mystery, moral complexity, and enduring questions:

- Was Snowden's decision to leak classified documents an act of treachery, or a courageous stand for democratic values?

- Can the violation of laws ever be justified in pursuit of a higher moral principle?

- How does society balance the need for security with the fundamental right to privacy?

Snowden's Judgment Core, shaped by his belief in transparency and accountability, guided him through one of the most consequential decisions of his life. His story challenges us to examine our own moral compasses. When faced with a choice between following the rules and doing what we believe is right, what path would we take?

As Snowden's life continues in exile, his actions remain a lightning rod for debate. He serves as a reminder that navigating the gray area requires not just courage but a willingness to bear the consequences of one's convictions. In the end, Snowden's story is less about whether he was right or wrong and more about the questions he forces us to ask about our own values, our governments, and the kind of world we want to live in.

So, what would you do if your principles collided with the law? Would your Judgment Core guide you to act, or would you remain silent, weighed down by fear and uncertainty? The answers lie not in Snowden's choices, but in the decisions each of us makes when faced with the gray areas of our own lives.

The Lifeboat Dilemma: A Haunting Choice

It was the summer of 1974, and Garrett Hardin, a philosopher and ecologist, sat at his desk in Santa Barbara, California, crafting a provocative essay that would leave an indelible mark on ethical discourse. "Lifeboat Ethics: The Case Against Helping the Poor" emerged not merely as an intellectual exercise but as a haunting exploration of moral ambiguity—a mirror held up to humanity's greatest dilemmas.

Now imagine yourself cast adrift in the middle of an endless ocean, the sun scorching down on a solitary lifeboat. It's December 1974, and a shipwreck has left you and 29 others floating in a small vessel designed to hold 50 people. All around you, the water teems with the desperate cries of those clinging to the last threads of life. The lifeboat can take 20 more souls before it tips into chaos, drowning everyone aboard.

As you grip the edge of the boat, scanning the sea of faces, the enormity of the decision ahead chills you more than the ocean's spray. If you try to save everyone, the boat will sink, ensuring the deaths of all. If you let no one else aboard, you guarantee the survival of your group but condemn the rest to perish. And then there's the third choice—allowing only 20 more people onboard—but how do you decide who deserves salvation? The young? The strong? The hopeful? Each option tears at the fabric of your humanity, forcing you to confront the fragility of your moral compass and the weight of your Judgment Core.

Hardin's lifeboat scenario isn't just a metaphor—it reflects countless real-world dilemmas where resources are finite, and the stakes are high. In 2020, as the world battled the COVID-19 pandemic, doctors in overcrowded hospitals faced an eerily similar predicament. With ventilators in short supply, medical teams were forced to decide who would receive life-saving treatment and who would not. These decisions weighed heavily on their moral cores, often leaving scars on their conscience long after the crisis had passed.

Imagine standing in an ICU ward, faced with two patients and only one ventilator. One is a 35-year-old mother of two with a high chance of recovery. The other is an elderly man, a beloved grandfather, but with multiple underlying conditions. Who do you save? Who do you let go? And how do you live with the aftermath of such a choice? The doctors' dilemma echoes the haunting uncertainty of Hardin's lifeboat: there is no right answer, only choices that ripple outward, shaping lives and reshaping moral compasses.

Hardin's essay forces us to confront uncomfortable truths about human nature, compassion, and the limits of altruism. It compels us to ask:

- How do we balance compassion and pragmatism when resources are limited?

- What principles guide our choices when every option comes with sacrifice?

- When faced with impossible decisions, how do we safeguard our humanity?

Navigating these gray areas requires a steadfast moral compass, grounded in empathy, fairness, and practicality. It demands that we acknowledge the inherent flaws in every decision while striving to minimize harm and uphold dignity. Our Judgment Core—the internal framework shaped by personal values and collective experiences—becomes our guide, helping us weigh competing interests and make the best choice in imperfect circumstances.

The lifeboat dilemma isn't merely a hypothetical scenario; it's a mirror reflecting the struggles of societies today. Whether it's allocating resources in a climate crisis, addressing income inequality, or managing refugee resettlement, we face countless variations of Hardin's lifeboat every day. The challenge is not just to survive but to do so in a way that preserves our shared humanity.

As you reflect on Hardin's lifeboat and its parallels to real-world crises, consider this:

- What would you do if you held the power to decide who lives and who dies?

- Would your decisions prioritize the many over the few, or the vulnerable over the strong?

- And how would you ensure that your choices, however imperfect, align with your moral compass?

The lifeboat forces us to grapple with the hardest truths about human existence. It reminds us that in the murky waters of ethical dilemmas, clarity is a luxury we rarely have. But within the uncertainty lies the opportunity to act with courage, integrity, and compassion, ensuring that even in the harshest storms, we remain anchored to the best parts of our shared humanity.

Conclusion - The Precarious Bridge: Navigating Life's Moral Gray Areas with Integrity

You're standing on a precarious bridge, shrouded in mist, suspended between two vast landscapes—one labeled "Right" and the other "Wrong." Beneath the bridge lies an abyss of uncertainty, where shadows shift, and clarity dissolves into complexity. Each step you take requires careful calculation, balancing your weight against the swaying structure, trusting only in the compass within you. This compass, your Judgment Core, is the quiet force that helps you navigate the gray areas of life, where no signposts exist, and every decision demands reflection.

In a world increasingly defined by its complexities, where absolutes are rare, navigating these moral gray zones becomes less about certainty and more about adaptability. The bridge represents the path we all must walk—a journey that tests the strength of our values, the depth of our empathy, and the resilience of our integrity.

Balancing right and wrong in these moments is far from simple. Life often demands that we make choices that seem flawed no matter which way we turn. Perhaps it's deciding whether to break a rule to protect someone vulnerable or whether to speak out against an injustice, knowing the personal cost could be immense. These are not hypothetical dilemmas; they are the daily realities of navigating a complex world.

In these ambiguous situations, your Judgment Core becomes more than a guide—it becomes a test of who you're. Consider these questions as you step into the fog:

- When faced with a choice that pits loyalty against justice, which principle will you honor most?

- Do you have the courage to challenge the rules when they conflict with your sense of fairness and humanity?

- How do you ensure that your decisions, though imperfect, minimize harm while staying true to your values?

Each answer reflects not just a momentary decision but the shaping of your moral compass. The gray area is not a place for indecision; it is a realm where action, guided by thoughtfulness, matters most.

The bridge of life demands balance. Too rigid, and you risk breaking under the strain of inflexible principles. Too permissive, and you lose the structure that keeps you grounded. True wisdom lies in recognizing that the world is neither black nor white but an intricate mosaic of context, intent, and consequences.

Empathy enables you to see beyond your perspective and consider the lives and experiences of those affected by your choices. Fairness reminds you that your decisions must strive for equity, even when perfection is unattainable. Integrity anchors you, ensuring that your actions reflect your deepest principles, even when the path forward is shrouded in ambiguity.

Navigating the gray area is not about finding perfect answers—it is about making principled choices in the face of imperfection. Reflect on your role in the decisions you make. Do you act with courage, knowing that the path is unclear? Do you strive to minimize harm, even when you cannot eliminate it entirely? And do you hold yourself accountable, ensuring that your choices align with your moral compass, even as the winds of uncertainty shift?

Every step on the bridge reshapes the traveler. Each choice you make in the gray areas of life strengthens your Judgment Core, teaching you not just to survive uncertainty but to grow within it. This journey demands vigilance, thoughtfulness, and the courage to act when clarity is a luxury.

As you step off the bridge and look back, what will your decisions say about you? Will they reflect compassion, fairness, and courage? Or will they reveal hesitation, fear, or neglect? The answers are not written in stone—they are shaped by every action you take, every choice you make, and every moment you face the complexity of life head-on.

So, when the fog thickens and the bridge sways beneath your feet, ask yourself:

- Will you walk with conviction, even when the path is unclear?

- How will your Judgment Core guide you when the stakes are highest?

- And when your journey ends, will you look back with pride, knowing you navigated the gray areas of life with integrity and heart?

The answers lie not in certainty but in the courage to act with purpose, compassion, and resilience. The bridge may be uncertain, but your Judgment Core can illuminate the way forward, ensuring that every step reflects the best of who you're.

7.14 Selfishness and the Double Standards: A Test of Integrity

You're standing in a crowded marketplace, holding a loaf of bread. Around you, hands reach out—some trembling with hunger, others steady and expectant. You have enough for yourself, but you hesitate. If you give freely, will others share with you when your own time of need arises? Or will you be left empty-handed, betrayed by those who took without giving back? This moment of decision reveals the delicate tension between self-preservation and fairness—a tension that defines the boundaries of selfishness and integrity.

Selfishness often hides behind the veil of justification. It whispers, "You deserve this more," or, "It's just self-care." While self-prioritization is essential for personal well-being, the line between healthy self-care and selfishness is thin and easily crossed. When personal needs consistently outweigh the needs of others, selfishness takes root, creating double standards that erode trust and distort relationships.

At the heart of this issue lies integrity—the alignment of actions with values. True integrity demands consistency: that we apply the same principles to ourselves as we do to others. Yet selfishness often bends this rule, creating scenarios where individuals expect understanding, generosity, and support without offering the same in return. This imbalance not only undermines relationships but also weakens our Judgment Core (JDC), the internal moral compass that guides our ethical decisions.

This section explores the subtle yet pervasive impact of selfishness and the double standards it fosters. It challenges you to reflect on your own actions:

- Are you holding yourself to the same standards you expect of others?

- Do your values guide your decisions, or do convenience and self-interest take precedence?

- How does your Judgment Core navigate the balance between self-prioritization and fairness?

As we delve into the complexities of selfishness and its impact on integrity, prepare to question your assumptions, confront uncomfortable truths, and refine the principles that guide your life. The answers lie not in what you believe about yourself, but in how you act when fairness and self-interest collide.

The Rise and Fall of Lance Armstrong: A Test of Ambition and Integrity

It was a brisk autumn evening in October 1999 in Austin, Texas. A crowd had gathered at a local sports bar, their eyes glued to the screen as Lance Armstrong, clad in the iconic yellow jersey, crossed the finish line of the Tour de France. The room erupted into cheers. For the people of Austin, and indeed for the world, Lance was more than just a cyclist. He was a symbol of resilience, having battled and beaten testicular cancer, and now he stood as a testament to the indomitable human spirit.

From 1999 to 2005, Armstrong would continue to make history, clinching seven consecutive Tour de France titles. His story seemed too good to be true: a hometown boy who had faced death and emerged not just alive but victorious. Through his Livestrong Foundation, Lance raised millions for cancer research, inspiring patients and families worldwide. To his fans, he was untouchable—a man of integrity, grit, and heart.

But beneath the golden glow of his achievements lay a shadow that would later unravel his legacy. Behind closed doors, Lance Armstrong was orchestrating one of the most intricate doping scandals in sports history. While he preached the values of hard work and clean competition, he was injecting EPO, undergoing blood transfusions, and using testosterone to secure his dominance on the cycling circuit.

In 2001, whispers of doping began circulating in cycling circles, but Armstrong was quick to dismiss them. His charm and determination made him a formidable force against any accuser. He fiercely denied any wrongdoing, often lashing out at those who dared question his integrity. Yet, as the years passed, the cracks in his facade began to widen.

Armstrong's double standard became glaringly evident. He publicly championed a drug-free sport while privately ensuring that his entire team participated in his doping program. Teammates who resisted faced intimidation and exclusion. Those who complied did so reluctantly, caught in a web of deceit spun by the very man they had idolized.

Frankie Andreu, a former teammate, and his wife Betsy were among the first to speak out. In 2004, they testified about Armstrong's doping practices, revealing details of what they had witnessed. Rather than owning up to the truth, Armstrong launched a campaign to discredit them. The Andreus were labeled as bitter and jealous, subjected to years of public ridicule and legal threats. Armstrong's relentless pursuit to protect his image at all costs highlighted a selfishness that would eventually lead to his undoing.

The turning point came in 2012 when the U.S. Anti-Doping Agency (USADA) released a comprehensive report exposing Armstrong's doping empire. The report described it as "the most sophisticated, professionalized, and successful doping program that sport has ever seen." Testimonies from former teammates corroborated the extent of his deception, and the truth could no longer be denied.

The fallout was swift and brutal. Armstrong was stripped of his seven Tour de France titles, banned from professional cycling for life, and abandoned by sponsors who had once celebrated him as their golden boy. His carefully curated image disintegrated, leaving fans and supporters grappling with the betrayal. Even the Livestrong Foundation, the charity that had become synonymous with hope, distanced itself from its founder.

The damage extended beyond Armstrong himself. The cycling world was left in disarray, its credibility tarnished. Fans questioned whether any victory could be trusted, and aspiring athletes were left disillusioned by the sport they loved.

Lance Armstrong's story is not just one of ambition and success but also of a deeply fractured moral compass. At what point did his Judgment Core—his internal guide for distinguishing right from wrong—begin to falter? Was it when he first succumbed to the pressures of competition, or when he chose to silence those who spoke the truth?

His actions force us to confront our own moral dilemmas:

- Would you compromise your values for success if the stakes were high enough?

- How do you justify decisions that benefit you but harm others?

- When faced with the truth, do you double down on deception, or find the courage to come clean?

Armstrong's fall serves as a stark reminder of the dangers of selfishness and hypocrisy. His unwillingness to align his actions with the values he publicly championed eroded not only his credibility but also the trust of millions. His story challenges us to reflect on our own Judgment Core and the choices we make when ambition and integrity collide.

In the end, Lance Armstrong's legacy is a cautionary tale: a once-revered hero undone by his own double standards. It reminds us that no matter how high we climb, our actions in the gray areas of life—when our moral compass is truly tested—ultimately define who we are. How will your Judgment Core guide you when faced with your own crossroads? The answer lies not in what you achieve but in how you achieve it.

Marie Antoinette: The Queen of Opulence and the Fall of a Nation

In May of 1770, a young Austrian princess named Marie Antoinette arrived in France, her carriage glittering with gold as it passed through the narrow streets of Versailles. At just 14 years old, she was thrust into the opulent world of the French court to marry the future king, Louis XVI, sealing a fragile alliance between Austria and France. For the French people, she was a symbol of hope, a new chapter in their monarchy. But for Marie, Versailles was a dazzling labyrinth of power, politics, and privilege that would soon become her gilded cage.

By 1774, at the tender age of 19, Marie Antoinette was crowned queen. To the outside world, her life seemed like a fairy tale—a young, beautiful queen ruling one of the most powerful nations in the world. But beneath the surface, whispers of discontent stirred in the countryside. Bread prices were climbing, poverty was spreading, and the people of France grew restless under the weight of their suffering. Meanwhile, in the glittering halls of Versailles, Marie Antoinette lived a life that seemed to mock their struggles.

Her most extravagant indulgence was the Petit Trianon, a hidden retreat on the palace grounds. It wasn't just a place to escape the formalities of court life—it was her fantasy world. In the 1780s, Marie commissioned the construction of a quaint hamlet within the retreat, complete with pastoral cottages and an idyllic farm. Here, she would don the costume of a shepherdess or milkmaid, playing at the simplicity of rural life while servants ensured that her milk pails were filled and her fields perfectly manicured. To the starving peasants of France, this whimsical escapism was an insult. Her "simple" life at the Petit Trianon cost a fortune, paid for by the very people whose lives she pretended to emulate.

The disconnect between queen and country was stark. As famine swept through France, families rioted for bread while Marie hosted lavish masquerades at Versailles. Rumors of her spending fueled political cartoons that depicted her as "Madame Déficit," a queen who drained the nation's coffers for jewels, gowns, and frivolities. The infamous phrase, "Let them eat cake," was falsely attributed to her, but it stuck because it captured the essence of her perceived indifference—a queen who couldn't understand the suffering of her people.

By 1789, the tension boiled over. The French Revolution began, and Versailles—once untouchable—became a symbol of everything the people despised. On October 5, 1789, a mob of thousands marched to the palace, driven by hunger and fury. They stormed its gates, forcing the royal family to abandon their sanctuary and relocate to Paris. For Marie Antoinette, it was the beginning of the end. The Petit Trianon, once her haven, was left behind, its artificial charm crumbling under the weight of the revolution.

In 1791, the royal family attempted to flee France, hoping to rally support from foreign monarchies. But they were captured and returned to Paris as prisoners. By 1793, the monarchy was abolished, and the guillotine became the symbol of justice for the revolution. On October 16, 1793, Marie Antoinette, stripped of her wigs and jewels, was led to her execution. She wore a simple white dress as she stood before the crowd at the Place de la Révolution. The queen who had once ruled over a world of silk and diamonds met her end with dignity, but her death was a stark reminder of her legacy.

Marie Antoinette's story is a cautionary tale of unchecked selfishness and the dangers of double standards. Her devotion to luxury, her insistence on maintaining a world of indulgence while her people starved, became her ultimate downfall. She reminds us that leadership demands empathy, accountability, and a connection to those who depend on you. Her life challenges us to reflect on our own Judgment Core:

- When faced with privilege, do we use it to uplift others, or do we retreat into selfishness?

- How do we ensure that our actions align with the values we claim to hold?

- Can we recognize when our pursuits of personal comfort come at the expense of others' well-being?

The haunting legacy of Marie Antoinette invites us to question our own moral compasses. Are we the architects of gilded illusions, blind to the suffering around us? Or can we navigate the gray areas of responsibility and privilege with compassion and integrity? Her life, both beautiful and tragic, stands as a mirror, reflecting the choices we all must make when power and empathy collide.

Conclusion - Beyond Me: Choosing Generosity Over Selfishness

You're standing in a room filled with echoes of "me, me, me" reverberating around you. The voices are not shouting, but their persistence is undeniable. They demand attention, prioritization, and indulgence. Now, ask yourself—how often do these echoes define your choices? Selfishness, after all, doesn't always wear a bold mask; it often lurks in subtle gestures, unspoken refusals, and a quiet insistence on self-preservation above all else.

At its heart, selfishness is a quiet thief. It rationalizes, whispers, and justifies, convincing us that our needs outweigh fairness, that our actions are somehow exempt from the principles we expect others to uphold. Yet, each act of selfishness chips away at the consistency of our values, leaving behind a fractured moral compass that struggles to point true north.

Selfishness is not limited to hoarding wealth or refusing financial help. Its reach extends to emotional giving—the warmth of a genuine welcome, the respect for someone's feelings, and the effort to care about the struggles others carry silently. It is in how we make others feel seen, valued, and respected. To embrace integrity means to shift from a mindset of "it's all about me" to one that acknowledges the interconnectedness of our actions with the well-being of others.

It doesn't take grand sacrifices to combat selfishness. A small gesture—offering a seat, lending an ear, or giving a modest amount—may seem insignificant to you but could transform someone else's day, week, or even life. Sharing with family, friends, or those in need won't leave you destitute, but withholding care and kindness can leave others feeling unseen and abandoned. Giving, whether emotional or material, is not about depleting yourself; it is about recognizing that our resources, when shared thoughtfully, amplify their impact.

Consider these questions as you reflect on the role selfishness plays in your life:

- Do you prioritize your feelings and needs at the expense of others' emotional well-being?

- When was the last time you extended kindness or generosity without expecting anything in return?

- Does your Judgment Core guide you toward actions that uplift others, or does it rationalize decisions centered on self-preservation?

Selfishness clouds judgment and creates an illusion of scarcity where none exists. It convinces us that withholding—whether affection, understanding, or material support—is necessary for survival, when in truth, generosity often strengthens us. Giving doesn't mean losing; it means contributing to a cycle of compassion and care that enriches everyone involved.

Integrity demands that we move beyond the confines of "me" and into a space of "we." It requires us to recognize that small acts of giving—whether a kind word, a helping hand, or a heartfelt gesture—carry the power to bridge divides, heal wounds, and nurture trust.

So, how will you navigate the whispers of selfishness when they tempt you to retreat into your own world? Will you allow your Judgment Core to guide you toward fairness, empathy, and connection? The answer lies in the choices you make every day, in the small but profound moments where selfishness can be replaced with generosity and integrity. Look within and ask: How can I give more—emotionally, financially, or spiritually—to create a world that is richer for everyone?

7.15 Kindness: A Powerful Virtue with Boundaries

You're standing at the edge of a quiet lake. You toss a single pebble into the water and watch as ripples cascade outward, touching every corner of the surface. Each ripple is small yet unmistakable, a reminder that even the smallest act of kindness can extend far beyond its origin. But what if the lake were not serene? What if the water was murky, hiding dangers beneath the surface? Would you still toss that pebble, knowing it might awaken something unexpected?

Kindness, like the ripple effect of that pebble, carries immense transformative power. It is a virtue celebrated across cultures, embodying empathy, compassion, and the ability to uplift others without expecting anything in return. Yet, in the unpredictable waters of human interactions, kindness requires discernment. Blindly offering kindness without considering the context or intentions of others can leave you vulnerable, exposing you to exploitation, betrayal, or emotional exhaustion.

At its best, kindness strengthens bonds, fosters trust, and affirms our shared humanity. A simple gesture—like comforting a stranger, listening to a friend, or helping someone in need—can ripple outward, creating a wave of positivity and connection. It reinforces the Judgment Core (JDC), our internal moral compass, encouraging us to act with empathy and fairness. But kindness is not synonymous with naivety. It must be tempered by wisdom to ensure that it uplifts rather than undermines.

The complexity of kindness lies in its duality. On one hand, it assumes the best in people, operating on the belief that most are inherently good until proven otherwise. This outlook fosters openness and trust, inviting genuine connections. On the other hand, unchecked kindness—offered indiscriminately or without boundaries—can lead to imbalance and harm.

Consider the wisdom in the saying, "If you honor the generous, you will own him, but if you honor the ignoble, he will rebel." It highlights the necessity of discernment in kindness. To those who appreciate it, kindness becomes a bridge to deeper trust and gratitude. To those who seek to exploit it, kindness is seen as a weakness to be manipulated.

To ensure kindness remains a source of strength, it must be paired with boundaries and observation. For example:

- An employee who covers for a colleague's repeated mistakes may think they are being kind. Yet over time, they may become overburdened, unrecognized, and even resented for their efforts.

- A friend who always says “yes” to every request, no matter how inconvenient, risks emotional burnout and strained relationships. Their well-meaning gestures may enable dependency or foster ungratefulness in others.

Kindness must be balanced with self-respect and fairness. Saying “no” is not a rejection of kindness but an act of integrity—ensuring that the virtue remains genuine and sustainable.

Reflecting on kindness through the lens of the Judgment Core invites self-examination:

- Do you start with kindness as your default, assuming the best in others until proven otherwise?

- How do you determine when kindness is appropriate, and when it might be enabling harmful behavior?

- Have you set boundaries that protect your well-being, or does your kindness leave you vulnerable to manipulation?

Kindness should not come at the expense of your emotional health or principles. Instead, it should reinforce your moral compass, guiding you to act thoughtfully and ethically, even in challenging situations.

Kindness, when balanced with discernment, creates ripples that touch everyone around you. It strengthens relationships, deepens empathy, and upholds the integrity of your Judgment Core. By pairing kindness with wisdom and boundaries, you ensure that this powerful virtue uplifts both yourself and those it reaches, creating a world grounded in mutual respect and genuine support.

So, the next time you hold that pebble of kindness, ask yourself: Are you casting it into calm waters, or are you ignoring the hidden depths? How will your kindness ripple outward, and will it truly align with your moral compass?

The Transformation of Daryl Davis

On a quiet evening in 1983, Daryl Davis, a Black pianist with an undeniable talent for rock ’n’ roll, was performing at a small bar in Frederick, Maryland. The crowd was lively, clapping along as Davis’s fingers danced across the keys, delivering a performance that captured the spirit of legends like Jerry Lee Lewis and Chuck Berry. After the set, a white man approached Davis, a mix of astonishment and admiration in his voice.

"I've never heard a Black man play like that," the man said, shaking his head in disbelief. Davis smiled politely.

The man continued, "You sound just like Jerry Lee Lewis!"

Davis chuckled and replied, "Well, where do you think Jerry Lee Lewis learned it from? He learned it from Black musicians."

The conversation took a surprising turn when the man admitted he was a member of the Ku Klux Klan - KKK is a white supremacist hate group that originated in the United States in 1865 during the Reconstruction era. It has a history of using violence, intimidation, and terrorism, particularly against African Americans, to uphold racist ideologies and maintain white dominance- Davis, though startled, chose not to walk away. Instead, he asked the man a question that would change the course of his life: "How can you hate me when you don't even know me?"

That interaction sparked something in Davis—a profound curiosity to understand the roots of such hatred. It was a question he couldn't let go. Over the coming years, Davis began what many would consider an unthinkable journey: he sought out and engaged with members of the KKK, not to argue or confront them, but to listen and understand.

Davis attended his first Klan meeting in 1984, held in a small town just outside of Baltimore. As he walked into the room, the air was thick with tension. Eyes bore into him, a Black man stepping into a space where he was not only unwelcome but actively despised. But Davis didn't waver. He greeted the members calmly, shook hands, and sat down.

He didn't come armed with accusations or anger. Instead, he came armed with kindness, patience, and a willingness to talk. Over time, Davis developed an approach that would disarm even the staunchest racists. He would sit down with Klan members, share meals with them, and have honest conversations about race, prejudice, and humanity.

One such conversation took place in Hagerstown, Maryland, with Roger Kelly, a Grand Dragon of the Klan. The two met repeatedly over the years, discussing their vastly different perspectives. Davis didn't try to change Kelly's mind through confrontation but simply by being himself—a Black man who defied every stereotype Kelly had been taught.

"I was just there to understand," Davis later said. "But understanding has a way of leading to change."

Davis's unwavering kindness and openness began to bear fruit. Over the years, more than 200 Klan members—including high-ranking leaders—

renounced their affiliations, many citing Davis as the catalyst for their transformation.

One by one, they handed him their Klan robes and hoods, symbolic gestures of leaving behind a life of hatred. Davis keeps these items in his home, not as trophies but as reminders of the power of dialogue and empathy. Among these robes is Roger Kelly's. The former Grand Dragon left the Klan after years of friendship with Davis, acknowledging that his beliefs were wrong.

"He treated me with respect," Kelly said in an interview years later. "And that made me think about what I was doing."

Davis chronicled his journey in his 2016 book, Klan-Destine Relationships, and his work has been featured in the documentary Accidental Courtesy. Through these platforms, Davis shares his belief that kindness, though often dismissed as a soft or naïve approach, is a transformative force. His story has reached audiences worldwide, inspiring people to engage with those they disagree with, not through confrontation but through connection.

"Kindness is not weakness," Davis often says. "It's strength."

Davis's journey also highlights an essential truth: you can't truly know someone's character—whether they are mean or kind—until they are tested. Davis approached every Klan member with the assumption that change was possible, choosing to extend kindness until their actions proved otherwise. This philosophy allowed him to forge unexpected connections and plant seeds of transformation where others saw only hate.

Today, Daryl Davis continues his work, speaking to communities, organizations, and schools about his experiences. His story is a testament to the belief that people are capable of change when confronted with empathy and understanding.

In a world often divided by fear and prejudice, Davis's example reminds us that the most profound transformations can begin with a simple question: "How can you hate me when you don't even know me?" Through kindness, patience, and a willingness to engage, Davis has shown that even the deepest hate can be unraveled, one conversation at a time.

Anna Sorokin (Anna Delvey)

New York City, Summer 2017. Rachel Williams couldn't believe her luck. She had been swept into a world she never thought she'd be part of—one of private jets, exclusive dinners, and luxurious getaways. Her newfound friend, Anna, was unlike anyone she had ever met: poised, sophisticated, and seemingly larger than life. Anna had an effortless charm and an eye for the finer things, yet she carried herself with a down-to-earth warmth that made Rachel feel like they were equals in this glittering world of privilege.

Their friendship had blossomed over a series of late-night dinners in New York's trendiest restaurants, where Anna would pick up the tab without hesitation. "It's nothing," Anna would say with a dismissive wave, brushing off Rachel's gratitude. Anna spoke of her plans to open an exclusive art foundation, a project she claimed would revolutionize the city's cultural scene. Rachel admired her drive, her vision, and her generosity.

When Anna invited Rachel on an all-expenses-paid trip to Morocco, Rachel didn't think twice. It felt like an adventure out of a movie: staying in a private riad at the famed La Mamounia Hotel, dining on Moroccan delicacies, and lounging by the pool as the sun dipped below the horizon. Anna assured Rachel that everything was taken care of—after all, she was a wealthy heiress with a trust fund worth millions.

But as the trip progressed, small cracks began to appear. Anna started making excuses about her credit cards not working and her bank having issues transferring funds. "It's so frustrating dealing with international banks," she would sigh. Then came the moment of truth. As the hotel staff politely but firmly demanded payment for the $62,000 bill, Anna turned to Rachel with an apologetic smile.

"Could you cover it for me? Just until I get this sorted out?"

Rachel hesitated but agreed, convincing herself it was a temporary inconvenience. Anna had been so generous before—surely this was just a small hiccup. But days turned into weeks, and the promised reimbursement never came. Each text, each phone call, brought a new excuse. The weight of the debt fell squarely on Rachel's shoulders, and the glamorous adventure quickly turned into a nightmare.

It wasn't just Rachel. As more people came forward, the true story of Anna Sorokin began to unravel. She wasn't the wealthy German heiress she claimed to be. Anna was a Russian-born con artist who had spent years weaving an elaborate web of lies to infiltrate New York City's elite social circles. From luxury hotels to private jets, Anna lived a life of unimaginable extravagance—funded entirely by the kindness and generosity of those she deceived.

With her fabricated backstory and undeniable charm, Anna had managed to con financial institutions, hoteliers, and even her closest friends into funding her lavish lifestyle. Her victims were left blindsided, their goodwill exploited by someone who saw their trust as an opportunity to fulfill her selfish desires.

Anna's lies came crashing down in 2018 when she was arrested and charged with multiple counts of theft and grand larceny. In her 2019 trial, prosecutors revealed how she had used her charm and fabricated identity to defraud her victims, leaving many in financial and emotional ruin.

Anna Sorokin's story is a cautionary tale about the thin line between kindness and being naive. Her victims weren't gullible; they were kind, generous people who believed they were helping someone in need. Yet, their compassion was weaponized against them by someone who saw it as an opportunity to serve her own ends.

Rachel Williams, who had acted out of friendship, was left with a $62,000 debt and a painful lesson about the dangers of misplaced trust. Anna's charm and sophistication masked her true intentions, reminding us that appearances can be deceiving and that kindness without boundaries can leave us vulnerable to manipulation.

While kindness is one of humanity's greatest virtues, Anna's story underscores the importance of exercising discernment. Trusting others and giving freely are noble qualities, but they must be tempered with vigilance and the ability to recognize when someone's intentions may not be genuine.

Anna Sorokin's tale is a powerful reminder: always extend kindness, but do so with eyes wide open. In a world where deception can hide behind a smile, the ability to balance compassion with caution is key to protecting oneself from those who seek to exploit our better nature.

A Chilling Encounter in the Bronx

March 2008, Bronx, New York City. The night air was sharp, the kind of cold that bit through layers and settled deep in your bones. Julio Diaz, a seasoned social worker in his late thirties, was heading home after another exhausting day. The subway platform was unusually desolate, its eerie quiet broken only by the faint hum of distant trains. The fluorescent lights flickered, casting restless shadows on the walls, matching the unease Diaz felt but couldn't explain.

As he walked toward the edge of the platform, he felt a presence behind him—a flicker of movement in his peripheral vision. Before he could react, a voice, low and trembling, broke the silence.

"Hand over your wallet."

Diaz turned slowly, his calm eyes meeting the desperate gaze of a teenage boy, no older than sixteen. In the boy's shaking hand was a knife, its blade glinting in the pale light. The moment stretched, the air thick with tension.

Without flinching, Diaz reached into his pocket and handed over his wallet. He moved deliberately, avoiding any sudden motions, and extended it toward the boy, whose grip on the knife tightened. Diaz noticed something behind the young man's hardened expression: a flicker of fear, desperation, maybe even shame.

As the boy began to back away, Diaz did something unexpected. "Wait," he called out, his voice steady and kind.

The boy froze, confusion flickering across his face.

"If you're out here robbing people tonight," Diaz said, pulling off his jacket, "you'll need this. It's freezing out."

The boy stared at him, unsure whether this was a trick. But Diaz's tone was unyielding in its sincerity. Tentatively, the boy took the coat, his hands brushing against the warm fabric as if testing its reality.

Before the boy could retreat into the night, Diaz added, "I was about to grab some dinner. Why don't you join me?"

The boy hesitated, his confusion deepening. He glanced at the knife in his hand, then at the man before him. There was no anger in Diaz's eyes, no fear—just an odd, disarming warmth. Against all logic, the boy nodded.

The two made their way to a nearby diner, a bustling little spot known for its comforting aromas of coffee and grilled sandwiches. As they entered, the regulars glanced curiously at the odd pair—a man in his work clothes and a nervous teenager clutching a knife in his pocket.

They slid into a booth. Diaz handed the boy a menu, acting as if they were old friends. "Order whatever you'd like," Diaz said, his tone casual.

As the boy hesitated, the tension slowly began to dissolve. Over burgers and hot coffee, Diaz didn't scold or interrogate. Instead, he asked questions about the boy's life—where he was from, who his family was, and what had led him to this point. Bit by bit, the boy opened up.

He spoke of a fractured home, nights without food, and the desperation that had driven him to pick up a knife and head into the cold streets. He admitted he hated what he was doing but didn't know another way.

The diner staff, familiar with Diaz's warm demeanor, watched from a distance. This was the man they knew—a customer who greeted everyone with a smile, now quietly breaking bread with someone who had just threatened him.

As they finished their meal, Diaz leaned back and smiled. "You know," he said lightly, "I can't pay for this. You still have my wallet."

The boy's eyes widened. Slowly, he reached into his pocket and handed the wallet back, along with the knife. "I'm sorry," he murmured, his voice cracking under the weight of his remorse.

Diaz took both without a word, his expression firm but forgiving. "You don't have to do this," he said gently. "There's always another way."

The boy nodded, tears brimming in his eyes. For the first time that night, he seemed to stand a little taller, as if a burden had been lifted.

The story of Julio Diaz and the teenager spread after it was featured on National Public Radio's This American Life. It resonated with listeners across the country, sparking conversations about the power of empathy and second chances.

For Diaz, it wasn't about being heroic. "I just wanted to understand," he said. His Judgment Core—the internal moral compass that guided him—was rooted in the belief that even in moments of fear, humanity could triumph over division.

That night in the Bronx, Diaz chose kindness over anger, understanding over judgment. His actions reminded the teenager—and everyone who heard the story—that redemption is always possible.

Julio Diaz's story isn't just about a chance encounter; it's about the choices we make when faced with fear and uncertainty. It challenges us to ask:

- How would we respond when threatened—would we react with anger, or with courage and compassion?

- Do we see others as the sum of their worst actions, or as human beings capable of change?

- How does our Judgment Core guide us to navigate the thin line between self-preservation and empathy?

That cold night in the Bronx, Diaz didn't just share a meal; he offered hope, proving that kindness, when paired with courage, can turn even the darkest moments into opportunities for transformation.

Conclusion: Beyond me

Picture a tree growing in the heart of a bustling city, its roots winding deep into the ground while its branches stretch outward, offering shade to strangers and passersby. The tree gives freely—shelter from the sun, a place to rest—yet it cannot thrive without strong roots anchoring it and drawing sustenance from the earth. Kindness is much like that tree: its branches extending outward to nurture others, but it must be grounded by wisdom and boundaries to remain strong and enduring.

Kindness is not merely a series of actions but a profound reflection of our Judgment Core (JDC)—the internal compass that helps us weigh our values against the complexities of life. It teaches us to balance compassion with accountability, generosity with self-preservation, and connection with discernment.

The beauty of kindness lies in its transformative power to heal and uplift, yet its strength can falter when offered without thought. Like an untended tree that overextends its branches, kindness without grounding risks being exploited or leaving us emotionally depleted. This delicate balance asks us to confront pivotal questions about our actions and intentions:

- Are your acts of kindness rooted in genuine compassion, or are they stretching you too thin?

- Do you nurture others while ensuring your roots remain strong and intact?

- How does your kindness align with your Judgment Core, guiding you to act thoughtfully even when faced with uncertainty?

Your Judgment Core serves as the foundation of integrity, helping you evaluate when kindness is an act of strength and when it risks enabling harm. Thoughtful kindness, guided by a well-calibrated JDC, not only uplifts others but also preserves the giver's emotional and moral balance.

To wield kindness wisely, consider these principles:

1. Ground Your Kindness in Strength: Approach others with compassion while maintaining a clear understanding of your own needs and limits.

2. Observe the Recipients: Like a gardener tending a tree, pay attention to how others respond to your kindness. Their reactions will reveal their intentions.

3. Prune When Necessary: Establish boundaries that protect your well-being and ensure your kindness fosters growth rather than dependency or harm.

4. Align Kindness with Core Values: Let empathy, fairness, and accountability guide your actions, ensuring they reflect the integrity of your JDC.

The tree's strength lies not just in its ability to offer shade but in the depth of its roots and the resilience of its trunk. Similarly, kindness gains its power from discernment and balance. It creates ripples of trust and connection, encouraging transformation while ensuring sustainability.

As you reflect on your own capacity for kindness, ask yourself:

- Are your actions deeply rooted, providing strength to both yourself and those you touch?

- Do you protect your inner reserves while offering shelter to others?

- How will your kindness shape the world around you, and will it align with the principles that define your moral compass?

Kindness, when grounded in wisdom, is a force that can weather storms, bridge divides, and inspire profound change. Let your kindness be like that tree—deeply rooted, offering shade and support while standing strong against the winds of life. Through thoughtful generosity and a well-tended Judgment Core, you can create a legacy of compassion and enduring connection, shaping a world that thrives in its shared humanity..

7.16 Remember That You're Being Watched

You're walking through an ancient library, its vast shelves lined with books detailing every action ever taken—some noble, others regrettable. Each page you turn represents a decision, a moment of choice. As you browse, you realize these aren't just random stories; they're yours, written by an unseen hand that records everything. Even in solitude, every word, every act is etched into the fabric of time, bearing witness to who you're when no one else is looking.

This concept is at the heart of the idea that we are always being watched—whether by the people around us, the consequences of our actions, or a higher power. This awareness challenges us to align our behaviors with integrity, recognizing that even our most private decisions ripple outward, shaping not only our lives but also the world around us.

A striking truth emerges when we examine the origins of suffering. Studies, such as a 2022 survey by the World Economic Forum, reveal that the majority of human pain and hardship is caused by human actions—dishonesty, selfishness, exploitation, and neglect. Only a small fraction of suffering results from uncontrollable events like natural disasters or acts of God. This finding underscores the profound responsibility each of us bears in creating or alleviating the burdens of others.

Consider the ripple effects of a careless decision: a promise broken, a trust betrayed, or a selfish act that harms another. These choices accumulate, spreading pain far beyond their immediate impact. Yet, the reverse is equally true: acts of kindness, fairness, and accountability create waves of healing and hope, reinforcing the interconnectedness of human lives.

The test of moral character lies in what we do when no one else can see. In moments of power over others—be it a subordinate, a stranger, or a child—our actions reveal the essence of our Judgment Core (JDC), the internal moral compass that guides us. Do we act with fairness and empathy, or do we exploit the situation for personal gain?

A recurring pattern in human behavior is the tendency to justify harmful acts when we feel unobserved or unaccountable. It's easy to rationalize bending the rules, breaking promises, or neglecting our responsibilities when we believe no one will know. Yet, true moral integrity demands consistency, requiring us to uphold the same standards in private as we do in public.

Religious teachings across cultures emphasize the concept of divine observation. Islam teaches that angels record every deed, good or bad, which will be presented on the Day of Judgment. Christianity reminds followers that God is omnipresent, knowing every thought and action. Hinduism and Buddhism highlight karma, where every action shapes one's spiritual balance and future.

Even outside religious contexts, the principle of accountability remains universal. Secularly, the consequences of our actions often circle back to us, shaping relationships, reputations, and emotional well-being. Dishonesty and selfishness erode trust, while compassion and integrity foster connection and mutual respect.

As we navigate our lives, we must reflect on the far-reaching impact of our actions:

- Do my choices contribute to the suffering or the healing of others?

- Am I consistent in my actions, treating others fairly even when no one is watching?

- Does my Judgment Core guide me to act with empathy and responsibility, recognizing the interconnectedness of humanity?

Our actions—no matter how small—are seldom isolated. They ripple outward, influencing the lives of those around us. Recognizing this interconnection compels us to act thoughtfully, avoiding harm and striving to uplift others.

The truth is both humbling and empowering: the majority of human suffering is preventable. It stems not from unknown forces or acts of God but from deliberate choices, neglect, and indifference. This reality places immense responsibility on each of us to ensure that our actions align with principles of fairness, empathy, and respect.

The next time you face a decision, ask yourself:

- Am I acting in a way that aligns with my values, even if no one else sees?

- Are my choices rooted in kindness and fairness, or do they prioritize self-interest at the expense of others?

- What legacy will my actions leave behind, both for those I know and for the broader world?

Remember, whether through divine observation, the impact on others, or the consequences that return to us, we are always being watched. This awareness is not meant to instill fear but to inspire integrity. Let your Judgment Core guide you to act in ways that reduce suffering, foster connection, and uphold the shared responsibility we all have in creating a just and compassionate world.

The Case of the Mysterious Hot Pickle: A Culinary Conundrum

Pensacola, Florida – May 2021. It was a sunny afternoon in Pensacola, and one woman's routine lunch at Burger King was about to make history—or at least, spark some serious head-scratching. Armed with a craving for a classic chicken sandwich, she slid into a booth and prepared to indulge in what should have been a simple, satisfying meal. But fate—or perhaps a particularly zealous pickle—had other plans.

As she took a bite, a lone pickle, heated with what can only be described as the fervor of a thousand suns, escaped its bun and landed dramatically on her lip. What followed was a scene worthy of a soap opera. She winced, recoiled, and, if we're being honest, likely questioned her life choices. The offending pickle, which had been cooked to molten perfection, allegedly left her with a burn that caused both physical pain and, as she later claimed, emotional distress. Yes, a pickle—something most of us encounter without incident—had somehow managed to ignite a legal and philosophical debate.

At first, the incident seemed minor, almost comical—an unfortunate pickle-related mishap destined to be forgotten by dinnertime. But this was no ordinary customer. A few weeks later, she filed a lawsuit against Burger King, asserting that the restaurant had been negligent in allowing the pickle to become "dangerously hot" without warning its unsuspecting patrons of the impending condiment peril.

The legal saga quickly gained traction, drawing the attention of curious onlookers and sparking debates over fast food, accountability, and, frankly, the logistics of pickle physics. The plaintiff's legal team argued that Burger King had a duty to ensure that every aspect of their food was safe—yes, even pickles. The implication was clear: Burger King had failed its customers by allowing such a spicy situation to unfold.

Burger King, unsurprisingly, defended itself with vigor. Their attorneys countered that their food preparation practices met industry standards and that this was nothing more than an isolated incident—a freak accident, if you will. No similar complaints had been lodged at any other locations, which raised the question: was this really a safety issue, or was someone simply trying to milk the pickle for all it was worth?

As the trial approached, the story took on a life of its own. Social media erupted with memes, hashtags like HotPickleGate trended, and late-night talk show hosts had a field day. "How hot could a pickle possibly be?" skeptics wondered aloud. Meanwhile, others asked, "If a pickle can be this dangerous, what else have we been underestimating in the fast-food world?"

Then, in December 2021, just as the public braced itself for what promised to be the culinary equivalent of the Scopes Monkey Trial, the case took an anticlimactic turn. Burger King opted to settle out of court. The terms of the settlement? Confidential, of course—because nothing stirs the imagination quite like an undisclosed agreement.

Was this a sign of corporate accountability, or did the fast-food giant simply want to avoid the spectacle of a protracted trial over a pickle? The mystery deepened, and the public was left to ponder what really happened behind closed doors.

While it's tempting to dismiss this as just another quirky lawsuit, the "hot pickle case" raises deeper questions about the interplay between personal responsibility and corporate accountability. It also puts the Judgment Core (JDC)—our internal moral compass—to the test.

- Fairness: Was the plaintiff genuinely seeking justice for an injury, or was she simply exploiting a bizarre incident for personal gain? Conversely, did Burger King settle because they recognized a flaw in their safety practices, or was it a strategic move to avoid scrutiny?

- Empathy: Could both parties have handled the situation differently? Did the plaintiff's claims stem from genuine distress, or was it a classic case of crying over spilled milk—or in this case, a rogue pickle?

- Consequences: How do cases like this shape our understanding of justice? Will it lead to better food safety standards, or encourage more lawsuits over the mundane misadventures of everyday life?

As the dust settles on this puzzling saga, we're left to consider the broader implications. Was this truly a battle for justice, or a pickle-sized example of playing the system? And, most importantly, what does this say about how we handle life's small but spicy inconveniences?

The next time you bite into a sandwich, think of the mysterious hot pickle and ask yourself: are we too quick to find fault in the mundane, or are these small battles a necessary stand for accountability? Let your Judgment Core guide you—and maybe keep an eye on those pickles. You never know when one might strike.

The Watchful Eye: The Redemption of Jean Valjean and the Story of Cosette

It was a cold winter evening in October 1815 when Jean Valjean trudged into the quiet, unwelcoming town of Digne. His clothes were tattered, his face weathered by years of relentless labor, and his eyes carried the hollow look of a man who had wrestled with fate and lost. His crime? Nineteen years in prison for stealing a loaf of bread—a single loaf taken from a baker's window to feed his sister's starving children. The original sentence had been five years, but multiple escape attempts turned it into nearly two decades of suffering.

With every door slammed in his face that night, Valjean felt society's silent verdict: once a criminal, always a criminal. It wasn't just the yellow ticket of leave branding him as a convict—it was the collective gaze of a world that saw him as irredeemable.

But then, fate intervened. The door of the Bishop of Digne, Monseigneur Myriel, opened. The bishop offered food and shelter without hesitation, treating Valjean as a guest rather than a dangerous ex-convict. Over dinner, the bishop spoke of mercy, dignity, and the potential for redemption. But years of suffering had hardened Valjean's heart. In the dead of night, he stole the bishop's silver and fled.

The next morning, when the police caught him and dragged him back to the bishop, Valjean braced for the inevitable return to prison. But what happened next shattered his understanding of the world. The bishop, holding the silver candlesticks, said, "Ah, Jean Valjean! You forgot these."

The police left, bewildered. Valjean stood speechless as the bishop leaned in and whispered, "With this silver, I have bought your soul for God. Go, and make yourself a new man."

Valjean did exactly that. He adopted a new name—Monsieur Madeleine—and, within a few years, became the prosperous mayor of Montreuil-sur-Mer. He built factories, created jobs, and was known for his generosity and fairness. Yet, despite his success, the ghost of his past trailed him like an invisible chain.

His Judgment Core—the internal compass that dictates right from wrong—grew stronger with each act of kindness. He believed in the bishop's words, in the idea that redemption was possible through good deeds. But even as he thrived, he remained acutely aware of the invisible eyes that watched him: the eyes of God, the memory of the bishop, and the moral code now rooted deep within him.

There was, however, another set of eyes that never stopped watching: those of Inspector Javert.

Inspector Javert was a man carved from stone—rigid, severe, and unshakably devoted to the law. Born in a prison to a fortune-teller mother and a convict father, Javert had clawed his way into law enforcement, determined to distance himself from the stigma of his birth. For him, the law was absolute. People were either good or bad; there was no gray in between.

He had encountered Valjean once during his time as a prison guard in Toulon and recognized something familiar about Mayor Madeleine. His suspicions grew into certainty: Madeleine was Valjean, the fugitive. And Javert, governed by his own moral code, was determined to bring him to justice.

In 1823, a man named Champmathieu was arrested and misidentified as Jean Valjean. Witnesses—including former prison guards—testified that Champmathieu was the escaped convict. Javert, certain he was right, presented this "evidence" to Mayor Madeleine.

This was Valjean's test. He stood at the crossroads of his conscience. If he stayed silent, an innocent man would be condemned in his place, and he could continue his life of prosperity and good deeds. No one would ever know. No human eyes would see through his deception.

But Valjean wasn't just being watched by society. He believed he was being watched by God, by the bishop's lingering mercy, and by his own Judgment Core. He knew that integrity isn't measured by what others see, but by the decisions we make when we are alone with our conscience.

That night, Valjean sat in his office with the silver candlesticks glowing softly on the mantelpiece. The bishop's words echoed in his mind: I have bought your soul for God.

The next morning, he walked into the courtroom and declared: "I am Jean Valjean." The room fell into stunned silence.

Valjean was immediately arrested, but he had done what he believed was right. His soul remained intact, even as his freedom was taken away. Yet fate was not done with him. He escaped custody and returned to fulfill a promise he had made to a dying worker, Fantine: to care for her daughter, Cosette.

Cosette was born into hardship. Her mother, Fantine, was a single working woman abandoned by her lover. Fantine worked tirelessly to provide for her child, leaving Cosette with the Thénardiers, a couple who ran a small inn in Montfermeil. The arrangement was supposed to be temporary, but the Thénardiers saw Cosette as a source of easy money.

They forced her to live as a servant, dressed in rags, and sent her into the forest each night to fetch water from a distant well. She became known in the village as L'Alouette—the lark—because she was always seen running, her small feet never stopping, her eyes always wary.

On Christmas Eve of 1823, Valjean arrived in Montfermeil. He found Cosette struggling to carry a heavy bucket of water through the dark woods. Her eyes, wide with fear, met his. Valjean gently took the bucket from her hands, carried it to the inn, and paid the Thénardiers a substantial sum to release her into his care.

Cosette's life transformed overnight. Valjean became the father she never had. He dressed her in warm clothes, taught her to read, and protected her fiercely. But even as they built a peaceful life together in Paris, Valjean was haunted by the knowledge that Javert was still watching.

In 1832, during the Paris uprising, Javert infiltrated the rebel barricade as a spy. He was caught and brought before Valjean, who had joined the rebels to protect Marius, the young man in love with Cosette. The tables had turned: Javert was now at Valjean's mercy.

Javert expected no leniency. The law showed none; why should Valjean? But Valjean, guided by the same Judgment Core that had compelled him to reveal his true identity in court, cut Javert's bonds and set him free.

Javert, unable to reconcile this act of mercy with his rigid worldview, stood on the Pont au Change that night, staring into the dark waters of the Seine. The man he had considered irredeemable had spared his life. The law was absolute, yet mercy had undone it. His Judgment Core, locked in an unyielding framework his entire life, fractured. In the early hours of the morning, Javert stepped off the bridge and disappeared into the river.

After the uprising, Valjean arranged for Cosette to marry Marius Pontmercy, a young revolutionary who had survived the barricades. Marius was from a family of distinction, but his political ideals aligned with the hopes of a brighter, fairer France. Cosette stepped into a world of comfort and love—one she had never imagined possible.

Valjean, however, did not stay to bask in the happiness of her new life. His conscience told him his task was done. He retreated to a small, solitary apartment, content in knowing that Cosette was safe and cared for.

As Valjean lay on his deathbed, the silver candlesticks stood beside him, their flames a reminder of the bishop's mercy and the enduring power of moral integrity. Cosette and Marius arrived just in time to hear his final words.

"To love another person is to see the face of God," he whispered. And then, with the peace of a man who had lived by his Judgment Core, Jean Valjean passed away.

Jean Valjean's life presents us with a series of moral challenges that resonate deeply with our own Judgment Core:

- Do we choose honesty even when deception would bring comfort?

- Are we guided by external judgments or by the internal compass that reminds us of right and wrong?

- Can we extend mercy to those who have wronged us, trusting that kindness is not weakness but strength?

Valjean knew that he was always being watched—not just by society or by Javert, but by the unyielding eyes of his conscience and the higher moral truths he believed in. His story teaches us that integrity is not built in moments of public recognition but in the quiet decisions we make when no one is looking.

In the end, the silver candlesticks were more than just objects of mercy—they were symbols of the Judgment Core that guided Valjean's life. And now, as you reflect on his story, the question remains:

When you stand at the crossroads of convenience and integrity, which path will your Judgment Core lead you to choose?

Conclusion: The Unseen Observer:

You're walking through a darkened theater, empty except for a single beam of light illuminating the stage. You step forward, believing you're alone, your actions hidden from the world. But then, a whisper echoes from the shadows: "I see you." You freeze, heart pounding, and realize the truth: the seats are filled with unseen watchers—your conscience, your moral compass, and the invisible ripple of consequences that stretch beyond the moment. This theater is life, and the Judgment Core (JDC) is the ever-present audience, quietly observing, always guiding.

This sense of being watched is not confined to moments of public scrutiny. It lingers in the quiet decisions made behind closed doors, in the words spoken when no one seems to hear, and in the actions taken when the law provides cover for self-serving behavior. The truth is, whether we believe in God or not, there is always an observer. For those who have faith, it is the divine presence that records every act—good or bad—for judgment in the afterlife. For those without religious conviction, it is the ripple of consequences that inevitably return to us in this life. No action, however hidden, remains without effect.

The idea that "no one will know" is a dangerous illusion. Our Judgment Core always knows. It stands as a silent witness to our choices, reminding us that integrity is not about external accountability but internal consistency. The JDC doesn't ask, Is this legal? It asks, Is this right?

In a world governed by human-made rules, we often find legal loopholes that permit behavior clearly unethical. The law might allow us to exploit a system, deceive a colleague, or mistreat someone who is powerless to resist. But just because something is allowed does not mean it is justified. Our moral compass should never take instructions from the law alone, for laws are imperfect, changing with time, politics, and societal norms. What is lawful today might be condemned tomorrow. But the principles of fairness, empathy, and accountability transcend legal systems—they are eternal anchors of human integrity.

When the law gives us an opening to act selfishly or abusively, we must pause and ask ourselves:

- Am I doing this simply because I can, or because it is the right thing to do?

- Does this action cause harm, even if it benefits me?

- Would I want to be on the receiving end of this decision if roles were reversed?

- If my hidden actions were made public, would I feel proud or ashamed?

This self-questioning isn't just about avoiding guilt; it's about recognizing that actions leave invisible marks—on ourselves, on others, and on the fabric of society. Abusing power, exploiting rights, or manipulating others for personal gain might yield temporary rewards, but the JDC records everything. Over time, the weight of disregarded principles corrodes our moral foundation, leaving us disconnected from the core of who we are meant to be.

For those who believe in divine justice, the consequences of hidden actions are not confined to this life. The Quran speaks of angels recording every deed, the Bible warns that every secret will be revealed, and karmic teachings in Hinduism and Buddhism assert that our actions, seen or unseen, shape our destiny. Even for those who reject the notion of an afterlife, the principle remains: cause and effect, action and consequence. Call it divine justice, karma, or the simple mechanics of human interaction—our actions, no matter how well concealed, inevitably yield results.

So the next time you're tempted to bend the truth, exploit a loophole, or harm someone because the law won't punish you, remember that the JDC demands more than mere legality. It demands integrity. It challenges you to act with fairness when power makes injustice easy, with kindness when cruelty goes unnoticed, and with accountability when anonymity tempts you into moral shortcuts.

In the quiet moments when no one seems to watch, when the world looks away, ask yourself:

- If no one ever found out, would I still feel at peace with this decision?

- Does my JDC align with this action, or am I suppressing its voice for my own gain?

- Am I guided by principles that endure beyond the shifting sands of convenience and legality?

Ultimately, whether we attribute it to God, universal law, or human conscience, we are always being watched. Not out of malice or punishment, but because the consequences of our choices are inescapable. The unseen observer is not an external force but the moral compass embedded within us.

The next decision you make—big or small—will either reinforce your integrity or erode it. The question is not whether someone will see, but whether you can look into the mirror of your conscience without flinching.

So, when that moment comes, listen for the whisper that follows every action: I see you. And then ask yourself:

Am I proud of what is being written in the invisible book of my life?

7.17 The Silent Influence of Environment: The Ink in the Water

A glass of crystal-clear water placed on a table before you. The water is pure, transparent, untouched. Now, picture someone adding a single drop of black ink into that glass. At first, the ink forms delicate tendrils, swirling and dancing through the water. It looks harmless, even beautiful. But as time passes, the ink dissolves, spreading until the entire glass is tinged with gray. If you continue to add a drop of ink each day, the water, once pristine, will eventually turn completely black.

This is how our environment influences us. The people we surround ourselves with, the communities we engage in, and the values we encounter every day are like those drops of ink. One comment, one behavior, one compromise at a time, the clarity of our moral compass begins to fade. It doesn't happen with a single, obvious moment of corruption; it happens through a series of small, almost imperceptible changes.

We often think of personal change as a dramatic event—a single decision or an abrupt shift in behavior. But in reality, transformation is far more subtle. The environment around us, whether positive or negative, infiltrates our Judgment Core (JDC) gradually. Each conversation, interaction, and influence acts like a drop of ink, merging with our beliefs and perceptions. If we are not vigilant, the clear water of our moral compass can become clouded, leaving us disoriented and vulnerable to choices we once would have rejected.

This process doesn't always appear sinister. It often starts with seemingly harmless acts. Imagine joining a group of friends who occasionally gossip. At first, you feel uneasy when they mock someone who's not present. Your JDC sounds a faint warning—a whisper reminding you of the values you were raised with: respect, empathy, integrity. But over time, as the gossip becomes a routine part of your social interactions, the discomfort fades. What once felt inappropriate now feels normal. The ink has spread further into the water.

Now consider more serious shifts. A professional who works in an environment where cutting ethical corners is common might, at first, refuse to engage. But after witnessing colleagues rewarded for dishonest practices, the resistance begins to weaken. "If everyone's doing it, it must be acceptable," the mind rationalizes. Another drop of ink. Eventually, the line between right and wrong blurs, and decisions once deemed unethical become everyday practice.

- How many drops of ink have seeped into your life without you noticing?

- What behaviors or beliefs have subtly shifted because of your surroundings?

- Is your JDC still calibrated to your core values, or has it been dyed by the environment you've allowed yourself to remain in?

The influence of our surroundings is insidious because it bypasses our defenses. We rarely notice the changes until the glass of water—our moral compass—is no longer clear. Left unchecked, we risk losing the ability to differentiate between right and wrong, convinced that our judgment remains intact when it has, in fact, been compromised.

This gradual transformation doesn't mean we should isolate ourselves from the world or live in constant suspicion. It means we must become more aware of the environments we choose and the people we allow close to us. Like water, our judgment is profoundly affected by what it is exposed to.

As we move through this section, we will explore how small influences accumulate into significant shifts in behavior, how to recognize the signs of environmental impact on your JDC, and practical strategies to maintain the clarity of your moral compass—even in murky waters.

Because the ink doesn't stop spreading until you remove it or change the water. And the question that remains is this:

How long will you let the ink spread before you reclaim the clarity of your judgment?

The Shadow of Wall Street

New York City, 1998 – Tom Harding had never seen a world like this.

The towering Lockwood & Co. headquarters on Wall Street reeked of power and ambition. Polished marble floors reflected the city skyline, and brokers in tailored suits moved like gods, commanding millions with a single phone call.

At just 22 years old, fresh out of Harvard, Harding had landed a job that was the envy of every finance graduate. He had grown up in Boston, raised by a father who was a schoolteacher and a mother who ran a small bookstore. They had taught him about honesty, hard work, and ethics—values he carried with him as he stepped into his dream job.

Harding's first year (1999) at Lockwood & Co. was a battlefield of ringing phones, shouting brokers, and numbers flashing across massive screens. He worked 20-hour days, fighting for his place among the financial elite.

Then came his first real test. One afternoon, his boss, Daniel Graves, called him into his office. Graves was a legend—ruthless, feared, and untouchable.

He slid a file across the desk.

"Tom, this is your first big deal. Valcor Energy. A client is considering investing. Your job is to sell them on it."

Harding flipped through the file. Valcor was a disaster. Their numbers were artificially inflated, and the company was hemorrhaging money. If his client bought in, they'd be throwing their fortune into a black hole.

"Sir," Harding hesitated, "these numbers don't look—"

Graves leaned forward. "Tom, your job isn't to warn the client. Your job is to make them believe in the deal."

A long pause. Harding felt a war inside him. His father's words echoed in his mind.

Then he looked at Graves' Rolex, his penthouse key fob, the power in his voice.

That night, Harding made the call. He spun the numbers. He sold the lie.

Two months later, Valcor collapsed. His client lost everything.

The next morning, Graves clapped him on the back. "Welcome to the real Wall Street, kid."

Harding's Judgment Core—the internal compass that once guided him—took its first hit.

Wall Street's transformation wasn't immediate. It chipped away at you, piece by piece.

Harding learned quickly that morality was fluid here. He told himself:

- "Everyone does it."

- "If I don't, someone else will."

- "It's only temporary."

Each year, the compromises grew larger:

- 2002: He manipulated stock values to secure million-dollar commissions.

- 2003: He sold mortgage-backed securities, knowing they were built on risky loans.

- 2004: He covered losses with falsified reports, keeping investors blind.

- 2006: He bribed analysts to suppress negative press on failing companies.

With every deal, his life transformed:

- A black Aston Martin in his garage.

- A penthouse with a view of Central Park.

- Private jets, VIP clubs, and an endless supply of luxury.

The kid from Boston who once believed in ethics and integrity had vanished.

By 2008, the market was built on deception, and Harding knew it.

The subprime mortgage crisis wasn't a shock—he had helped create it.

Then, in September 2008, his phone rang.

"SEC Investigation Underway. DELETE ALL FILES."

The walls collapsed overnight.

Lockwood & Co. crumbled.

Billions were lost.

Clients were ruined.

Harding sat alone in his penthouse, watching the world he built turn to ashes.

His father's voice echoed again. "Make money, but make it the right way."

For the first time in a decade, Harding felt shame.

Harding struck a plea deal—but he was banned from finance forever.

With no career, no reputation, and no future, he fled to Vermont, hoping silence would give him answers.

For months, he did nothing. No stock tickers. No late-night deals. Just emptiness.

Then, one day, he saw a headline:

"Another Wall Street executive indicted for fraud."

It was a kid just like him. Fresh-faced. Hungry. About to make the same mistakes.

Harding stared at his reflection in the café window.

For the first time, he asked himself:

- When did I stop recognizing myself?

- Was it the first lie? The second? Or did it happen so slowly that I never saw it?

- If I had walked away earlier, could I have saved myself?

Harding couldn't erase the past, but he could warn others.

By 2013, he started speaking at universities and finance schools, exposing the slow corruption of Wall Street.

- He mentored young traders, teaching them how to navigate corporate pressure.

- He advised whistleblowers, guiding them on ethical dilemmas.

- He wrote "The Slow Corruption: How Corporate Greed Nearly Destroyed Me."

He would never undo the damage he had done, but he would make sure no one else followed the same path.

Can You See It Happening Before It's Too Late?

Harding didn't wake up one day as a liar and a fraud, it happened slowly, one small lie, one small justification, one tiny compromise, until one day, there was nothing left to lose.

Now, ask yourself:

- If your job rewarded dishonesty, would you recognize the slow corruption?

- Would you have the courage to leave before you became someone you don't recognize?

- Or would you convince yourself—like Harding once did—that 'it's just business' until it's too late?

Because in the wrong environment, anyone can change—and sometimes, you don't even see it happening.

The Tale of Power, Deception, and Conscience

Michael Dawson arrived in Washington, D.C., in the summer of 1996, fresh out of Georgetown University, armed with a degree in political science and a heart full of ambition. He had dreamed of working in public service since he was a boy, watching his father, a high school history teacher in Chicago, fight tirelessly for better education policies.

Politics, to Dawson, was about change. About justice. About doing what was right, even when it was hard.

When he landed a coveted position as a legislative aide to Senator James Holloway, he believed he was stepping onto the path of righteousness. Holloway, known as a man of integrity, had built his career on fighting corporate corruption.

On his first day, Dawson's father called him. "Make money, but make it the right way, son. Never forget why you started this journey."

Dawson promised he wouldn't.

But Washington had a way of breaking promises.

Three years later, Dawson had climbed the ranks, becoming Senior Policy Advisor to the senator. He had learned the game—the intricate dance of policy, negotiation, and power.

One afternoon, Robert Tate, the senator's chief strategist, called him into his office.

Tate had been in Washington for two decades. He wasn't just a political operator; he was a kingmaker, the kind of man who knew everyone's secrets and used them as currency.

"Michael, we need to secure this bill. The donors are watching," Tate said, sliding a thick folder across the desk.

Dawson opened it and felt his stomach turn.

The bill was supposed to lower prescription drug costs for seniors. But this version was riddled with loopholes—ones that would allow pharmaceutical giants to hike prices even higher.

Dawson frowned. "This… this isn't what we promised voters."

Tate smirked, leaning back. "Michael, let me give you some advice. Politics isn't about what's right. It's about what's possible."

Dawson hesitated. He could push back. He could say no.

But then he thought about his career.

- The corner office he was close to getting.

- The influence he was building.

- The calls from major donors who had started remembering his name.

That night, he signed off on the bill, it was his first real compromise, And it wouldn't be the last.

Washington didn't change people overnight. It eroded them, piece by piece.

- 2002: Dawson rewrote environmental reports to downplay concerns for a corporate donor.

- 2004: He helped block a reform bill that would have ended tax loopholes for billionaires.

- 2006: He funneled corporate donations into shadow PACs, keeping their influence hidden from the public.

- 2008: He silenced a whistleblower who tried to expose unethical deals.

Each compromise came easier than the last. With every deal, his life transformed:

- A million-dollar brownstone in Georgetown.

- Weekend getaways in the Hamptons.

- Private dinners with CEOs and lobbyists who now called him "Mike" instead of "Mr. Dawson."

He stopped asking himself if he was doing the right thing, because as long as no one knew the truth, did it even matter?

Breaking News: Senator Holloway's Office Under Federal Investigation

Dawson woke up to his phone exploding with calls, a leak had exposed emails detailing how his team had funneled government contracts to major donors in exchange for political contributions. His name was all over the documents.

His phone wouldn't stop ringing. Reporters, federal investigators, former colleagues—everyone wanted answers.

Holloway, his mentor, was forced to resign in disgrace, And Dawson? He had two options:

Fight and risk prison, or cooperate and lose everything.

He took the plea deal.

His punishment? A lifetime ban from politics.

In one day, his career was over.

For the first time in 15 years, Dawson had nothing.

No more meetings with senators.

No more high-stakes deals.

No more power.

He returned to Chicago, moving into a modest apartment on the South Side, miles away from the life he had built.

For months, he barely left the house.

Then, one evening, he walked past his old high school.

Inside, a group of students sat, listening to a guest speaker talk about public service.

Dawson stopped. That was supposed to be him.

And for the first time, he asked himself:

- When did I stop being the person I set out to be?

- Was it the first lie? The first deal? Or did it happen so slowly I never noticed?

- If I had walked away earlier, could I have saved myself?

The answer was painfully clear.

Dawson spent the next four years rebuilding.

- He volunteered at government transparency organizations, working against the very system he once protected.

- He mentored young political aides, warning them about the slow corruption of power.

- He wrote a book: “Politics and Poison: How Washington Changed Me.”

He would never undo the damage.

But he could stop others from making the same mistakes.

The Lesson: Would You See It Before It’s Too Late?

Dawson didn't wake up one morning as a corrupt official.

It happened slowly.

- One bill.

- One favor.

- One justification.

Until one day, he no longer recognized himself.

Now, ask yourself:

- If your job rewarded dishonesty, would you recognize the slow corruption?

- Would you have the courage to leave before you became someone you don't recognize?

- Or would you convince yourself—like Dawson once did—that 'this is just how the game is played'?

Because in the wrong environment, anyone can change—and sometimes, you don't even see it happening.

Conclusion: The Unseen Drift:

Picture yourself standing at a crossroads, a heavy fog rolling in around you. The path behind you is clear—marked with the values, ethics, and principles you once held with conviction. But ahead, the road is obscured, shrouded in the silent influence of your environment. With each step forward, the surroundings shift, subtly altering your perception of right and wrong. You tell yourself you're still the same person, but are you?

The slow corruption of one's moral compass rarely announces itself with flashing red lights or a single moment of obvious betrayal. It happens gradually, like ink seeping into water—one small drop at a time. A minor compromise here. A justification there. A decision made to "fit in" rather than to do what's right. And before you know it, the water that was once crystal clear is now murky.

The real danger is that you won't even notice the change.

Your Judgment Core (JDC)—that internal guide that once kept you anchored to fairness, honesty, and integrity—can be quietly rewritten by the people, places, and values that surround you. A dishonest workplace, a manipulative friend group, a toxic online community—each of these can act as ink, darkening your sense of right and wrong in ways you don't realize until it's too late.

But this isn't just a warning—it's a call to action.

Look around you. Who are the people influencing your thoughts and decisions? What ideas and values have subtly become "normal" in your world that once seemed wrong? Have you already accepted behaviors you once swore you never would?

Because once the ink spreads, clearing the water isn't easy.

And yet, it is possible.

The antidote to corruption isn't isolation—it's awareness and intentionality. You must question your surroundings, challenge your influences, and recalibrate your JDC before the changes become irreversible. You must have the courage to step away from environments that no longer serve your values, no matter how difficult that choice may be.

So ask yourself:

- How many drops of ink have already entered your life without you noticing?

- Are you still in control of your moral compass, or has it quietly been rewritten by those around you?

- If you had to defend your choices to your past self, would you be proud—or would you struggle to explain how you got here?

Because whether you believe in divine justice, the judgment of history, or the simple reality that our actions shape our future—you're always being watched.

By the people who trust you.

By the ripple effects of your choices.

By the legacy you leave behind.

And most importantly, by your own conscience.

So the final question remains:

Will you reclaim the clarity of your judgment before it's too late?

7.18 Envy, the Poisoned Arrow

Imagine yourself in an ancient chamber, dimly illuminated by the gentle glow of countless treasures. Each treasure represents dreams you silently cherish—wealth, recognition, success, love. Yet, as your eyes wander, they settle upon treasures more dazzling than your own, held in the reflection of another's life. In your hand, hidden yet potent, rests a poisoned arrow—envy. You now face a critical and deeply personal choice: Will you release the arrow, allowing its toxin to corrupt relationships, fracture dignity, and shatter your moral compass? Or will you resist, choosing instead to embrace gratitude, humility, and empathy?

Envy is not merely an emotion—it is a slow-acting poison, quietly eroding integrity, corrupting your Judgment Core, and blinding you to your own inherent worth. It silently whispers, convincing you that your value diminishes with another's success, tempting you to deny others their rights, recognition, and dignity. But consider this: When envy takes hold, who truly suffers—the one envied, or you?

Pause, look inward, and honestly ask yourself:

- Have you ever allowed envy to quietly shape your actions, turning your respect into resentment?

- Has envy ever driven you to deny someone recognition or undermine their happiness?

- Can you see how envy, unchecked, can lead you across moral boundaries, causing emotional or physical harm, and permanently damaging trust?

Your Judgment Core (JDC)—the heart of your moral compass—must remain acutely aware of envy's corrosive power. Only by recognizing and resisting this hidden poison can you uphold the ethical commitment to honor the rights, dignity, and well-being of those around you.

The choice lies solely in your hands: Will you set envy aside, embracing appreciation and gratitude, or will you let it poison your judgment, eroding your integrity from within?

Here's a more elaborate, historically enriched, and compelling rewrite of the section, including vivid details, historical context, and engaging dialogue to deeply challenge the reader's Judgment Core:

The Poisoned Arrow: The Tragic Betrayal of Selena Quintanilla

In the early 1990s, the name Selena Quintanilla echoed through packed stadiums and humble households alike, her captivating voice breaking barriers of language and culture, turning a Tejano singer into a global icon. Known as the "Queen of Tejano music," Selena's vibrant performances and genuine warmth made her not only a beloved artist but a symbol of hope and inspiration for millions, especially within the Latino community. From small family gatherings in Lake Jackson, Texas, to massive concerts across America, Selena carried an aura of humility and kindness, treating each fan like family.

But as Selena's star continued to rise, envy—a silent, hidden poison—lurked closer than anyone could have imagined. Its vessel was Yolanda Saldívar, who initially appeared as Selena's dedicated fan, later becoming president of her official fan club and manager of her boutiques. To the outside world, Yolanda was a fiercely loyal protector of Selena's image, diligently managing her fan club with tireless dedication. Yet beneath that façade, envy began quietly twisting her perception, planting seeds of resentment that would soon bear tragic fruit.

By early 1995, Selena's career was soaring. Her groundbreaking album, Amor Prohibido, had captured the hearts of millions, pushing her into mainstream recognition. She was working on her first English-language album, poised to achieve global superstardom. At the same time, disturbing reports of financial discrepancies emerged from within her fan club. Funds had vanished, leaving unanswered questions swirling around Yolanda's management. Reluctantly, Selena confronted the issue directly, trusting Yolanda to provide clarity and honesty.

On March 31, 1995, Selena agreed to meet Yolanda privately at a Days Inn motel room in Corpus Christi, Texas, to discuss the unsettling financial irregularities. The room felt unnaturally cold despite the Texas heat outside, tension filling every corner. Selena, ever hopeful for reconciliation, approached Yolanda gently, her voice calm but firm.

"Yolanda," Selena spoke softly, her voice holding an edge of sorrow. "You know I've always trusted you. Why didn't you come to me if you needed help?"

Yolanda's face twisted in anguish—envy finally stripped bare. Her voice trembled, revealing resentment hidden for far too long. "You don't understand, Selena! Everything comes easy to you! Fame, love, money—everything! And what about me? I'm left behind, forgotten!"

Selena paused, pain filling her eyes, softened with compassion despite the accusations. "It's never been easy, Yolanda. It took years of struggle, work, and sacrifice. We trusted you. I trusted you."

But envy had fully corrupted Yolanda's Judgment Core. Blinded by jealousy and bitterness, she reached a tragic point of no return. From beneath her purse, Yolanda drew a revolver, her hand shaking, her eyes clouded by bitterness and desperation.

"Yolanda… no…" Selena whispered, her eyes wide with disbelief and sorrow, stepping back slowly. "This isn't you."

"You made me this way!" Yolanda cried, her voice breaking. A single, fatal shot echoed through the motel, silencing Selena's radiant voice forever and tearing apart the hearts of millions worldwide.

In a single moment of envy-driven madness, Yolanda extinguished a life filled with potential, love, and light, plunging the entire Latino community—and fans worldwide—into profound grief. Selena, only twenty-three years old, had become the victim of envy's ultimate betrayal.

As the tragic news spread, thousands mourned openly, their tears mixing with unanswered questions: How could envy twist human love into murderous resentment? How had Yolanda allowed envy to overwhelm her Judgment Core, poisoning her morality so thoroughly that she destroyed the very person she once admired?

Reflect deeply on this devastating truth:

- How often have you let envy quietly whisper its toxic message into your heart, making you forget the blessings already in your grasp?

- Can you recognize envy's insidious power before it darkens your soul, leading you toward irreversible actions?

- Are you strong enough to reject envy's silent whispers, choosing instead appreciation, gratitude, and kindness—even when faced with your own insecurities and desires?

This heartbreaking betrayal offers a powerful lesson about the Judgment Core within each of us. Selena's legacy is one of compassion, generosity, and dignity—a legacy permanently overshadowed by envy's deadly consequence. Yolanda's fate—a lifetime burdened by remorse and regret—stands as a sobering reminder of envy's destructive power.

The story of Selena Quintanilla's untimely death is not merely history—it is a timeless warning. The envy you harbor today, even quietly, can corrupt your decisions tomorrow. The line between admiration and resentment is thin; your moral compass must be ever vigilant, your Judgment Core steadfastly committed to integrity, compassion, and gratitude.

Now ask yourself deeply and honestly:

- Will you release your poisoned arrow of envy, allowing it to wreak havoc upon others, or will you set it aside, choosing the nobler path of kindness and respect?

- If envy ever tempts you toward harm, will your Judgment Core have the strength to resist, preserving your humanity and dignity?

The decision rests firmly in your hands, guided by your Judgment Core—your choice today shapes not just your own life but the lives you touch tomorrow.

Here's your rewritten story in the same detailed, engaging, historically enriched style, with added dialogue and emotional depth, clearly aligned with the previous story's approach:

The Hidden Price: Mozart, Salieri, and the Symphony of Envy

Vienna in the late 18th century was a city alive with music. Elegant palaces echoed with melodies, theatres buzzed with operas, and composers competed fiercely to capture the ears—and hearts—of European royalty. At the heart of this vibrant world stood Antonio Salieri, a respected and influential composer, admired not only for his musical brilliance but also for his impeccable taste and refined character.

Yet, in the autumn of 1781, the vibrant Viennese scene was disrupted by a dazzling newcomer: the young, irreverent, and prodigiously gifted Wolfgang Amadeus Mozart. Mozart arrived like a whirlwind, composing masterpieces with astonishing ease, melodies flowing effortlessly from his fingertips, captivating audiences and patrons alike. His genius was undeniable, his success meteoric, leaving many—including Salieri—both astonished and disturbed.

At first, Salieri warmly admired Mozart's extraordinary talent. Yet slowly, admiration began to give way to something darker. With every new acclaim Mozart received, Salieri felt his own accomplishments diminished. His inner voice, once supportive, now whispered envy's quiet, corrosive poison.

One chilly evening in December 1785, Salieri found himself attending a lavish salon in a grand Viennese mansion. Guests eagerly awaited Mozart's performance, murmuring in admiration before the composer even touched the keys. Salieri stood quietly near a gilded column, bitterness burning beneath his polite smile.

"Maestro Salieri," remarked Countess Isabella softly, noticing his tense expression, "isn't Mozart's talent extraordinary? Truly divine."

Salieri nodded, masking his turmoil. "Yes, indeed. Mozart's gift is…remarkable." The words came reluctantly, envy tightening his throat. "Though, one wonders if such effortless brilliance is truly fair. After all, art demands sacrifice, does it not?"

Isabella smiled gently, unaware of his inner torment. "Perhaps some gifts simply defy fairness," she replied, moving closer to listen as Mozart began to play.

Mozart's music filled the room, a melody so pure, so perfect, it moved listeners to tears. Yet Salieri's envy twisted the beauty into bitterness. Why had such brilliance come to this impulsive, carefree young man, who appeared to treat his talent so lightly, while Salieri had struggled, sacrificed, and toiled tirelessly for every measure he composed?

In the following years, Salieri's envy quietly influenced his choices, subtle yet profound. Historical accounts suggest that he began to undermine Mozart discreetly—quietly discouraging wealthy patrons, planting seeds of doubt, and ensuring lucrative positions passed Mozart by. Though Salieri never physically harmed Mozart, his envy silently eroded the younger composer's chances, gradually isolating him from potential success.

By the time Mozart lay ill, desperately poor, and nearly forgotten in December 1791, Salieri's envy had exacted its hidden price—not only on Mozart, but on Salieri's own soul. As Mozart's funeral passed through the cold Viennese streets, attended by only a few mourners, Salieri felt the bitter emptiness of his envy keenly.

Decades later, confined to his room, Salieri's heart heavy with regret, he reflected painfully upon his choices. In his final days, he whispered, haunted by remorse:

"Mozart...forgive me. Your genius was never my enemy—it was envy that poisoned me."

Salieri's story stands as a haunting lesson for your own Judgment Core:

- Are you allowing envy to quietly corrode your moral compass, leading you to undermine rather than uplift?

- Have you withheld recognition or opportunities out of resentment, quietly diminishing the happiness and rights of others?

- Do you realize the true cost of envy—not only the harm you cause to others, but the permanent damage inflicted on your own spirit and integrity?

Envy's poisoned arrow may never be visibly shot, but its wounds—both inflicted and suffered—run deep, often irreparable. Your Judgment Core demands constant vigilance, guiding you toward appreciation, fairness, and humility.

Now, the question remains: Will you release envy's poisoned arrow, silently destroying yourself and others, or will you set it down, choosing kindness, generosity, and moral clarity instead?

The answer lies solely within your conscience.

Conclusion: The Crossroads of Your Judgment Core

Now pause, close your eyes, and picture yourself standing again in that ancient chamber, the poisoned arrow of envy trembling slightly in your grasp. Ask yourself deeply and honestly: Will you allow jealousy—a natural yet dangerous part of human nature—to quietly twist into envy, or will you acknowledge and master it before it consumes you?

Jealousy, by itself, is not a crime or sin; it is simply human. Yet it requires your honesty and courage to recognize it within yourself and choose consciously not to let it become envy, the destructive force that corrodes your Judgment Core. Can you admit when you feel jealous, using that acknowledgment to protect your integrity rather than harming others?

Look carefully around you now: consider your life, your family, your health, your loved ones. Do you have a mother or father whose love you can still feel, siblings who stand by your side, a partner who supports you unconditionally, or children whose smiles illuminate your world? Perhaps you have good health, steady friendships, or simple blessings that millions around the world long for desperately.

Ask yourself:

- When was the last time you truly stopped to recognize your blessings instead of envying others?

- Do you understand that envy can only thrive if gratitude and conviction are missing from your heart?

- Can you commit, right now, to seeing the treasures that already exist in your life, embracing gratitude as your shield against envy's poison?

Your Judgment Core is calling you urgently to action—not tomorrow, not someday, but right now. Decide at this crossroads to embrace conviction over envy, gratitude over resentment, and joy in what you already possess rather than bitterness over what others have.

You hold the arrow.

Will you choose to set it aside and cherish your blessings, safeguarding your moral compass?

Or will you let envy's silent poison corrupt you, clouding your Judgment Core and endangering your relationships, dignity, and self-worth?

The choice—and the responsibility—is entirely yours.

What path will you take?

Chapter 8: Integrating These Principles into Your Judgment Core (JDC)

You're standing on the deck of a ship, the vast ocean stretching endlessly before you. The sky is clear, the horizon sharp, and you feel a sense of direction, purpose, clarity. In your hands, a compass—your guide, ensuring that no matter how turbulent the waters become, you stay on course.

Now, imagine that compass slowly shifting, almost imperceptibly. A single degree off-course seems meaningless at first. You don't notice it in an hour, or even a day. But weeks, months, or years later, that small miscalibration has taken you miles away from where you intended to go. By the time you realize it, you're lost—adrift in a sea of uncertainty, wondering how you ended up here.

This is how moral judgment works. It isn't lost in a single moment of failure, nor is it defined by one great act of virtue. It is shaped, day by day, by the decisions we make, the influences we allow, and the questions we dare—or fail—to ask.

Your Judgment Core (JDC) is your internal compass, guiding you through life's moral complexities. But how often do you stop to check if it is still aligned with your true values? How do you ensure it remains sharp, relevant, and capable of leading you in the right direction?

In this final chapter, we bring together the principles explored throughout this book—not as rigid rules, but as dynamic, adaptable tools to refine and strengthen your moral compass.

1. Reflect Regularly: The Art of Recalibrating Your JDC

A compass left unchecked can easily become unreliable. The same is true for your JDC. Without regular reflection, your values can be subtly influenced by external pressures, personal biases, or social trends.

Ask yourself:

- Am I making decisions based on principles, or am I just following the path of least resistance?

- Are my judgments fair, or have I unconsciously absorbed biases from my environment?

- When I look back on my choices, do I feel at peace, or do I sense something is off?

Reflection isn't about self-condemnation; it's about recalibration. The most dangerous moral drift is the one we don't notice.

2. Seek Different Perspectives: Challenge Your Own Beliefs

We do not grow in isolation. The strongest JDC is not the one that rigidly resists change, but the one that is tested, questioned, and refined through interaction with others.

Engaging with different perspectives helps expose blind spots. It prevents our moral compass from becoming an echo chamber, where our beliefs are never challenged, only reinforced.

Ask yourself:

- Do I listen only to voices that confirm what I already believe?

- Have I genuinely considered the viewpoints of those with different experiences?

- Am I open to changing my perspective when new knowledge emerges?

Your JDC should be both firm and flexible—anchored in principles, yet adaptable in understanding.

3. Stay Open to Growth: Morality as a Journey, Not a Destination

One of the greatest moral failures is the belief that we have already arrived at the perfect understanding of right and wrong.

True wisdom lies in the ability to acknowledge that we are always learning. Morality evolves—not in the sense that principles lose meaning, but in how they are applied to an ever-changing world.

Ask yourself:

- Am I willing to admit when I was wrong?

- Do I allow my experiences to shape my moral understanding, or do I resist change out of fear or pride?

- Have I mistaken certainty for truth?

The moment we believe we have all the answers is the moment we stop growing.

4. Act with Intent: The Choices That Shape Your JDC

Every decision you make strengthens or weakens your moral compass. The more often you choose integrity, the stronger your JDC becomes. The more you justify small compromises, the easier it becomes to stray further from what is right.

Ask yourself:

- Am I making this decision out of convenience or out of conviction?

- Would I still make this choice if someone I deeply respect were watching?

- Does this action align with the values I claim to hold?

Your JDC is not just about what you believe—it is about what you do when the moment of choice arrives.

5. The Most Important Rule: Avoid Harming Others

If there is one principle that should never be compromised, it is this: Do no harm.

While morality can be complex, and right and wrong are often debated, the prevention of suffering should always be a priority.

- Are my actions causing harm—physically, emotionally, or psychologically—to another person?

- Am I using my power, knowledge, or influence to manipulate or exploit someone?

- Am I justifying harm under the guise of ambition, personal gain, or societal norms?

The moment we allow ourselves to ignore the suffering of others, we risk losing the essence of our humanity. Our JDC becomes warped, and we begin justifying the unjustifiable.

In a world where cruelty and exploitation often go unnoticed or even rewarded, we must remain vigilant in ensuring that our morality is not dictated by what is legally permissible, but by what is fundamentally right.

Revisiting the Core Insights: The Principles That Shape a Strong JDC

Throughout this book, we have questioned the foundations of morality, seeking to understand how right and wrong are defined and redefined across cultures, laws, and personal experiences.

Here are the five principles that must remain at the core of a strong JDC:

1. Morality is Fluid, But Integrity is Constant

Right and wrong are not fixed absolutes; they are shaped by culture, history, and context. But integrity—the commitment to act in alignment with one's deepest values—remains constant.

2. Context, Intent, and Consequences Matter

No action exists in isolation. To judge fairly, we must consider why something was done, the circumstances surrounding it, and the outcomes that followed.

3. Empathy, Fairness, and Collective Well-being Are Key

A moral framework that ignores the impact of our actions on others is incomplete. True morality extends beyond self-interest and considers the greater good.

4. Beware of Extremes—Balance Is Essential

Too much of any virtue—kindness, honesty, ambition—without balance can become destructive. A strong JDC is one that seeks equilibrium.

5. Living in the Gray Area Requires Awareness, Not Fear

Moral dilemmas are rarely black and white. Instead of fearing uncertainty, we must develop the ability to navigate complexity with wisdom and thoughtfulness.

The Final Question: Who Decides What Is Right?

Throughout this book, we have challenged the question: "Who says this is wrong?"

At first, it may have seemed that the answer lay in external forces—laws, religions, cultures, or governments. But in the end, the responsibility falls upon you.

Your Judgment Core is the final judge of your actions. It is shaped by your choices, your willingness to learn, and your commitment to doing what is right—even when no one else is watching.

So now, the final question is not who says this is wrong—but rather:

What does your Judgment Core say? And are you willing to listen?

References

- Ilibagiza, I. (2006). Left to Tell: Discovering God Amidst the Rwandan Holocaust. Hay House.
- Abagnale, F., & Redding, S. (1980). Catch Me If You Can. Grosset & Dunlap.
- Hugo, V. (1862). Les Misérables. A. Lacroix, Verboeckhoven & Cie.
- Lee, H. (1960). To Kill a Mockingbird. J.B. Lippincott & Co.
- Gladwell, M. (2008). Outliers: The Story of Success. Little, Brown and Company.
- Al-Tabari, M. (1989). History of Al-Tabari. State University of New York Press.
- Murray, L. (2010). Breaking Night: A Memoir of Forgiveness, Survival, and My Journey from Homeless to Harvard. Hyperion.
- Albom, M. (2003). The Five People You Meet in Heaven. Hyperion.
- U.S. Department of Justice. (2009). The Case of Bernie Madoff.
- Armstrong, L. (2013). Admission of Guilt Interview. Oprah Winfrey Network.
- Sanders, H. (1974). Colonel Sanders: The Autobiography of the Original Celebrity Chef. Doubleday.
- Collins, M. (1982). Marva Collins' Way. St. Martin's Paperbacks.
- Robertson, J. (2015). Commute Story in Detroit. Detroit Free Press.
- Bridges, L. (1960). Civil Rights Movement and Desegregation. National Archives.
- U.S. Securities and Exchange Commission (SEC). (2010). Fraud Prevention and Enforcement Cases.
- Sandberg, S. (2013). Lean In: Women, Work, and the Will to Lead. Knopf.
- Kahneman, D. (2011). Thinking, Fast and Slow. Farrar, Straus and Giroux.
- Friedman, T. (2005). The World Is Flat: A Brief History of the Twenty-First Century. Farrar, Straus and Giroux.
- Pink, D. H. (2009). Drive: The Surprising Truth About What Motivates Us. Riverhead Books.
- Zimbardo, P. (2007). The Lucifer Effect: Understanding How Good People Turn Evil. Random House.
- Baumeister, R. (1997). Evil: Inside Human Violence and Cruelty. W.H. Freeman.
- Lewis, C.S. (1942). The Screwtape Letters. Geoffrey Bles.
- Singer, P. (1975). Animal Liberation. HarperCollins.

- Frankl, V. (1946). Man's Search for Meaning. Beacon Press.
- Arendt, H. (1963). Eichmann in Jerusalem: A Report on the Banality of Evil. Viking Press.
- Nietzsche, F. (1887). On the Genealogy of Morality.
- Greene, R. (1998). The 48 Laws of Power. Viking Press.
- Browder, B. (2015). Red Notice: A True Story of High Finance, Murder, and One Man's Fight for Justice. Simon & Schuster.
- Carnegie, D. (1936). How to Win Friends and Influence People. Simon & Schuster.
- Machiavelli, N. (1532). The Prince.
- Sun Tzu. (5th century BCE). The Art of War.
- Gandhi, M. (1927). The Story of My Experiments with Truth. Navajivan Trust.
- King, M.L. Jr. (1963). Letter from Birmingham Jail.
- Mandela, N. (1994). Long Walk to Freedom: The Autobiography of Nelson Mandela. Little, Brown and Company.
- Hosseini, K. (2003). The Kite Runner. Riverhead Books.
- Hedges, C. (2002). War Is a Force That Gives Us Meaning. PublicAffairs.
- Chomsky, N. (1999). Profit Over People: Neoliberalism and Global Order. Seven Stories Press.
- Foucault, M. (1975). Discipline and Punish: The Birth of the Prison. Pantheon Books.
- Pinker, S. (2011). The Better Angels of Our Nature: Why Violence Has Declined. Viking.
- Sen, A. (1999). Development as Freedom. Oxford University Press.

Made in the USA
Columbia, SC
18 June 2025

59537095R00195